FORGOTTEN MEN AND FALLEN WOMEN

FORGOTTEN MEN AND FALLEN WOMEN

THE CULTURAL POLITICS OF NEW DEAL NARRATIVES

HOLLY ALLEN

CORNELL UNIVERSITY
Ithaca and London

Copyright © 2015 by Cornell University

All rights reserved. Except for brief quotations in a review, this book, or parts thereof, must not be reproduced in any form without permission in writing from the publisher. For information, address Cornell University Press, Sage House, 512 East State Street, Ithaca, New York 14850.

First published 2015 by Cornell University Press

Printed in the United States of America

Library of Congress Cataloging-in-Publication Data

Allen, Holly, 1965– author.
  Forgotten men and fallen women : the cultural politics of New Deal narratives / Holly Allen.
       pages cm
  Includes bibliographical references and index.
  ISBN 978-0-8014-5357-1 (cloth : alk. paper)
 1. New Deal, 1933-1939—Personal narratives.
2. United States—Social conditions—1933–1945.
3. Politics and culture—United States—History—20th century.   4. Sex role—United States—History—20th century.   5. United States—Race relations—History—20th century.   I. Title.

E806.A44 2015
973.917—dc23
                                                                       2014039031

Cornell University Press strives to use environmentally responsible suppliers and materials to the fullest extent possible in the publishing of its books. Such materials include vegetable-based, low-VOC inks and acid-free papers that are recycled, totally chlorine-free, or partly composed of nonwood fibers. For further information, visit our website at www.cornellpress.cornell.edu.

Cloth printing   10 9 8 7 6 5 4 3 2 1

*To the memory of my mother,
Candace Claire Mueller*

*and to her granddaughters,
Maisie, Claire, and Lily*

Contents

"More Terrible than the Sword": Emotions, Facts, and Gendered New Deal Narratives — 1

1. The War to Save the Forgotten Man: Gender, Citizenship, and the Politics of Work Relief — 11

2. "Uncle Sam's Wayside Inns": Transient Narratives and the Sexual Politics of the Emergent Welfare State — 49

3. "Builder of Men": Homosociality and the Nationalist Accents of the Civilian Conservation Corps — 68

4. "To Wallop the Ladies": Woman Blaming and Nation Saving in the Rhetoric of Emergency Relief — 96

5. Civilian Protectors and Meddlesome Women: Gendering the War Effort through the Office of Civilian Defense — 134

6. The Citizen-Soldier and the Citizen-Internee: Fraternity, Race, and American Nationhood, 1942–46 — 169

Stories of Homecoming: Deserving GIs and Faithless Service Wives — 203

Notes 211

Index 247

FORGOTTEN MEN AND FALLEN WOMEN

"More Terrible than the Sword"
Emotions, Facts, and Gendered New Deal Narratives

In the spring of 1932, more than twenty thousand jobless men converged on Washington, DC, demanding early payment of cash bonuses to which they were entitled as veterans of the Great War.[1] Calling themselves the "Bonus Expeditionary Force," some accompanied by wives and children, they camped out in Hoovervilles and demonstrated on Capitol grounds while legislators considered the Patman Bonus Bill.[2] When the Senate failed to pass Bonus legislation in mid-June, some veterans left Washington, but many stayed behind, vowing to continue their protests until their demand for early veterans' compensation had been met.

Remarkably, the ranks of Bonus veterans swelled in the weeks following the defeat of the Patman Bill. Disconcerted by marchers' vows to remain in Washington until their demands were satisfied, President Herbert Hoover ordered General Douglas MacArthur to disperse the marchers by force. In an event that furnished some of the most arresting images of political crisis in twentieth-century America, MacArthur mobilized whippet tanks, saber-wielding cavalrymen, and foot soldiers armed with tear gas and bayonets to force the marchers out of Washington.

Marchers called their encounter with federal troops on July 28, 1932, the "Battle of Washington." Together with sympathetic journalists, they characterized the battle as an assault on their rights as veterans and as family men. Popular accounts of the battle centered on federal troops' assault on marchers' wives and children and the destruction of their makeshift homes. With typical gendered sensationalism, one journalist narrated, "Bayonets, sabers, gas—a night attack—put to the torch—screaming women—crying babies—wild-eyed men."[3] Another journalist told of soldiers "rousting men, women and children out of bed, drenching them with tear gas, ruthlessly burning their poor shelters and whatever personal property they could not carry on their backs."[4] Yet another related seeing "dozens of women grab their children and stagger out of the area with streaming, blinded eyes while the bombs fizzed and popped all around them."[5]

After the Battle of Washington, welfare administrator J. Prentice Murphy visited a large encampment of retreating marchers in Johnstown, Pennsylvania, and was amazed by the stories marchers told. What astonished and frankly frightened Murphy were not just the overblown reports of atrocities marchers described—an ear sliced from the head of a retreating veteran, a child bayoneted while attempting to rescue his pet rabbit, veterans barred from rescuing tear-gassed wives and children. Rather, what concerned Murphy even more was the power such stories had to foment social revolution. "One could see how far such tale[s] would run, how difficult it would be to keep [them] within the facts," Murphy commented. He added, "Emotions do strange things to facts. They can set them on fire so that they can become more terrible than the sword." Murphy lamented that atrocity stories stemming from the Bonus rout were "abroad in the land, being told at this fireside or in that store, or at some family table." He concluded, "We must bestir ourselves to see that we do not give occasion for the makings of more such stories."[6]

Murphy's resolve notwithstanding, such stories proliferated throughout the 1930s by word of mouth, in print, in political rhetoric, and even in popular music and film. They were joined by other sensational gendered narratives in the Great Depression, some focusing on unemployed breadwinners, others on wandering youth and homosexual transients, and still others on "pantry-snooping" female caseworkers and emasculating wives. As the Depression gave way to war and economic conditions improved, a new set of sensational narratives emerged: stories of heroic white male air-raid wardens and meddlesome civilian women, of idealized white male soldiers and disloyal Japanese American men.

How do we make sense of such stories? What might they tell us about the gender and racial contours of U.S. civic culture in the New Deal years? A central premise of this book is that stories are a crucial means through which ordinary people understand their place within systems of national political power. During the Great Depression, as Americans grappled with the effects of economic crisis and the expansion of federal governmental bureaucracy to combat it, politicians and ordinary people alike developed a range of "civic stories" in their efforts to comprehend and adapt to the emergent U.S. welfare state.[7] Significantly, the stories that gained the most traction dramatized the effects of expansive governmental authority on long-standing civic ideals, such as the small-town community and the white-male-headed home. Stories of jobless white breadwinners restored to civic respectability through federal public works and of white wandering youth restored to masculine virility through emergency conservation work invoked traditional notions of white male civic authority, while introducing Americans to new concepts of social citizenship and welfare statehood that might otherwise seem threatening. Civic stories that celebrated virile white manhood, hard at work on New Deal relief projects, helped to align residual white male authority with the emergent welfare state, even as the growth of a federal relief bureaucracy compromised existing state, local, and familial sources of civic power.

The apparent tension between residual and emergent sources of civic authority was elided in such narratives through the emotionally satisfying convention of scapegoating gender outlaws, such as unsavory "loafers" and transient "perverts," selfish women workers and emasculating wives. Even as mass unemployment and the advent of a federal relief bureaucracy seemed to compromise masculine self-reliance and local civic autonomy, stories in which transient "wolves" seduced impressionable youth or in which selfish wives nagged and demoralized husbands diverted public scrutiny from the expansion of federal power to the scandalous conduct of gender and sexual outsiders. Particular sensational narratives recurred so frequently that we might regard them not as isolated civic *stories*, but rather as civic *genres*. Lauren Berlant defines genre as "an aesthetic structure of affective expectation . . . that absorbs all kinds of small variations . . . while promising that the persons transacting with it will experience the pleasure of encountering what they expected, with details varying the theme."[8] During the New Deal years, a series of gendered "civic genres" emerged—each offering "affective intensities and assurances" to a gendered New Deal public and operating through recurring characters, plot developments, and audience expectations. For example, in the heat of the economic crisis, stories of "forgotten manhood" assured anxious Americans that jobless white male householders were not threatening civic outcasts, but rather privileged members of a virile nation imagined in fraternal and familial terms. Such stories centered on the jobless white man's affective transformation from bitterness, despair, and civic alienation to renewed pride, purposefulness, and patriotism as beneficiaries of federally sponsored work relief. They also offered affective assurance that the New Deal, despite its expansive bureaucratic authority and apparent disregard for local civic traditions, was a champion of the very political conventions it seemed most to upset: local civic autonomy and the self-reliant white-male-headed home.

Emotions, as Murphy noted, do strange things to facts. In the case of forgotten-man stories, positive feelings of sympathy, pride, and reassurance combined with negative regard for feminized and racialized outsiders to engender support for the New Deal state, despite the anxiety many Americans felt over the expansion of federal power that New Deal policies entailed. Yet Murphy also noted that stories can run out of control; as they proceed from "fireside" to "store" to "family table," their emotional and political impact can change. Certainly, in the case of forgotten-man narratives, what New Deal officials authored as a heartwarming story about the civic regeneration of jobless white breadwinners would become an alarming narrative of civic *degeneration* when reauthored by conservative critics of the New Deal. Yet regardless of whether forgotten-man stories cast the New Deal in a positive or a negative light, they invariably affirmed the ideal of white heterosexual masculine authority in the household and the public square. Moreover, they helped to constitute a gendered, raced, and sexed U.S. public whose members derived pleasure from the genre's repeated portrayal of white male breadwinners who triumphed over economic and personal adversity.

On one hand, this work considers a series of emotionally charged civic narratives, each of which speaks to the gender, racial, and sexual dimensions of the emergent U.S. welfare state. Yet it complements that discursive emphasis with a focus on the institutional histories of several federal agencies. Beginning with the Federal Emergency Relief Administration (FERA) and Civilian Conservation Corps (CCC) in 1933, continuing through the Works Progress Administration (WPA), and concluding with the Office of Civilian Defense and the War Relocation Authority (WRA) in World War II, it analyzes institutional sources to explore how gender, racial, and sexual differences informed Americans' lived experience of citizenship in the Depression and World War II.[9] Each chapter has a particular federal agency, or a series of agencies, as its focus. Yet as Eve Sedgwick observes, in order to fully understand the relationship of gender, race, and sexuality to political power, "an analysis of representation is also necessary." In particular, Sedgwick argues, narrative analysis is crucial if we wish to apprehend "the really very different intuitions of political immediacy that come to us from the sexual realm."[10]

Certainly, studying the narrative operations of New Deal hegemony enriches our understanding of the sexual politics of the emergent welfare state. Stories of intergenerational transient perversion, of prostitutes and punishing wives, of erotically charged CCC youth, of sexually indeterminate Kibei "troublemakers" and faithless service wives animated public discourse and policy throughout the Great Depression and World War II.

Historians have noted that the early decades of the twentieth century were a period of increasing public scrutiny of homosexual practices. Antihomosexual campaigns sought to regulate sexual, ethnic, and class differences by targeting members of a highly mobile, ethnically diverse subculture composed of migrant workers, seamen, and urban laborers.[11] The intersectionality of class, ethnic, and sexual anxieties that animated early twentieth-century antihomosexual campaigns extended into the 1930s, as economic hardship forced increasing numbers of unemployed men into the ranks of the ethnically diverse working-class bachelor subculture. Simultaneously, concerns about prostitution that had languished since the Progressive era resurfaced in the early 1930s, as Americans speculated that mass unemployment would lead many working-class women, no longer restrained by male providers, to engage in sexual commerce. Simultaneously, fears that impressionable masculine youth, deprived of legitimate opportunities to make their way in the world, would fall prey to sexual degenerates added another dimension to what might be described as the sex panic of the early Depression.[12] Finally, the widespread belief that wives of unemployed men would sexually punish their husbands added to a general climate of sexual anxiety in which New Deal relief policy unfolded.

Despite the prominence of sexual anxieties in Depression-era public discourse, few scholars have addressed the sexual politics of the New Deal.[13] Margot Canaday offers the most thorough analysis of sexuality and New Deal politics, but she restricts her focus to the status of homosexuals within particular federal programs.[14] This book, in contrast, considers how emergent concepts of social citizenship and New Deal statehood engaged a range of sexual meanings and identities throughout the Depression and wartime years. In particular, it looks at how New Dealers and other contestants for political power mobilized perceptions of sexual danger to enlist support for their leadership claims. Civic stories that elaborated new expectations of civic participation and federal leadership, while working to contain sexual threats, continued into the wartime years, as Americans contemplated a host of new sexual anxieties: the promiscuity and homosexuality that might result when millions of young men were mobilized for military service, as well as the illicit couplings that might occur when civilian women and men were thrown together in chaotic war production centers. Perceptions of sexual incontinence intersected with fears of national and racial disloyalty throughout World War II. This book considers how those sexual anxieties entered into compelling civic narratives, and how those narratives, in turn, shaped federal policy developments.

Focusing on civic storytelling also illuminates the racial dimensions of New Deal hegemony. Even as New Deal policies preserved state and local civic hierarchies that favored white male breadwinners, not all nonwhite Americans accepted their ascribed status as inferior claimants to New Deal and wartime social policy. African American civil rights leaders, in particular, contested the discriminatory practices of state and local New Deal administrators by invoking the liberal, equalitarian implications of federal policy statements.[15] Other nonwhite groups also identified with the emergent ideal of New Deal social citizenship throughout the Roosevelt years. Long relegated to low-wage seasonal and domestic labor, some Mexican Americans embraced federal relief policies that, in principle at least, enabled them to refuse exploitative labor at starvation wages. How such New Deal policies worked in practice was often disappointing because federal politicians and administrators were loath to alienate powerful Southern Democrats and so conceded to racially discriminatory administration of New Deal civic benefits. For their part, Southern Democrats emphatically resisted any civic transformation that would undermine white control over African Americans in the South and Mexican Americans in the Southwest.[16] All parties to the contest over the racialization of New Deal civic benefits used civic storytelling to advance their political claims.

Looking at how racial themes played out in popular civic narratives affords new insight into the complexities and contradictions of New Deal racial politics. Whether featuring a jobless white breadwinner whose civic regeneration entailed wielding authority over white women and "foreigners," an African American lynch victim unprotected by indifferent federal lawmakers, or a Mexican American worker thrown off the relief rolls to perform seasonal labor at below-subsistence wages, the contested narrative of forgotten manhood worked to define national citizenship in racially significant ways. Wartime civic narratives similarly defined loyalty in racial terms. The white air-raid warden, that celebrated icon of home-front civic virtue, wielded authority over weak-willed women and delinquent nonwhite youth, and the certain loyalty of white citizen-soldiers was defined against the uncertain loyalty of young Japanese American men.[17]

Civic stories gained much of their affective charge when sexual, racial, *and* gender boundaries were transgressed simultaneously: when white wives usurped their jobless husbands' economic power and belittled them sexually; when intergenerational homosexual seduction was also interracial seduction; and when racial otherness, as in the case of Kibei "troublemakers," was compounded by gender and sexual indeterminacy. Civic stories that carried positive affective charges—stories of "loosely clad forestry workers" who formed a "great white chain of camps," and of heroic white civilian defenders who maintained home-front vigilance during the war, likewise drew on the connected pleasures of masculine virility and embodied whiteness.

The shifting contours of U.S. citizenship—of who was, and who was not, entitled to claim full membership in the New Deal nation—are also addressed in this study. New Deal welfare policies expanded citizenship to include not just political rights, but social and economic rights as well; as feminist scholars have shown, each of these domains of citizenship rights is gendered.[18] Administrators' efforts to fashion a workable concept of social citizenship—one that would maximize public support for the New Deal—resulted in an American welfare state that meaningfully transformed the obligations and entitlements binding citizens to the nation-state, simultaneously grafting residual gender, sexual, and racial exclusions onto the emergent concept of U.S. social citizenship.

In addition to expanding the social and economic rights of citizens, the New Deal also revised the concept of citizenship as obligation. Civic obligation has long been unequally distributed in U.S. history; during the Depression and World War II, gendered and racialized concepts of civic obligation animated U.S. civic narratives and social policies.[19] From welfare policymakers who rationalized discriminatory relief provisions on the grounds that men had a greater civic obligation to work than women, to wartime administrators who exacted racially specific forms of civic sacrifice from Japanese American men, the gendered and racialized meanings of citizenship-as-obligation animated civic narratives and social policies of the New Deal state.

In crafting compelling narratives of U.S. civic identity, New Dealers also invoked the republican notion of citizenship as active participation in public affairs.[20] Throughout the Depression and World War II, white heterosexual men were idealized as active participants in well-ordered civic communities, even as actual federal policies belied the image of the small, well-ordered republic with ever-larger scales of domestic and foreign policy administration. The persistence of the civic republican ideal of the white male householder wielding authority over gendered and racialized dependents may seem at odds with the nation-building project of the New Deal state, but it was, in fact, integral to it. Preserving that reassuring gendered and racialized ideal helped Americans adjust to new and potentially unsettling political realities on the national and global stage.

Finally, New Dealers invoked the idea of citizenship as ascribed status.[21] According to the tradition of ascriptive Americanism, Rogers Smith argues, "'true' Americans are 'chosen' by God, history, or nature to possess superior moral and intellectual traits associated with their race, ethnicity, religion, gender, and sexual orientation."[22] Suzanne Mettler notes that ascriptive Americanism is strongest at state and local levels; it thus has great significance for New Deal and wartime civilian agencies, which operated through a complex interplay of federal, state, and local governance.[23] Indeed, New Deal and wartime policymakers buffered the transformative impact of federal social policy by tacitly consenting to, and sometimes actively invoking, the civic inferiority ascribed to white women, nonwhite women and men, and nonfamily individuals at the state and local levels.

Contemplating the civic transformation wrought by New Deal social policy also entails examining how national identities are formed. Kinship metaphors are central to mid-twentieth-century imaginings of U.S. national community.[24] Many Depression and wartime civic narratives imagined the nation in idealized *heterosexual* terms, as a well-ordered male-headed home. But some narratives imagined the nation in idealized *homosocial* terms, as a military fraternity. Tensions *between* homosocial-fraternal and heterosexual-familial models of national community animated many Depression-era and wartime civic narratives, which also had meaningful consequences for the gender, racial, and sexual dimensions of U.S. civic membership.

Imagining the nation as a symbolic kinship has racial implications because idealized kinship structures in the mid-twentieth-century United States were racially endogamous.[25] The forgotten man of the Depression and the mature civilian defender of World War II embodied gendered notions of patriarchal power, but they also embodied whiteness. Similarly, Depression-era CCC youth and virtuous citizen-soldiers embodied racially exclusive ideals of military brotherhood. Thus the centrality of kinship metaphors to New Deal and wartime civic culture diminished the membership claims of many groups: white women and homosexuals certainly, but also African Americans, Mexican Americans, Japanese Americans, and other nonwhite groups.

As witnesses before a committee contemplating Japanese American internment testified in 1942, national identity is also "heartfelt" and entails "an upswelling of emotion."[26] The mobilization of hatred or ill will toward civic outsiders is a crucial means of delineating a common national identity. As Sara Ahmed notes, scapegoating outsiders promotes both negative and positive attachments: "The passion of . . . negative attachments to others is redefined simultaneously as a positive attachment" to those who can claim membership in the privileged social group. Ahmed puts it this way, "*Together we hate, and this hate is what makes us together.*"[27] During the Depression and World War II, gender, racial, and sexual scapegoating were central to the emotionally charged civic narratives by which New Dealers mobilized popular support for their nation-building project.

Although kinship metaphors and scapegoating are crucial resources in imagining the collective body of the nation, so too are individual human bodies, with all of their markings of cultural difference. Thinking about the relationship of individual bodies to the body of the nation is crucial to understanding the affective dimensions of U.S. national citizenship. Several Depression and wartime civic narratives center on the disposition of individual bodies in relation to established hierarchies of gender, sexuality, race, and class. Many center on the deviant bodies of prostitutes, hoboes, juvenile delinquents, and misbehaving wives. During the tumultuous Depression and World War II, civic narratives that focused on sexually deviant outsiders enabled a community of civic insiders to cohere. Such stories also evoked intense, often pleasurable, emotional responses, for as Michel Foucault observes, discourses of sexual deviance "function with a double impetus: pleasure and power."[28]

"Emotions do strange things to facts," J. Prentice Murphy remarked in response to sensational narratives of the Bonus march. "They set them on fire so that they can become more terrible than the sword." Certainly, emotionally charged civic narratives were a potent means by which Roosevelt officials interpreted the "facts" of the Depression and World War II and framed federal policies to combat them. During the Depression, New Deal storytellers sought to counter widespread demoralization and despair by stressing the hopeful effects of federal relief policy. They elaborated a vision of U.S. civic community that centered on affective bonds between local civic leaders, male householders, and relief applicants on the one hand, and between white male authority figures and their feminized and racialized dependents on the other. Similarly, during World War II, civic narratives of "total warfare" idealized white male civilian defenders and the well-ordered civic communities they protected while scapegoating meddlesome civilian women, Japanese American citizens, and youths of other nonwhite groups.

Such stories were not simply instruments by which New Deal officials justified policy. Multiple authorship meant that sensational civic narratives were often out of New Dealers' control. Moreover, stories were not simply means of emotional persuasion; they were materially significant in the shape that federal social policy took. For all of their potential to instill hope in white male householders, the trajectory of New Deal social policy was unfortunate for women, African Americans, Japanese Americans, and other groups who could not claim the social and symbolic privileges of white heterosexual manhood. For such groups, New Deal civic stories really did set the horizon of political possibility in unjust and unfortunate ways.

Chapter 1

The War to Save the Forgotten Man
Gender, Citizenship, and the Politics of Work Relief

In an Albany radio address in the spring of 1932, Franklin Roosevelt introduced the "forgotten man" into the nation's political imagination. In a speech on national economic policy, he proclaimed, "These unhappy times call for the building of plans that . . . put faith once more in the forgotten man at the bottom of the economic pyramid." In describing the forgotten man, he referred to the nation's unemployed, but also to modest farmers, homeowners, and small investors whose buying and saving power was failing due to the "top-down" policies of the Hoover administration. If elected, Roosevelt declared, he would make resolving the troubles of such "forgotten men" a priority. He would rebuild the nation's fortunes "from the bottom up," he claimed, just as an earlier generation of military leaders had done in 1917.[1]

Although initially representing a much broader group of ordinary Americans, the forgotten man quickly became a figure for the Depression unemployed and particularly for jobless white men dependent on relief. After Roosevelt's inauguration in March 1933, his administration touted the federal government's role in recuperating the forgotten man, converting him from a national liability into a harbinger of national recovery. Over the course of the New Deal years, the forgotten man came to represent a combination of old and new American principles: the reassuringly familiar principles of productivity, family providership, and responsible civic membership, and the potentially alarming principle of federal action to protect citizens' social and economic rights. By aligning emergent federal policies with traditional gender and racial ideals, forgotten-man stories worked to alleviate public anxiety about the expansive bureaucratic authority of the New Deal state.

The New Deal narrative of forgotten manhood was by no means static, and it underwent multiple challenges and revisions over the course of the 1930s. Indeed, an indicator of its effectiveness is the extent to which it captured the popular imagination as well as that of the New Deal's conservative opposition. As the principles embedded in the forgotten-man narrative gained acceptance, the narrative itself grew more varied. The forgotten-man story spiraled outward from its official origins, finding its way into opposition rhetoric as well as into advertising, popular literature and film, and the correspondence and conversation of ordinary Americans. Those unofficial variations, in turn, reverberated inward, affecting not only New Deal narratives but the actual relief policies with which those narratives were linked. Examining the evolution and variety of forgotten-man stories thus affords us the opportunity not only to consider the gender and racial implications of federal relief policy from a different perspective but also to examine how a particular, emotionally charged story about collective white masculine identity contributed to the hegemonic power of the New Deal state.[2] How did various contestants for authorship of the forgotten-man narrative use emotionally charged gender and racial imagery to promote "a useful sense of civic identity"? What "preexisting senses of common identity" did they invoke? And how were federal relief policy and concepts of national citizenship and governmental authority correspondingly changed?

In posing these questions, this chapter approaches forgotten-man narratives as an important genre of civic storytelling during the New Deal years.[3] Operating through recurring characters, plot developments, and audience expectations, forgotten-man stories reassured anxious Americans that jobless male householders might be down and out, but they were still privileged members of a virile, white nation imagined in fraternal and familial terms. Such narratives centered on the jobless white man's affective transformation from bitterness and despair to renewed pride and purposefulness as participants in federally sponsored work relief. They also offered affective assurance that the New Deal was a champion of the very political conventions that its expansive bureaucracy seemed most to upset: local civic autonomy and the self-reliant white-male-headed home.

Within the wide-ranging narrative and iconography of forgotten manhood, three interconnected strands are evident: (1) official narratives that appeared in government publications and in the public addresses and writings of New Deal leaders, (2) unofficial narratives that elaborated sympathetically on official New Deal versions, and (3) conservative counternarratives that used the same basic story line to critique the New Deal. Each kind of story influenced the others as well as the policymaking process.[4]

In most civic narratives of forgotten manhood, the protagonist was racialized as white. Yet members of other racial groups also identified with the "forgotten man . . . at the bottom of the economic pyramid" whom Roosevelt had pledged to "remember" in his 1932 campaign. African Americans and Mexican Americans supported and benefited from New Deal programs, but they also endured considerable racism as claimants to New Deal civic membership. As a result, they generated forgotten-man narratives that reflected their own, racially specific experiences of New Deal relief. Considering their stories, along with more prevalent white narratives, illuminates the gender and racial inequities embedded in the stories themselves and in relief policies and concepts of social citizenship that those stories helped to mediate.

The institutional history of federal emergency relief is also intertwined with the broader narrative of forgotten manhood. More than just a context for the other narratives, it stands as another story of forgotten manhood— one that interacted with the others in fascinating ways. What distinguishes the institutional history from the other stories is that its actors include many men and women for whom the vagaries of the Depression and relief were all too real. As clients within a changing system of federal relief, they all had pressing material needs, but not all could conform to the shifting civic ideals embedded in white forgotten-man narratives and in relief policies that emerged in dialogue with them. The contested narrative of forgotten manhood was particularly consequential for them.

➤ Popular Narratives

Introduced in April 1932, Roosevelt's campaign version of forgotten manhood quickly began to generate alternative narratives. When the Hoover administration forcibly dispersed Bonus veterans in July 1932, commentators labeled the retreating marchers "forgotten men." When private citizens sent letters to newspapers and public officials, they often signed themselves "The Forgotten Man." In the year 1933 alone, several books were published under the titles "Forgotten Man" and "Forgotten Men," to say nothing of articles, opinion pieces, short stories, and verse.[5] The frequency of forgotten-man references prompted one magazine editor to wonder whether the "forgotten man," like other "phrases and expressions [that] suddenly become popular," would be "overworked and pass away almost as rapidly as [it] sprang into being."[6] Far from passing away quickly, "the forgotten man" remained phenomenally popular throughout the New Deal years. And although it continued to apply to many different groups, its primary referent quickly became jobless white men struggling to provide for their families.

"Who was this Forgotten Man of Mr. Roosevelt's?," Julian Aronson, a writer for *Scholastic* magazine, asked in February 1934. He continued, "He was the man who had no job and was told to rely on charity for relief...."[7] Having been forgotten "in the great blizzard of prosperity that blinded us all to the insane nature of our catch-as-catch-can system," the forgotten man was not responsible for his unemployment, but was rather a victim of forces beyond his control. He was also a householder with family dependents. Aronson continued, "Anybody who had seen... the sheriff confront him with a warrant for non-payment of rent, his children go to school unfed, could now identify with the Forgotten Man."

Without explicitly naming the forgotten man, sociologist Pauline Young also narrated his composite experience in 1933. Through no fault of their own, she suggested, men who lost their livelihoods in the Depression had been "uprooted from the soil that previously sustained them." As a result, many "became despondent to the breaking point." They lost "the sense of their personal worth" and faced "a breach in family relationships." As Young described him, the forgotten man was not only economically but emotionally destitute: "not only a worker without a job, [he was]... a citizen without courage, a husband without the moral support of his wife, a father without control over his children."[8] His joblessness spelled disaster not only for his family's finances but for a whole range of American values and institutions that depended on the emotional hardihood of the white male breadwinner ideal.[9]

Fictional narratives of forgotten manhood also abounded. In "Fred Salo—Forgotten Man," Tom Jones Parry describes a white forgotten man who leads a modest yet comfortable life until he falls victim to the economic crisis. Unemployed through no fault of his own, Fred Salo initially meets misfortune with optimism, claiming, "I'll find something... I've never been idle long in my life, you bet."[10] Yet gradually, as his efforts to find work meet with disappointment, he grows demoralized and disaffected. Parry writes, "Fred listlessly walked the streets. He made few calls now, and sometimes whole days would pass without him mustering up courage for one interview." His family situation deteriorates, leaving Fred "ashamed to go home."[11] He spends more and more time associating with other jobless men at the headquarters of the Unemployed League, whose subversive views he gradually adopts. Salo's desperation and increasingly radical views only alleviate when his former employer invites him back to work. No longer idle but pleasantly exhausted after his first day back on the job, Salo is effectively restored to productive breadwinning manhood. Domestic harmony is restored as his wife recovers her role tending to his domestic needs. Salo's renewed optimism suggested the necessary means to national recovery: hard, productive labor for America's white male breadwinners to keep them from idleness and the demoralization and subversive fraternization that idleness fosters.

The poet Nels Francis Nordstrom similarly depicted the plight of "forgotten" steelworkers. "There are men everywhere. Strange—different. / Their faces are clean, pale, lost." He likened them to rusting machinery, forced to "serve . . . days of waiting." Idle by day, such men were troublesome by night, having no outlet except "the poolrooms, the gang."[12] Like Parry's story, Nordstrom's poem raises the specter of improper fraternization that results from jobless men's demoralization. "There are men everywhere," Nordstrom comments; women and the stabilizing influence of family ties are absent from the bleak picture he paints.

Other writers likewise depicted the forgotten man as a potentially subversive, homosocial figure who increasingly gravitated to the fraternal "army of the unemployed" in preference to his destitute and unhappy home. "Uprooted from the social soil which previously sustained them, they lose their sense of balance," Pauline Young observed. One man who described himself as "28 years old with a wife and child to support," informed the editor of the *New York Times* that he was "frantic" for work. "I must have a position before I literally go to pieces," he declared, signing his letter "The Forgotten Man." People who "went to pieces" behaved in unpredictable ways. "An undercurrent of resentment, disaffection, and threats [is becoming] more prevalent," one social worker observed. He added, "Fears are expressed that a mounting unrest may begin to assume more violent forms of expression."[13] Prior to the advent of New Deal relief, the individual "forgotten man" was often linked with the aggregate "army of the unemployed," which posed a threat to American political and social institutions.

✒ Federal Relief

Just as unofficial narratives emphasized the white forgotten man's joblessness and demoralization in the months following the 1932 campaign, New Deal insiders focused their rhetoric of forgotten manhood more squarely on the unemployed in 1933. In his March 21 message to Congress titled "Three Essentials for Unemployment Relief," Roosevelt embellished his campaign vision of forgotten manhood. "The overwhelming majority of unemployed Americans, who are now walking the streets and receiving private or public relief, would infinitely prefer to work," he declared. Through a combination of federal grants of aid to the states, emergency conservation work, and federal public works, Roosevelt pledged to "eliminate to some extent at least the threat that enforced idleness brings to spiritual and moral stability."[14]

Assisting the forgotten man to recover emotional and economic equilibrium became a crucial rationale for the Federal Emergency Relief Administration (FERA), established in May 1933. Directed by Harry Hopkins, the FERA was a massive undertaking that brought the federal government directly into the lives of millions of ordinary citizens. Not only individuals, but state and local governments and private welfare agencies were compelled to yield, at least to some extent, to the strong hand of the New Deal administration under the new relief agency. Of course, the FERA was a limited beginning based on the premise that the economic emergency was temporary and joblessness would soon abate. Nevertheless, the agency shifted the balance of power between federal, state, and local civic authorities and challenged the masculine civic ideal of self-reliance by offering jobless Americans a federal helping hand.

The FERA began a fundamental transformation of American relief practices. It began its work at a time when state and local relief agencies had been overtaxed and the infusion of federal funds explicitly for the purpose of emergency relief transformed the relief picture. It imposed a national structure on the administration of general relief, helping to set up state-level relief offices for the first time in forty of the forty-eight states. Prior to the FERA, old-style poor relief—punitive, inadequate, and discriminatory—was the norm in many communities. In it place, FERA imposed professional social work standards in exchange for federal funding. As much as possible, agency administrators tried to enforce employment of trained social workers at every level of public relief administration. Welfare historian William Brock notes that its professional formula for relief giving was remarkably successful. Using its power as a funding agency to encourage compliance, the FERA created a new, federal blueprint for relief administration.[15]

Although states and localities complied with some facets of the new relief program, many balked at distributing relief equitably across racial lines. In the South and Southwest, where a majority of African Americans and Mexican Americans lived, state and local relief committees, composed entirely of whites, reserved the lion's share of federal relief funds for white applicants, even though nonwhite applicants suffered disproportionately from Depression unemployment.[16] African American community leaders wrote to administrators in Washington requesting that blacks be appointed to state and local relief committees because white administrators so thoroughly disregarded their relief needs. In letters to the President and Mrs. Roosevelt, many African Americans described how white relief administrators subjected them to cruel and humiliating treatment. Forrester B. Washington, formerly the president of the all-black Atlanta School of Social Work, was appointed to represent African American interests in the FERA in the winter of 1934. It was his job to read the letters of suffering and humiliation that African American relief applicants sent to Washington. Citing those letters as a factor in his decision, Washington resigned his FERA post after only six months because he felt ineffective in advocating for African American relief needs.[17] Unwilling to alienate powerful Southern Democrats, federal administrators in Washington often turned a blind eye to FERA racial discrimination.[18] Their tacit consent to discriminatory relief practices lends credence to the notion that the forgotten man was a white figure and not a racially inclusive one.

Despite full knowledge of FERA racial discrimination, Hopkins and other New Deal officials cast the FERA as a central example of the New Deal's commitment to "human rather than material values." Invoking Roosevelt's pledge to remember the forgotten man, they touted the agency's support, not for the salvaging of "railroads, banks, and insurance companies alone" but also "for the salvaging of human beings."[19] Agencies such as FERA, Harold Ickes asserted, were making "this country a better place to live in for the average man and woman."[20] The aid the FERA provided was temporary, intended to tide jobless citizens over until New Deal recovery measures had improved the nation's economic outlook. The FERA was always emphatically an *emergency* agency, one that made it the responsibility of the federal government to see that Americans' temporary subsistence needs were met.

Even though New Deal officials promoted the FERA as a nation-saving enterprise—one that extended a lifeline to "the average man and woman"—the agency was controversial, in part because it overturned widely accepted methods of relief giving and interfered with state and local autonomy. The FERA's practice of granting funds only to public agencies alienated many in the private welfare establishment. Its insistence on professional social work standards displaced many relief workers who lacked the necessary professional training. Federal guidelines challenging racial discrimination engendered conflict, particularly in the Southern states. Over the course of its tenure, the FERA also became much more than a simple mechanism for reviewing grants of aid to the states. FERA branches and departments proliferated, separate programs such as the Federal Transient Program were established, and administrative costs soared. Finally, its methods of relief giving, particularly direct relief, became increasingly unpopular. That unpopularity was sometimes expressed through references to forgotten manhood. As sociologist E. Wight Bakke observed, direct relief reduced "the chief breadwinner . . . from . . . being a worker and a provider to [being] . . . a messenger boy to and from the relief office."[21] While "make work" projects such as leaf-raking or ditch-digging allowed relief clients to "earn" their allotments, even such "working" clients generally received grocery orders rather than cash wages, which detracted from their authority as family providers.

Critics of the FERA claimed that its policies compromised masculine authority in the home. Under the FERA, every individual who applied for federal unemployment relief was subject to casework methodology as a precondition for receiving benefits. Applicants—always figured as male—first underwent a "means test," usually administered by a female social worker, which many applicants found degrading. Routine practices such as home visits by social workers and careful monitoring of grocery orders caused considerable resentment. These policies came to be known derisively as "pantry-snooping," and the female social worker who nosed her way into the homes of unemployed men became the object of considerable hostility.[22] Such practices were objectionable because they undermined the conventional distribution of power and authority in the home. Not only was the federal government meddling in the affairs of private households; its proxy in that meddling was a woman who repudiated women's traditional domestic role to pursue paid work as a social worker at a time when many men were jobless.[23] As relief specialists Marie Dresden Lane and Francis Steegmuller observed, "Under the FERA the income of millions of American families was being distributed not as they wished, but as tens of thousands of social workers thought best. . . . [I]t was the social workers who ran the households." They concluded that "the system was not one which fitted easily into the frame of the American tradition."[24]

Federal administrators rapidly capitulated to the view that direct relief was out of keeping with gendered American principles of work and self-reliance. As FERA administrator Hopkins himself would later explain, "I came to believe more and more that we should not undertake to care for unemployed persons by means of the dole or grocery order while the heads of families remained at home in idleness. It was an extremely demoralizing thing."[25] Echoing popular narratives of forgotten manhood, he contended that prolonged dependency on the part of family breadwinners encouraged "an unwholesome attitude toward the Nation and the States" and was creating "a dependent class in America."[26] Roosevelt agreed. Reiterating sentiments expressed by Hoover, he stated, "The dole method of relief for unemployment is not only repugnant to all sound principles of social economics, but is contrary to every principle of American citizenship and sound government."[27] The answer, he asserted, was not federal nonintervention, but federal sponsorship of masculine work relief.

✒ Changing the Official Story

Hopkins responded to criticism of emergency relief by intervening in the evolving narrative of forgotten manhood. In an October 1933 radio address, he drew on popular elements of the forgotten-man story. The typical relief applicant was not a pauper, he stated, but rather an upstanding American man who had exhausted all other resources and found it emotionally difficult to approach the relief office: "He had come to relief reluctantly . . . in stages, first losing his job, then using up his savings, then cashing in his insurance policies. The landlords had stopped extending the rent, the grocers had cut off his credit, friends and relatives had become unable to support his family. Despair pressed in. His children became hungry, then very hungry. One night he and his wife talked it over and decided to apply for relief. But two blocks from the relief office he turned back. In the end, though, he had no choice."[28]

Thus noting the forgotten man's emotional distress, Hopkins concluded, "Relief practices should not further humiliate people like this." Such people "knew how to work, how to handle money. They needed jobs and cash wages to spend." Hopkins intended his brief portrayal of the forgotten man to pave the way for a major shift in relief policy. In the fall of 1933, he and other top New Deal administrators also began imagining alternatives to FERA-style relief. Their first new departure in federal emergency relief was the Civil Works Administration (CWA), which began operation in November 1933 and continued through the early months of 1934. A short-lived experiment in federal public works, CWA used funding from the Public Works Administration along with FERA administrative resources to provide morale-building public employment to 400,000 unemployed Americans, almost all of them white male citizens.[29]

Reflecting New Deal sensitivity to criticisms of FERA, CWA eliminated the means test as a precondition for relief. As Hopkins explained to a group of CWA administrators, "We have got, at one stroke, to divorce ourselves from . . . an inquiring point of view . . . and think in terms of affirmative action, in terms of real jobs for real people."[30] In addition to eliminating the means test and the stereotypically female relief investigator who administered it, the CWA drew only half of its workers from the relief rolls, while the other half was drawn from the nonrelief population. CWA projects were concentrated in the construction field—a field that largely excluded women and nonwhite men. Highly visible and characterized by physically arduous work, such projects provided tangible evidence of the government's commitment to regenerating white forgotten manhood. According to New Deal officials, CWA projects also demonstrated the white forgotten man's virtuous nature and his contributions to the national welfare.[31] "Long after the workers of CWA are dead and gone," Hopkins wrote, "their effort will be remembered by permanent useful works in every county of every state. People will ride over bridges they made, travel on their highways, attend schools they built, navigate waterways they improved, do their public business in courthouses and state capitols which workers from CWA rescued from despair."[32]

Other Roosevelt officials were equally quick to tout the CWA's dramatic national benefits. Significantly, their claims hinged as much on the program's emotional and spiritual benefits as on its material accomplishments. Harold Ickes declared, "The effect of this bold stroke on the morale of the country has been marvelous." Thanks to the CWA, he added, "we are coming through the winter of 1933–34 as a people in the best physical and spiritual condition since the crash that brought us to our knees in 1929."[33] Hopkins commented that the CWA "let loose great forces, both economic and spiritual."[34]

As a symbol of national unity, the CWA was distinctly gendered. Suggesting the masculine contours of the agency, Hopkins characterized the unemployed who were eligible for CWA employment as "citizens and the sons and grandsons of citizens."[35] Given the agency's emphasis on construction projects, women had few choices for CWA employment. Projects that had targeted unemployed women under FERA, such as sewing rooms, were relegated to the separate and lesser-paid Civil Works Service (CWS) after the advent of CWA.[36]

African Americans and Mexican Americans also derived little benefit from the CWA. If federal oversight of FERA had been flawed, allowing state and local relief bureaus to discriminate against people of color, CWA oversight was even more so. Intended for quick and dramatic implementation, the agency privileged speed over accountability in the execution of projects. African Americans and Mexican Americans who had been disadvantaged as applicants for direct relief were even likelier to be excluded from CWA's more generous, masculinizing benefits. Like white women, nearly all nonwhite women and men were relegated to the obscure and considerably less remunerative CWS.[37]

New Deal administrators cast the CWA as a harbinger of national recovery and a political antidote to criticisms of FERA-style direct relief. The white, masculine CWA worker who built bridges, highways, and schools was anything but a domestic errand-boy "to and from the relief office." Indeed, his affect was altogether different: according to New Deal officials, he was a proud and purposeful participant in a common national enterprise. Like the indispensable and hardworking "forgotten men" whom Roosevelt had invoked in his campaign rhetoric, CWA workers also embodied a positive and productive vision of military fraternity. In improving the nation's public roads, buildings, and waterways, they acted as vigorous and determined foot soldiers in the New Deal war on the Depression.

Yet as Hopkins acknowledged, the CWA was a short-lived agency. In the spring of 1934, it succumbed to charges of graft and political corruption and to its own spiraling administrative costs. New Deal administrators were also frustrated that the public continued to confuse CWA with straightforward relief.[38] The division of CWA workers into relief and nonrelief categories also had unintended negative consequences. When informed that the nonrelief quota for CWA employment was filled on a given project, some workers applied for relief in order to qualify for project employment as relief clients. Thus CWA actually increased applications for relief, despite official claims that it was effective as a national recovery measure. Reports of CWA graft and political corruption, many of them justified, fueled allegations that the Roosevelt administration was building a vast political machine on the backs of the forgotten men. Public concerns that CWA had unhealthy political consequences were increased when, in the face of project closures in the early months of 1934, many CWA workers joined massive protests in an effort to keep the agency going.[39] In the wake of such protests, images of massive CWA demonstrations competed with other images in the contested construction of forgotten manhood. From the perspective of some political traditionalists, needs consciousness was spiraling out of control as the forgotten man's appetite for government handouts exceeded even the unprecedented generosity of the New Deal administration.[40]

☛ Mid-Decade Popular Narratives

Such changing perceptions of relief are reflected in popular narratives of white forgotten manhood that emerged in the mid-1930s. Without explicitly naming FERA or the Roosevelt administration, such narratives criticized federal emergency relief for its destructive impact on U.S. civic culture. The failings of the federal relief administration were dramatized as a struggle between jobless white breadwinners and the treacherous women who made their lives more miserable. Narrative closure occurred when the hero either triumphed over bad women in positions of authority, or in counternarratives of forgotten manhood, became thoroughly feminized by relief.

"Bill Meade: Brass-Tag Man: A Story of Emergency Relief" is one such story. Written by Elizabeth Frazer, it appeared in the widely circulated *Saturday Evening Post* in March 1934.[41] Like other fictional forgotten men, Bill Meade, a white jobless breadwinner, is initially too proud to apply for relief. Yet he is ultimately driven to it by a sense of family obligation. Once on relief, he continues his search for work, including work relief, but his morale gradually worsens. Reflecting a broader cultural hostility toward female relief investigators, Bill Meade deeply resents the social worker who intrudes on his domestic privacy. When she walks into his apartment uninvited, he regards her with hostility: "It was clear that he resented this unceremonious intrusion upon his privacy. His irate glance said plainly, 'What the hell do you mean butting into my home this way?'" Of this exchange, the narrator comments, "I liked his resentment. After all, it was his home, and despite the poverty, it had a clean, easy, intimate air."[42]

While Bill maintains a dignified reticence, his wife Mabel is more forthcoming with the family's story. As in other white forgotten-man narratives, it is she who pushes Bill to overcome his scruples and apply for relief: "It was hard for Bill to apply for relief; it shamed and humiliated him. But he had arrived at the end of his financial rope, and Mabel finally persuaded him." Over the course of the narrative, relief becomes a point of contention in Bill's relationship with his wife, and he begins spending more time in the fraternal company of other jobless men. More so than Bill himself, the jobless men with whom he associates are thoroughly demoralized and unmanned by prolonged relief dependency: "Their initiative and sense of responsibility had slackened; slowly but surely they were becoming pauperized." When Bill tells another relief client that he prefers work over direct relief, the other man is dumbfounded. Demonstrating a stereotypically feminine disregard for the public good, he responds, "The way I look at it, the country owes us guys a living. Think of all the good jobs we lost. And we didn't make this here depression."[43]

Bill is more resilient, and he eventually obtains work on a municipal relief project. His relief assignment boosts his morale and brings him into contact with other self-respecting men, but it is not long before maladministration brings the project to a close. The project closure further demoralizes Bill, as does Mabel's nagging. In a desperate state, he attends a radical meeting, only to find that the orator's heavy accent and un-American ideas deeply offend him. Bill assaults the speaker because, "Like most native American workmen, he entertained a hearty contempt for aliens."[44] The incident helps him to regain his common sense, and soon thereafter, he obtains a job on a private work-relief project. Bill's initiative and self-respect receive a boost from his new job, and he finds supplemental work as a craftsman. In the course of that work, Bill puts a miserly female client in her place. Bill tells the narrator, "Women . . . always drove harder bargains than men; they haggled, jewed you down or tried to vamp you so you'd work for nothing." When Bill insists that the miserly client pay him a fair price, she nearly "burst a blood vessel, she got so foaming mad; but in the end she paid."[45]

Although the private work bureau goes out of business and Bill is once again receiving direct relief at the end of the narrative, he has demonstrated emotional resilience in the face of previous setbacks, and his personal outlook is hopeful. The outlook for other jobless men whom Bill encountered in the course of his relief journey might be less hopeful, the narrative implies, unless federal relief funds are rechanneled into "the creation of useful, paid employment." In terms that invoke a distinctly masculine model of collective civic identity, Frazer moralizes, "To maintain the self-respect of the unemployed individual, to set him back to working for himself as soon as possible with a pay envelope so that he can provide for himself and his family and become a normal citizen again—that I conceive to be the main function of all emergency relief." She adds, "We don't want this country being turned into a national almshouse. . . . What we want is a nation of free men, using their own private initiative and drive to take care of themselves and their families."[46]

Overall, Frazer's story of Bill Meade was an object lesson in the virtues of work and the destructive impact of direct relief on the emotional fiber of upstanding white American manhood. In that sense, the narrative touched on ideas that were deeply embedded in Depression-era public discourse. Other forgotten-man stories similarly emphasized the importance of work to curbing the forgotten man's restless energy, restoring his self-respect, and returning him to proper political and familial relations.[47]

Yet if Bill Meade's story and others like it dramatized the importance of work to the forgotten man's morale, it also presented a picture of the proper gender and racial ordering of society. In the narrative, masculine citizenship is defined by breadwinning and the proper exercise of domestic authority. As Bill Meade's story shows us, such characteristics were difficult to maintain when social workers meddled in domestic affairs and determined the budgetary needs of the family. Bill's hostile response to the intruding social worker is an important moment in the narrative. His continued reticence about his family life is an assertion of his rightful claim to domestic privacy. Mabel's role in the narrative, particularly her willingness to compromise that same domestic privacy and her nagging disposition, are consistent with the general characterization of wives as contributors to jobless white men's demoralization in the Depression. Another significant moment is Bill's victory over the miserly woman for whom he builds some cabinetry. That incident affords Bill the opportunity to restate a common generalization: that women were "hagglers" and "vamps" who would "jew you down . . . so you'd work for nothing."

Frazer's narrative is also none too favorable in its depiction of aliens. At a time when many Americans scapegoated aliens for the shortage of jobs and the high cost of relief, Bill assaults a "flannel-mouthed foreigner" intent on "injecting Red microbes" into his vulnerable system. Bill Meade's regeneration thus depends not only on his access to productive employment, but also on scapegoating women and aliens as a means of reasserting his white masculine prerogatives.

"Bill Meade: Brass Tag Man" dramatized many concerns about emergency relief that were growing in the spring of 1934. Frazer's negative characterization of female relief investigators was shared by many others, including a number of prominent social work professionals. *The Survey* columnist Gertrude Springer lamented the arrogance and insensitivity of inexperienced female caseworkers, and Hopkins himself invented the derogatory term "pantry-snoopers" to refer to such women.[48] Frazer's depiction of collective white male demoralization was also reflected elsewhere. The pauperized men who surround Bill Meade, standing in breadlines and loitering in lunch rooms, were pervasive figures in popular accounts of the Depression. In Frazer's narrative, Bill Meade might have joined their ranks except that a combination of personal initiative, occasional work opportunities, and hostile encounters with women and aliens helped him to maintain a healthier, more "American" perspective.

Frazer's narrative appeared in the spring of 1934 at a time when the CWA was being demobilized, and the public was becoming weary of "emergency" rhetoric and was beginning to contemplate the problem of "permanent unemployment." The abrupt end of the CWA had been jarring to many, including CWA workers, some of whom mobilized in protest against project closures. Images of mass demonstrations by CWA workers, along with press reports detailing CWA graft and corruption, were fodder for the New Deal's critics.[49] The messy conversion from CWA back to FERA led to allegations of New Deal inefficiency and lack of long-range planning. By virtue of their own declared preference for work relief, New Deal officials found it difficult to justify the return to FERA-style relief in the spring of 1934. Instead, they emphasized the continuation of CWA-style work activities under the FERA's newly created Emergency Work Program. They also promised the creation of a new, improved public works program to replace FERA in the near future.

✒ Counternarratives

Charges of CWA graft, corruption, and federal mismanagement shaped conservative counternarratives of forgotten manhood. So too did pervasive reports of mass demonstrations by CWA workers. The widely held belief that direct relief demoralized and pauperized the unemployed, which New Dealers reinforced when they abandoned FERA in favor of CWA in the fall of 1933, also influenced the shape of conservative forgotten-man counternarratives. In contrast to official representations that emphasized individual forgotten men's restoration to productive citizenship through work relief, counternarratives accentuated the creation of a federal relief "machine" that generated votes for New Deal politicians while increasing the "needs consciousness" of an ever-more disruptive relief population. In conservative counternarratives of forgotten manhood, prolonged relief dependency had devastating consequences for the American way of life, turning a significant proportion of the nation's most vital political members—its self-reliant white male breadwinners—into effeminate, relief-dependent paupers. The federal government, formerly a distant entity that respected local civic autonomy, had become an overly indulgent national "parent" whose commands were carried out by an army of vindictive female "pantry-snoopers."

Yet for all of its differences from more positive versions of the forgotten-man story, such negative tales of pauperization and emasculation were clearly in dialogue with them. Both positive and negative stories of forgotten manhood conflated gender and politics and placed the white-male-headed household at the center of American political life. Both also accorded affective power to white male citizens, although they sought to avert negative emotional outcomes such as alienation, demoralization, and despair. Yet counternarratives of forgotten manhood differed from positive versions in their critique of a growing federal bureaucracy and its negative consequences for the white-male-headed home. By placing the family and local community even more squarely at the center of U.S. civic culture and by dramatizing the emasculating effects of federally administered relief, conservative critics of the New Deal shifted the terms of national political debate and influenced the shape of subsequent official rhetoric and practice.

An exemplary counternarrative is Priscilla Wayne's "Does the World Owe John Doe a Living?" which appeared in the *Saturday Evening Post* in May 1935. Wayne's narrative centers on an unemployed white workman named Harold Marsh. Prior to the Depression, Marsh had been an adequate worker and family provider, but Wayne is quick to point out that he was *only* average and that he had failed to save for the future. Like other fictional forgotten men, he had been reluctant to apply for relief, only doing so when his wife implored him. At first, Marsh has difficulty accepting direct relief, and his pride prevents him from talking about his family's predicament. Fairly rapidly, however, he grows more accepting of his relief status, and then he becomes demanding. When asked if he is employed on a work-relief project, Marsh declares, "Not me. Go down there and work in that river bed muck? I should say not." He explains to his caseworker, "the Government's pouring out money by the millions. Wouldn't I be a fool not to take my share of it?"[50]

As this exchange suggests, Harold Marsh is pauperized by FERA-style relief. In the story, Marsh loses all sense of civic responsibility and becomes politically passive. Significantly, as he deteriorates politically, he also becomes effeminate. Over the course of the narrative, he ceases to be a proud tradesman and breadwinner and is thoroughly domesticated. He stays home, takes to wearing an apron, and becomes petty and demanding in his encounters with relief officials. Entirely gone from Marsh's persona is any sense of the larger civic good. In fact, he is the antithesis of the official forgotten man: selfish rather than self-sacrificing, weak-willed rather than resolute in his desire for reemployment, dependent rather than self-reliant, mercurial rather than steady and authoritative. In all, he stands opposed to the ideal of white masculine citizenship in the Depression.

Wayne's story was part of a broader challenge to federal emergency relief in the mid-1930s. According to critics of New Deal relief, Marsh's deterioration was shared by others whose chronic neediness made them unwitting participants in the New Deal's efforts to "remake, regiment, collectivise the country, and bring centralization triumphant to Washington."[51] The vast majority of unemployed Americans, most of whom had been self-reliant and politically independent prior to the New Deal, were becoming cogs in "a vast Democratic political machine."[52] By pouring billions of dollars into relief, the federal government was creating an effeminate, dependent class whose members could no longer afford to be free-thinking because they relied on the largesse of the Roosevelt administration.

Although the fictional forgotten man was usually white, African Americans and Mexican Americans sometimes appeared as paupers in narratives critical of New Deal relief. Particularly in the South, but also in Northern cities where whites customarily paid below-subsistence wages for African American labor, some writers depicted black workers who were "ruined" by the beneficence of the New Deal administration. In such narratives, relief dependency pauperized African American women and men, making them lazy and disrespectful and prompting them to refuse private employment as agricultural and domestic laborers in preference to staying on relief.[53] In the Southwest, Mexican Americans were similarly cast as "chiselers" who preferred relief to their usual low-waged occupations. Anti-Mexican allegations were distinguished by the racist, nativist assumption that all needy Mexican Americans were undeserving aliens who should be repatriated to Mexico. Regarding African Americans and Mexican Americans in Texas, FERA field investigator Lorena Hickok commented, "An awful lot of the trouble here . . . seems to be that Mexican and Negro farm labor won't work for the prevailing wages if they can get on relief. And they've come to town to get relief."[54]

Called "chiselers" and "loafers" for refusing exploitative wages and working conditions, such African American and Mexican American relief clients joined Harold Marsh and other white paupers in conservative counternarratives of forgotten manhood. In all such stories, the expansive New Deal state imperiled U.S. civic culture by dislodging particular social groups from their traditional civic roles: white men from their roles as authoritative and self-reliant male householders, and African American and Mexican American men and women from their roles as humble subjects of white male power.

Lieutenant General Robert Lee Bullard created a stir in 1935 when, after a "nationwide survey of the relief situation," he asserted that "we have recognized in this country a new 'inalienable right'—the right of an individual to indefinite support at public expense and regardless of private employment available." He continued, "It indicates a breakdown in the primary characteristics of the American citizen—initiative, independence, self-reliance." Bullard asserted that 75 percent of those on relief were content to stay there.[55] That relief recipients "lived the life of Reilly at government expense" was a common refrain in the mid-1930s. Yet in spite of the New Deal's ill-advised largesse, the relief population was anything but grateful. "We are not increasing content," Margaret Culkin Banning commented. "On the contrary, we seem to be increasing discontent." She added, "It will soon be too much for everybody, even the Government, if these organized bands of unemployed begin to dictate methods and amounts of relief, and if politicians listen."[56]

As these comments suggest, critics of the New Deal cast the relief situation as a fundamental threat to America's most cherished political traditions, including the white masculine civic ideals of "initiative, independence, self-reliance." They also criticized federal relief for tampering with the authority of the states and local communities. As Banning explained, "A community ought to decide—because a community is apt to know—which of its members should get free potatoes and coal, and which members have the right to become pensioners on the others."[57] Federally administered relief undermined the forgotten man's accountability to his neighbors, forcing him to trade masculine civic respectability for effeminate dependency on a paternalistic federal government.

WPA Storytelling

Faced with allegations that relief dependency was damaging national morale and emasculating its breadwinners, New Deal administrators next devised a massive system of federal work relief: the Works Progress Administration (WPA). In response to charges that FERA and CWA represented the overreaching grasp of federal authority, the WPA distributed a greater share of power and responsibility to the states and localities.[58] State and local sponsors would be required to assume more of the material and financial costs of WPA projects. New Deal officials were also eager to share the *symbolic* costs of relief administration. They expressed frustration that the federal government was taking the blame for administrative irregularities for which, in their view, states and localities shared much of the responsibility.

The transition from FERA to WPA was gradual and confusing. New Deal relief administrators began outlining a new, work-based program of federal relief as early as March 1934 in the midst of CWA demobilization. Yet actual congressional approval of the WPA did not occur until May 1935, and the new agency was not fully operational until early 1936. At that time, the FERA ceased operation and the Roosevelt administration fulfilled its pledge to "quit this business of relief." In what one welfare historian has termed "a deliberate decision to resurrect local responsibility" and lay claim to "traditional values," New Deal officials returned the problem of general relief to the states.[59] Its program, officials stated, would concentrate exclusively on providing work to three million able-bodied breadwinners, thereby restoring their self-respect, domestic authority, and active role in the civic life of their communities.[60]

From the outset, Roosevelt officials touted WPA as a genuinely *American* alternative to relief. Whereas the FERA had essentially been a dole, administrators acknowledged, the WPA would offer real wages in exchange for work accomplished. In accordance with WPA sponsorship stipulations, states and localities would initiate and help to administer the projects to be undertaken. They would also resume responsibility for general relief. Noting that the federal government had never intended to assume responsibility for "unemployable" Americans who had always depended on public aid, Roosevelt officials rededicated themselves to helping only those "employable" Americans whose joblessness resulted from national economic conditions. Eligibility for WPA was also restricted to able-bodied breadwinners. By means of this restriction, administrators argued, the agency would assist a maximum number of American families to resume "living as Americans should."[61]

In creating the WPA, New Deal officials also sought to reclaim authorship of public representations of relief, which had suffered massively in the hands of administration critics. From the outset, WPA included a large public relations staff. Hopkins held frequent press conferences, and press releases accompanied each new shift in WPA administration.[62] In addition to their other work, artists employed on WPA graphically depicted the agency's success in rebuilding white American manhood. The resulting visual works accentuated the pride and purposefulness of the recuperated forgotten man. In addition, the WPA Office of Information issued pamphlets explaining the agency's work and responding to public criticisms. During the 1936 election year, top WPA officials toured the nation's political circuit giving pro-WPA speeches and generally touting the human accomplishments of the New Deal.

In all of its official releases, the Roosevelt administration emphasized WPA's Americanism, its commitment to sharing power with states and localities, and its benefits for the male-headed home. In this way, New Deal officials laid claim to political values that critics of federal relief had used so often. They also intervened in the conservative counternarrative of pauperized forgotten manhood. In his announcement that the federal government would "end this business of relief," Roosevelt acknowledged that direct relief had induced "a spiritual and moral disintegration fundamentally destructive to the national fiber." He admitted that "the vitality of our people . . . [had been] sapped by the giving of cash, of market baskets, of a few hours of weekly work cutting grass." While such practices had been "in violation of the traditions of America," Roosevelt maintained, federal work relief would revitalize America's forgotten men. It would preserve their "self-respect, their self-reliance and courage and determination."[63]

FIGURE 1. Work Projects Administration Poster created by the Federal Art Project, New York, between 1936 and 1941. Prints and Photographs Division, Library of Congress.

Similarly, in a 1936 campaign address, WPA assistant administrator Ellen Woodward stated that "the philosophy of the work program is based upon an appreciation of the true character of the American people." Americans were self-reliant and productive by nature, she argued. "Our country . . . was settled by builders and workers," she stated. "Are we to deny the quality and character of this country and its people?"[64] In a speech titled, "What is the American Way?," Hopkins also emphasized the WPA's role in preserving American traditions. "The American people," Hopkins stated, "have declared themselves in favor of a work program and will not go back to the socially unproductive and individually demoralizing principle of the dole." America's greatness derived from the rights and opportunities it granted its citizens, including "the right to earn an honorable living." In a statement suggesting that men's right to honorable livelihoods was more at stake than women's, Hopkins declared, "Here the rights a man might enjoy, the heights he might scale, [are] not limited by his family tree but by his own individual liberty."[65]

Hopkins also intervened in the narrative of pauperized forgotten manhood. In a December 1934 radio address, he characterized the able-bodied unemployed as more eager than any other group to see an end to direct relief. "The unemployed themselves want work," he stated. "We do not have to tell them that not having a job spoils a man for work. They go soft, they lose skill, they lose work habits. But they know it before you and I know it and it is their lives that are being wrecked, not ours." Hopkins declared that the nation could not afford "a continued situation through which its citizens lose their sense of independence and strength and their sense of individual destiny." A federal works program was necessary, he maintained, because "It preserves a man's morale. It saves his skill. It gives him a chance to do something socially useful."[66] Thus jobless men, and not the unemployed of both sexes, were at the center of Hopkins's relief agenda. Also at its center was the emotional recuperation of the forgotten man: his transformation from shame and despair to optimism and self-respect as a result of federal work relief.

New Deal officials' effort to rewrite the narrative of forgotten manhood is also evident in Hopkins's *Spending to Save*, significantly subtitled "The *Complete* Story of Relief" (emphasis added). At a time when Hopkins believed that the WPA was coming to represent the New Deal, his book-length account of federal relief policy was an effort to claim authorship of "the story of relief" from the New Deal's detractors. *Spending to Save* tells the story of federal relief policy from the final years of the Hoover administration to 1936. It is a celebratory narrative of increasingly effective federal policy culminating in the WPA.

The typical WPA worker, Hopkins stated, was "a white man, thirty-eight years of age and the head of a household." He was also a skilled or semi-skilled worker who found his place easily on the WPA's construction program. Hopkins stated that "the bulk of the WPA program has been a construction program." WPA workers built farm-to-market roads; built or repaired water and sewer systems, schools, and other public buildings; and installed or repaired electrical utilities. According to Hopkins, such projects elicited strong pride from "workers, public officials, and citizens alike."[67] Throughout the history of the WPA, New Deal officials emphasized the

WPA's construction projects over other kinds of work relief. Highly visible, tangibly productive, and affirming of project workers' masculinity, construction projects dominated the rhetoric and iconography of federal work relief. In contrast, white-collar and women's projects, including the service projects on which African American women and men predominated, received relatively little publicity.

Hopkins was careful to note that when family circumstances "compelled" women to apply for WPA work, they entered a program that had "been built around their traditional skills." He commented, "Thousands of women [have been taught] to make clothes, to can and to cook with knowledge of food values."[68] When publicists did address the work of the Women's Division, they focused on traditional women's projects such as housekeeping aides, handicrafts, and the hot school lunch program. Publicists paid considerably less attention to the sewing rooms, which were the mainstay of women's work relief.

Hopkins concluded his discussion of WPA by reiterating the nation's commitment to preserving the skill and regenerating the civic spirit of the unemployed worker. He stated, "Our work must be done for the worker by the worker. He is the first figure. He must be the first and last digit in all government accounting." Emphasizing the unemployed worker's potential value to the nation, he also commented, "The regeneration of the individual worker no longer needs to be the only concern of a national work program for the unemployed. We have come to a second concept, which is that his work is necessary to enrich the national life."[69] According to Hopkins, the forgotten man, restored to productivity on the WPA, was a national asset and a distinct contributor to national recovery. He contributed directly to the nation through useful public work, particularly through the construction of roads, buildings, and other public works.

Yet at the same time, Hopkins was quick to point out the WPA worker's contributions to his family and local community. Far from being a cog in a vast federal machine, the WPA worker was a breadwinner and participant in local community affairs. His restored breadwinning power brought him renewed respect and authority in the home. The work he performed was locally sponsored, and it was the local community that could best determine its lasting value. Thus Hopkins aligned WPA not only with masculine self-reliance, but with the related principles of local community governance and the male-headed home.[70]

Published in 1936 as a handbook for WPA workers, *Our Job with the WPA* can be read as another official narrative of forgotten manhood.[71] Like *Spending to Save*, the pamphlet accentuates many of the election-year talking points of the New Deal administration. In a section on frequently asked questions, the handbook informs the reader that WPA work is not the same as relief, and that eligibility for WPA employment is generally restricted to "the head of the family." In response to the question "Does the Federal Government select the projects on which we work?" the handbook states, "No. Practically a hundred percent of the work projects are selected, planned, and supervised by the local community where they are being done." The pamphlet thus aligned the WPA with localism and the male-headed home.[72]

Our Job with the WPA was also a conventional story of forgotten manhood restored to productive citizenship through the WPA. In text and image, it characterized the typical WPA worker as an able-bodied breadwinner whose joblessness was the result of national economic conditions. The slow pace of business recovery, technological unemployment, and competition from "young men and women just out of school" all contributed to his economic plight. Such conditions were beyond the jobless individual's control, but they were not beyond the control of the federal government. "What can Uncle Sam do?," the pamphlet asks. In terms that accentuate the masculinity of the typical WPA worker, it answers,

Let us starve—Not in this man's country
Give us a dole—But who wants a handout?
Let us work—Which is every man's right.

In its visual response to the question, the pamphlet presents two contrasting types of forgotten manhood. One is a slope-shouldered figure whose grocery basket marks him as an applicant for direct relief. The other is a square-shouldered worker who wields the implements of his trade. The pamphlet goes on to tell the story of the slope-shouldered relief applicant. "When we are on the dole . . . we lose our self-respect; we loaf on street corners; we lose our skill; we have family rows; finally we lose hope."[73] An image of jobless men gathered by a street lamp appears just above a scene of domestic conflict. In terms that recall earlier stories of forgotten manhood, all images accentuate the emasculation and emotional deterioration of the unemployed worker forced to accept direct relief.

The pamphlet then goes on to depict the regenerative power of WPA employment. Although professional workers appear alongside skilled and semi-skilled tradesmen, all three groups have been restored to masculine potency as a result of their WPA employment. The only female figure to appear in the section on WPA work is an actress who shrinks behind her male counterpart. As with other official accounts of WPA, the pamphlet emphasizes the national benefits of the WPA's construction program: "The country will

34   CHAPTER 1

What happens to us when we are on the dole

WE LOSE OUR SELF RESPECT

WE LOAF ON STREET CORNERS

WE LOSE OUR SKILL

FINALLY WE LOSE HOPE

WE HAVE FAMILY ROWS

Now let's look at what work does for us

FIGURE 2.   U.S. Works Progress Administration, *Our Job with the WPA* (Washington, DC: U.S. Government Printing Office, 1936), 26.

be richer if we build: roads, schools, airports, sewer systems, water systems, parks, playgrounds, public buildings." In a section on WPA accomplishments, the pamphlet again stresses the physical accomplishments of WPA's predominantly white male construction workers.

Our Job with the WPA is presented in a colloquial, question-and-answer format. With many pictures to accompany the simple text, the handbook was designed to be accessible even to marginally literate WPA workers. It informed them about basic WPA employment policies, but it also established their place in the nation-building politics of the New Deal. Reflecting the publicity consciousness of federal administrators, the pamphlet prepared workers for possible public criticism of their WPA work project. If they faced allegations that their project represented the overextended reach of the federal government, they were to know that it had been locally selected and sponsored by a local public agency. If they felt their WPA work was valuable, they were exhorted to declare their views publicly. The pamphlet stated, "If your union or your group wants to hold a celebration when the project is finished, ask your supervisor and he will arrange it, and invite other citizens to come and see it." It added, "You have added wealth to your community that no depression can take away."[74]

Most curiously of all, in *Our Job with the WPA*, workers were told their own story, and it was a conventionalized story of forgotten manhood. Whatever their actual past might have been, their symbolic past included the demoralization, family breakdown, and alienation from masculine civic conventions that characterized the forgotten man's response to unemployment and direct relief. Whatever their current situation, their symbolic situation was one of masculine revitalization as productive WPA workers. Thus *Our Job with the WPA* reflects the ways in which actual jobless Americans came to serve as a symbolic resource in the nation-building politics of the New Deal.

In WPA publicity, the official story of forgotten manhood adopted counternarrative conventions such as support for localism and the male-headed home. A story that was originally about America's "economic infantry" and the bold new experiment undertaken by the nation's peacetime generalship had evolved, by the later years of the Depression, into a very different tale about the restoration of white jobless men to their rightful place as family breadwinners and active participants in local civic life. By shifting the focus to the civic revitalization of America's forgotten breadwinners, New Dealers more effectively masked their own claims to national power as a defense of the traditional "American way of life." The new narrative of forgotten manhood was mirrored in relief policy that privileged white men over other social groups, particularly white women, people of color, and aliens who sought a share of WPA relief. It was also mirrored in a practice that William Leuchtenberg calls "cooperative federalism," wherein federal relief administrators shared power with states and localities, often with discriminatory results.[75] Federal relief officials often bemoaned the inegalitarianism of local sponsorship and certification boards. Yet they deliberately ceded authority to local administrative units as part of their broader strategy to create a uniquely American system of relief. The affective capacity of a local civic leader to instill feelings of guilt and accountability in relief applicants, like the capacity of a male breadwinner to command respect from his dependents, furnished the basis for civic community as it was imagined in official versions of the forgotten-man story after 1935. Reflecting the importance of narrative to federal policymaking in the Depression, those same civic ideals significantly informed eligibility criteria for WPA relief.

☙ "Unemployables" and WPA

The shift to WPA was not simply a positive affirmation of the nation's able-bodied unemployed. It was also negative, as Roosevelt repudiated the nation's involvement in "this business of relief." In announcing the change, Roosevelt did more than cast aspersions on direct relief. He also cast aspersions on a whole category of unemployed Americans—those whom he defined as *not* ordinarily self-reliant and courageous and determined.

Indeed, the viability of the WPA depended on a politics of exclusion. Even as Roosevelt announced his commitment to providing work for the nation's "able-bodied but destitute workers," he proposed returning the care of one-and-a-half-million "unemployables" to local relief. If the "employables" were "the victim[s] of a nation-wide depression caused by conditions which were . . . national," then the "unemployables" were jobless for reasons that were personal or local.[76] Hopkins stated that "the purpose of the Works Progress Administration is . . . not . . . to provide work for everybody."[77] He characterized the newly defined unemployable group as "old people, widows, persons who were breadwinners but are now in T.B. institutions, insane asylums, the crippled, and the handicapped."[78] Mothers with dependent children, some domestic servants, and many agricultural workers were also generally classified with the "unemployable" group. Taken together, administrators contended, the unemployables represented a cross section of the "chronic relief" population. As such, they possessed no legitimate claim on the nation's beneficence in time of crisis. Their presence compromised the integrity and purpose of New Deal relief, which was intended as "a temporary bridge to self-support" for the able-bodied unemployed—the forgotten men—who were the *true* victims of nationwide depression.

Many private and local relief administrators questioned the logic behind this "rough and ready classification of employables and unemployables by WPA." As one relief worker commented, "No one knows now just where employability begins or ends, either in WPA or direct relief rolls." Another lamented that "categories . . . seem to be crystallizing as our accepted system of public assistance." Indicating that many social workers opposed this trend, he asked, "Why should family men be given preference" over other needy groups, such as "widows with children" and "single men and single women"?[79] African American community leaders also objected that blacks were disproportionately categorized as "unemployable" in the transition to WPA. In the South, the plight of black "unemployables" was particularly dire because, without federal support, they had very little access to relief.[80]

From the perspective of the New Deal leadership, categories were vital in order to secure claims about the self-reliance and virtue of the unemployed breadwinner. Ambivalence about failed breadwinning meant that the image of the forgotten man restored to productivity on the WPA could not stand on his own; he had to be defined *against* emotionally charged counter-images of the dependent and undeserving unemployed. Effectively, jobless Americans who came to be lumped together as "unemployables"—older women and mothers of dependent children, nonwhite domestic and agricultural workers, people with disabilities—came to symbolize the inadequacies of earlier relief programs. Their exclusion from WPA served to deflect allegations of chronic dependency from federal relief administrators' preferred clients: white, able-bodied "forgotten men."

Central among those excluded in the shift to WPA were large numbers of unemployed women. From the outset of the Depression, women had faced discrimination in the job market, in legislation, and in federal unemployment relief. Women counted for only a quarter of the Depression workforce, yet they represented a third of the unemployed. Until its repeal in 1937, Section 213 of the 1932 National Economy Act prohibited women's civil service employment if their husbands also held government jobs.[81] In many localities, female teachers and other public employees were routinely dismissed following marriage throughout the 1930s. While the FERA did not categorically exclude married women from benefits, women comprised only eight percent of FERA recipients from 1933 to 1935. The Women's Division of FERA had been poorly integrated into the broader relief framework and was closely tied to traditional poor relief.[82]

Despite discrimination against female relief applicants prior to the WPA, administrators for the new agency resolved to further tighten gender restrictions. A shortcoming of the CWA, WPA administrators contended, was that it had sometimes granted relief to unemployed wives who were not heads of households. In contrast, the WPA stipulated that only one person per family would be eligible for work relief, ideally the male breadwinner. According to Donald S. Howard, when reviewing the relief applications of needy women, WPA officials were careful to determine whether they were "indeed economic heads of their families, genuinely employable and eligible in other respects" before granting benefits. In general, WPA officials sought "to avoid substituting the wife for the husband" in making work-relief assignments. Howard notes that relief officials who denied relief to needy women were motivated by a punitive desire "to put some break upon women's eagerness to be the family breadwinner, wage recipient, and controller of the family pocketbook."[83]

Administrators also sought to discourage single mothers with dependent children from seeking WPA benefits. Under the Social Security Act of 1935, single mothers were eligible for a new kind of federally mandated direct relief—one that emphasized their emotional ties to the home. At local and national levels, many WPA administrators believed that single mothers "should . . . be cut off WPA" even when it meant taking "a social security benefit at a much lesser amount."[84]

Even women who were ineligible for social security benefits and did not have able-bodied husbands or fathers to support them had difficulty obtaining WPA relief. Relief boards were quicker to grant the "employability" and breadwinner status of relief applicants if they were male than if they were female. Women who were single and lacked dependents were particularly hard-pressed under WPA eligibility requirements. In 1937, settlement house worker Mary Simkhovitch complained that single women without dependents were "just discards."[85] Her sentiment was echoed by many single, needy women. In a letter to Eleanor Roosevelt, Pearl Lindner of Buffalo, New York wrote, "Thinking you may use your influence . . . to bring about better conditions for unfortunate people who have no home or dependents, but are willing to work." Lindner explained that she was "a former employee of the Buffalo Knitting and Sewing Project," but was thrown off when eligibility requirements were restricted to family heads. As a result of her removal from work relief, she was receiving "welfare aid" but she complained that "to me [it] is slow death, I dislike it so. I can barely eat the food after I get it."[86]

More often categorized as "unemployable," needy women like Lindner were forced to rely on the sparse resources of local and private relief. Although WPA administrators contended that local and private charity seriously undermined the morale of unemployed men, they apparently harbored no such fears concerning unemployed women. The plight of women such as Lindner prompted another of Eleanor Roosevelt's correspondents to ask, "Why should everything be done for the men, everywhere, and . . . so very little done for the girls and women?"[87]

African Americans and Mexican Americans were also subject to more frequent classification as "unemployables." Even though the executive order establishing the WPA upheld the principle of nondiscrimination, the agency was far from race neutral in practice. The system of cooperative federalism that disadvantaged needy women by subjecting their relief claims to the approbation of state and local relief officials similarly disadvantaged people of color, particularly African Americans in the rural and small-town South. African Americans who applied for WPA relief confronted discriminatory eligibility criteria, unofficial quotas, and significant delays in receiving project assignments. Wage discrimination was also commonplace. A study of WPA wages in Atlanta, for example, found that average monthly relief checks to blacks totaled $19.29, whereas whites received an average of $32.66 per month.[88]

The WPA's commitment to state and local civic autonomy also adversely affected African American relief clients. Clark Forman, who analyzed the racial aspects of federal relief policy for the Roosevelt administration, noted that "the greater the area of government, the less it will be influenced by local prejudices." Although blacks received "their fairest treatment from the Federal government," Forman noted, state and local WPA officials routinely discriminated against them.[89] Southern segregationists rationalized discriminatory relief practices in affective terms, stressing whites' intimate knowledge of and friendly regard for African American neighbors and servants. Just as one forgotten-man counternarrator commented that "a community ought to decide—because a community is apt to know—which of its members should . . . have a right to become pensioners on the others," Southern racists argued that their long-standing personal connections with blacks qualified them to determine African Americans' real relief needs.[90] "The Negroes . . . have no better friends than the white people among whom they live and who will not willingly see them done an injustice," one segregationist wrote.[91] Southern whites defended wage differentials in New Deal programs on the basis of their friendly feelings for blacks, who they argued would be disadvantaged by a policy of equal pay for equal work. As one white newspaper editorialized, "Unless [wage] differentials are granted, the Negro is certain to suffer, because many would lose employment if a common minimum wage for both white and Negro labor was enforced."[92] As in relationships between men and women, the affective ties between whites and African Americans were hardly benevolent, even when whites cast them in friendly terms. Too often, those relations were overtly malevolent, as when Southern whites forced African American relief clients under threat of arrest or violence to accept seasonal employment at exploitative wages. African Americans' unwillingness to leave relief rolls to work for less money than their relief allotments led to a number of racial incidents. Some Southern counties went as far as to jail African American relief workers who refused white farmers' offers of employment. Expressing the sentiment that federal relief had "spoiled" black residents and compromised their affective ties with whites, one white farmer lamented, "This relief work has got the men so sorry you can't get them to do a thing."[93] Yet African Americans generally complied with racially discriminatory practices out of fear for their lives. As one African American in Birmingham, Alabama, explained, "We would tell about these things but we are scared to; these white folks would come to our house at night and mob us and kill us."⁹⁴

While Southern whites were administering relief in ways calculated to preserve white economic power, the WPA's Division of Social Research in Washington was preparing a report that attributed African Americans' economic travails not to racism but to their own compromised family structures. Published in 1938, *The Negro on Relief* asserts African Americans' compromised relationship to the civic ideal of the cohesive and orderly male-headed home. In explaining why African Americans were more chronically unemployed than whites, the research team stated, "An examination of the family and personal characteristics of the Negroes on the [relief] rolls . . . reveals some striking differences with those of whites." The report continued, "The hardships of the Negroes which cause them to become relief recipients arise, in part, from their family and marital difficulties. The normal family, with father, mother, and children living together, is more typical of whites than Negroes. The broken family, with its psychological and economic handicaps, is more general among Negroes. Of all Negro cases on relief it was found that 18% were made up of broken families, as compared with only 12% for whites."⁹⁵

Thus long before Senator Patrick Moynihan published *The Negro Family: The Case for National Action* in 1965, U.S. government officials were pathologizing African American families in order to rationalize the racially discriminatory aspects of federal social policy. In characterizing black families and particularly black men as pathologically weak, New Deal officials ignored racist employment and relief practices and deflected like allegations of weakness and dependency away from the families of white forgotten men.

❧ "No Forgotten Races"?

A week before the 1936 presidential election, Roosevelt declared to an African American audience, "As far as it was humanly possible, the government has followed the policy that among American citizens there should be no forgotten men and no forgotten races."⁹⁶ Roosevelt's claim that his administration did everything "humanly possible" to combat racial discrimination is easily disputed, but his African American supporters were willing to overlook the New Deal's imperfections and endorsed his candidacy in the press. The *Atlanta Daily World* declared, "Roosevelt not only promised to help the 'forgotten man,' but he has done so in a very big way. So much until our group has been helped the country over, 'and we were the most forgotten of the forgotten men.'"[97]

How well African Americans fared as New Deal relief clients depended considerably on where they lived. African Americans living in Northern states with high concentrations of African Americans such as New York, Ohio, and Illinois fared better than their counterparts in Georgia, Mississippi, Florida, and other Southern states. For some African Americans in the North, federal relief projects gave them opportunities to work alongside whites, receive equal pay, and occasionally be appointed to white-collar or supervisory positions. Although such opportunities were exceptional in the North, they were virtually unheard of in the Jim Crow South, where state and local relief officials worked hard to implement federal relief in ways that reinforced, rather than subverted, existing racial and gender hierarchies.

African American leaders knew very well that the administration of federal emergency relief, whether in the form of FERA, CWA, or WPA, was highly discriminatory against African Americans and other people of color. Yet at the same time, they seized on the principle of federal power that was embedded in New Deal relief policy. In his support for Roosevelt's reelection campaign, Kelly Miller, dean emeritus of Howard University, stated that the African American "has been the chief beneficiary of Federal power over the provincial restrictions of states' rights."[98] For African Americans in the South who could not vote, serve on juries, or otherwise exercise the rights and responsibilities of political citizenship, New Deal policies introduced the notion of federally sponsored social citizenship. In opposition to state and local traditions, the Baltimore *Afro-American* editorialized, the New Deal "brought the 44-hour week to thousands of workers for the first time in their lives, old-age pensions, unemployment insurance, cheap heat, light, and power, low-cost housing, and a WPA job or relief" to needy millions, including African Americans.[99] Historian Anthony Badger observes that while race discrimination was pervasive in the relief administration in the South, African Americans were still "grateful to Roosevelt because what they did receive from the New Deal was vastly greater than any assistance they . . . were likely to receive from white state and local governments."[100]

Just as Roosevelt proclaimed that "there should be no forgotten men and no forgotten races," New Deal publicists championed a racially specific version of the forgotten man directed at black audiences. Such writers touted the masculinizing effects of relief work for black men who could now, thanks to the New Deal, lay claim to the ideal of the virile worker-hero. "The Negro has been and is being enabled by the Works Progress Administration to

FIGURE 3. Alfred Edgar Smith, "Negro Project Workers, 1936," Report of Activities of Alfred Edgar Smith for February 1–28, April 1–30, and May 1–30, 1937. Records of the WPA, General Files, File 102, 1936–37, R.G. 69, National Archives.

hold up his head in the self-respect that emanates from earning daily bread by doing a useful task," a government pamphlet intended for black audiences proclaimed.[101] In a promotional article titled "What WPA Means to the Negro Worker in New York State," James A. Ross wrote, "You will find members of our group building roads with pick and shovel, deepening, repairing and assisting in building sewers, laying out streets, doing painting, carpentry work, bricklaying, and all kinds of skilled and unskilled labor in places where a member would not think of asking for employment before."[102]

The kinds of physically arduous tasks that Ross describes not only resulted in admirable civic improvements, but also in a muscular African American physique. The cover of Alfred E. Smith's 1936 Annual Report features a manly black worker with muscular forearms exposed.

Although the male figure on the cover of *Negro Project Workers* shares commonalities with images of white forgotten manhood in New Deal promotional literature, the nature of his task as an industrial worker meant something different in the black community. On the one hand, African Americans celebrated the opportunity to subvert the racialized occupational hierarchy that had long excluded blacks from many private industrial jobs. On the other hand, African Americans recognized that the ideal depicted on the cover of Smith's report differed profoundly from most black WPA workers' reality. In reality, occupational discrimination in private industry too often carried over to WPA jobs, especially when all-white local relief boards determined project assignments.

Also, although Smith's pamphlet shares certain conventions with other WPA publicity, its production values are lower. The image of the African American man is crudely reproduced, and Smith's name, institutional affiliation, and the date are handwritten in block letters on the pamphlet's cover. If the pamphlet had been intended for general circulation, these features would have been typeset.

Even so, male African-American writers embraced the masculine conventions of the forgotten-man story presented in Smith's report. Victor Cools, a black social worker, described how one WPA worker "with a family of five" thanked him "for having given him an opportunity to work for an honest living." According to Cools, the worker added, "Now I can look my children straight in the eyes. I've regained my self-respect. Relief is all right to keep one from starving but, well—it takes something from you. Sitting around and waiting for your case worker to bring you a check, and the kids in the house find that you contribute nothing toward their support, very soon they begin to lose respect for you. It's different now. I'm the breadwinner of the house and everybody respects me."[103]

Cools adds, "This is a very simple story. It is typical of what one hears every day from WPA workers." But promotional materials notwithstanding, it was not typical for African American project workers. According to a relief census of October 1933, a majority of African Americans on relief under the age of forty-five were women. Thus a more accurate narrative of African American relief might have featured a "forgotten woman" rather than a "forgotten man."[104] Black journalists and civil rights leaders, most of whom were men, were less hostile to women's wage-earning than their white male counterparts, but they still downplayed black women's breadwinning status. They also sought to protect the femininity of black womanhood by protesting the Southern practice of placing black women on outdoor manual labor projects rather than assigning them to stereotypically feminine indoor work.

Overall, the male-dominated African-American press touted the benefits of the WPA and urged that the program be continued indefinitely. As one paper editorialized, "The government must be urged to continue the colored citizens in WPA jobs until the bulk of private industry has recognized their ability, laid down its racial antipathy, and is prepared to accept Negro workers on the basis of ability alone and five them the positions for which they have fitted themselves."[105]

At the end of the decade, even as many whites left WPA for jobs in war-stimulated private industries, blacks continued to struggle to obtain private employment and became an increasing proportion of the relief population. As this happened, Congress curtailed the WPA more and more, against the protests of African American leaders. Thinking about African Americans' paradoxical relationship to WPA—an agency at once so enabling and so discriminatory—thus illuminates the complexity of U.S. race relations, and of federal, state, and local power sharing, in the New Deal era.

If one version of African American forgotten manhood mirrored the conventional white forgotten-man story, depicting the jobless black breadwinner restored to paternal authority and civic respectability on federal work relief, another version was racially specific. Centered on lynching and on the everyday practices of racial intimidation and violence that infused local relief administrations, that other story also illuminates how gender and race shaped the nation-building project of the New Deal state.

In the spring of 1935, the *Chicago Defender* addressed a public missive to "the Honorable Franklin Delano Roosevelt" regarding the forgotten man. It read: "The forgotten man appeals asking that you use your great influence to save him from the lynchers' rope." It continued, "This man, Mr. President, is the real forgotten man, who has for the past fifty years been a victim of the same beastly influences which precipitated the Civil War. He lives in the South, Mr. President, a section of this nation which has not as yet come into the Union."[106]

The *Chicago Defender*, along with other black newspapers, lamented that "lynching goes steadily on" under the New Deal administration, and it urged Roosevelt to throw his support behind Costigan-Wagner antilynching bill.[107] Indeed, lynchings had climbed since 1930 and spiked in 1933 during the New Deal's first year. A federal antilynching law was absolutely vital, civil rights leaders argued, because "lynching, the most heinous crime in America today, will not be stopped by the state governments." If the federal government could extend its reach in the field of social welfare to save the forgotten man, then why could it not also use its power to "blot out the shame of America"?[108]

Lynching and federal relief policy may seem unconnected, but they were closely intertwined. Certainly, Southern white civic authorities saw them as connected. Referring to the New Deal as a "second Reconstruction," Southern white officials resisted federal efforts to curtail state and local prerogatives in matters of racial violence and in the disposition of relief. Senator Josiah Bailey of North Carolina declared that the Costigian-Wagner antilynching bill was "not for the purpose of preventing lynching, but for the purpose of introducing the policy of Federal interference in local affairs." In defiance both of federal relief policy and of efforts to enact an antilynching law, conservatives in Congress pledged to maintain "state rights, home rule, and local self-government" and to administer unemployment relief "with maximum local responsibility."[109] They relied on the everyday threat of racial violence, fortified by the periodic terror of lynching, to ensure black compliance with discriminatory relief practices. Jobless African Americans in the South certainly experienced continuity between discriminatory relief policies enforced by threat of violence and the pervasive fear of the lynch mob.

Top officials in the New Deal relief administration also must have seen the overlapping implications of unequal federal relief administration and the practice of lynching. In both cases, federal administrators made strategic decisions about when and how to enforce federal power or to respect state and local sovereignty. In the case of relief, as the transition from FERA to CWA to WPA reveals, New Deal administrators increasingly pursued a policy of cooperative federalism, sharing power and responsibility with states and localities even as they forged an ever more expansive federal relief bureaucracy.[110] In the process, they also invited states to enforce local ascriptivist traditions. In the case of antilynching legislation, Roosevelt similarly chose to respect state and local sovereignty, with highly discriminatory results. In calculating the interests of the federal government, Roosevelt saw only disadvantages in recognizing lynching as a federal crime, which would have alienated Southern Democrats and confirmed their suspicions, already heightened by federal relief policy, that the New Deal administration wanted to overturn long-standing civic traditions and install a hostile centralized government in Washington.

Contemplating the lynch victim as a forgotten man also enriches our thinking about the affective dimensions of federal power in the New Deal years. Conventional white forgotten-man narratives, which afforded audiences the pleasure of seeing jobless white men restored to authority on New Deal relief, carried one kind of affective charge. Stories of black forgotten men,

CHAPTER 1

allowed to die horrible deaths in part because New Deal officials refused to back federal antilynching legislation, carried quite another. In the latter case, as David Garland and Amy Louise Wood observe, lynchings were affectively dense, multisensory rituals that enforced community cohesion at the expense of a much-reviled black victim and against the forces of outside federal authority. Garland notes that lynchings occupied the extreme end of a continuum of everyday gender and racial violence.[111] On this point, federal relief policy, typically narrated in stories of white-men-as-jobless-breadwinners, meets the problem of federal antilynching legislation, narrated in stories of black-men-as-lynch-victims. Federal relief policy explicitly ceded certain prerogatives, including the prerogative to enforce gender and racial differences, to the states; in the South, that power-sharing arrangement entailed the federal government's tacit consent to violently enforced discriminatory relief practices. Those practices were effective, in part, because of the pervasive fear of lynching. Moreover, federal relief policy worked to shore up the power and authority of white male householders; as Trudier Harris has argued, lynching did the same.[112] Needless to say, Roosevelt did not endorse federal antilynching legislation, nor did New Deal relief administrators meaningfully enforce equal claims to federal social citizenship for all social groups.

On July 19, 1935, Rubin Stacy was lynched for "threatening and frightening a white woman" in Fort Lauderdale, Florida. Stacy was a homeless African American tenant farmer, thirty-three years old, who had approached the house of Marion Jones, a thirty-year-old white housewife, probably to request food or drink. Stacy was one of tens of thousands of black tenant farmers who had been displaced from their homes and livelihoods in the thirties when the Agricultural Adjustment Administration (AAA) made it more lucrative for white landowners to leave ground fallow than to plant crops. In the city of Fort Lauderdale, federal emergency relief had never been fairly distributed. The *Pittsburgh Courier* published excerpts of a letter written by an African American Fort Lauderdale resident in December 1933. Addressed to Harry Hopkins, the letter complained that blacks were being deprived of public work and relief. The man described to Hopkins how local police had used "rifle and pistol" to force "hundreds of Negroes . . . to work for a white farmer." He stated that those who complained to federal officials were put in jail.[113]

Rubin Stacy might indeed be considered a kind of forgotten man—in the parlance of the race leaders, as "the most forgotten of all forgotten men." Had the AAA not favored white landowners over black tenant farmers, Stacy might have benefited from its provisions. Had formal sources of unemployment relief been available to Stacy in Fort Lauderdale, he might not have sought assistance from the private home of Marion Jones. Had local relief administrators not discriminated against men like Stacy on the grounds of race, he might have found work on a relief project. Perhaps, had a federal antilynching law been established, Stacy might have received due process for the crime of seeking food and frightening a white woman. But none of these conditions pertained, either for Stacy or for countless other African Americans who lived in the Depression-era South. White Southern politicians defended lynching and racially discriminatory relief practices on the shared grounds of states' rights. In its commitment to wedding the federal relief policy to traditional gender and racial ideals, the New Deal administration tacitly consented to lynching and to the "more routine racial controls" that lynching reinforced.

New Deal relief policy sought to meet an overwhelming public need and stood at the forefront of Roosevelt's recovery program. Americans on relief and others who sympathized with their plight voted overwhelmingly for Roosevelt in 1936 and again in 1940. Images of forgotten manhood, so closely tied to federal relief policy in the beginning, were harnessed to a variety of causes as the Depression wore on, including the marketing of consumer products. Even the New Deal's most vocal critics were forced to concede late in the decade that "the country had been irrevocably committed to the essentials of the social program of the New Deal."[114] In 1940, Wendell Willkie, the Republican candidate for president, declared, "We believe in federal relief. . . . Our Administration, if we are elected, will continue and will reinforce federal relief so long as any man in America is without a job."[115]

Yet in spite of its dramatic impact on American political life (and in some senses *because* of it), the New Deal relief administration was also perpetually on the defensive. New Deal relief challenged many civic conventions, including the interrelated principles of masculine self-reliance, limited government, and local civic autonomy. Almost all Americans were familiar with the federal relief setup and most had opinions about it. As Robert Staughton Lynd and Helen Merrell Lynd found in their study of Middletown, those opinions were by no means uniformly favorable. According to the Lynds, most businessmen and professionals in Middle America were distinctly hostile to federal relief and to the jobless Americans who received it. Conservative critics regarded relief as an imposition on the American taxpayer and a threat to the American way of life.[116] In response to positive depictions of forgotten manhood, they produced sensationalized counternarratives that stressed the negative gender and political consequences of a massive relief bureaucracy and a growing relief population.

New Deal leaders were extremely responsive to criticisms of the relief administration. Counternarratives that accentuated the New Deal's disruption of traditional gender, racial, and political roles often led to shifts in federal relief policy. In addition, certain counternarrative conventions were incorporated into the official relief story. From the beginning, counternarratives of relief detailed the emasculating effects of direct relief. That detail also became conventional in official versions of the story well before it was reflected in actual relief policy. Authors of forgotten-man counternarratives also took the lead in placing the white-male-headed home and close-knit civic community squarely at the center of the American way of life. Their stories detailed the devastation that ensued when New Deal officials replaced traditional family- and community-based authority structures with a paternalistic central government. Represented as an assault on the integrity of the white American home, the critique of New Deal–style centralized government proved irresistible to federal relief officials. Their response was to craft narratives and policies that emphasized local autonomy in relief matters and that invested considerable emotional value in the white-male-headed home.

As a narrative device, the valorization of the traditional white-male-headed home solved several problems for New Deal relief administrators. It enabled them to lay claim to a larger set of civic ideals that together composed a compelling vision of the American way of life. Rogers Smith and Suzanne Mettler note that the civic ideal of the male-headed home is part of a broader ascriptivist tradition that also places value in local community governance and in white men's direct participation in the civic life of their communities.[117] Forgotten-man narratives that valorized the male-headed home also typically endorsed the related ascriptivist ideals of class, ethnic, and racial hierarchy.

Because of its traditional association with other civic ideals, most notably localism, the ideal of the male-headed home was an effective means of combating one of the New Deal's stickiest political problems: repeated allegations that the New Deal was building a dangerous centralized bureaucracy on the backs of relief-dependent citizens while undermining constituted authority at the state and local levels. In the rhetorical and practical shift to WPA at mid-decade, New Deal administrators were able to represent what was actually an expansive federal policy as a return to localism and related civic ideals. In the process, they restored white male breadwinners to civic and familial respectability at the expense of women, African Americans, Mexican Americans, and others. As the next chapter reveals, among those others were transients, who figured in a different, emotionally charged civic narrative in the Depression: the narrative of intergenerational transient perversion.

☙ CHAPTER 2

"Uncle Sam's Wayside Inns"
Transient Narratives and the Sexual Politics of the Emergent Welfare State

An elderly African American transient graces the cover of the October 19, 1935, edition of the *Saturday Evening Post*. A road sign for U.S. Route 1 in New York State suggests his journey southward. The hobo's complacent demeanor and the migratory birds at his sides imply that he does not seek permanent settlement elsewhere, but is rather engaged in a cycle of continuous migration.[1] An ornate signature occupies a bottom corner of the image, informing *Post* readers that this arresting image is the work of J. C. Leyendecker, a long-time *Post* illustrator who was well known for his attractive—some would say homoerotic—portrayals of youthful white manhood.[2] The transient in this illustration is neither white, nor young, nor conventionally attractive. Old, black, and visibly impoverished, yet seemingly unperturbed by those conditions, he might not connote homosexuality at all except for the migratory ducks—both male—that balance the composition.

Removed from its 1930s context, the illustration's allusion to transient homosexuality might still go unnoticed. But to *Post* readers in 1935, both the sexual threat that inveterate transients posed and the rhetorical conventions by which that threat was expressed were readily discernible.[3]

That Leyendecker chose to depict his transient as African American is also noteworthy. If transients in general were theatening, African American transients were all the more so, given the long racist tradition of casting African

FIGURE 4. J. C. Leyendecker, "Southbound Hitchhiker," *Saturday Evening Post*, October 19, 1935. *Southbound Hitchhiker* illustration ©SEPS licensed by Curtis Licensing Indianapolis, IN. All rights reserved.

American men as sexual predators. That Leyendecker's African American transient was journeying from New York—the cradle of New Deal relief—toward the more traditional, segregated South is also significant. It implied the New Deal's disruption of regional and local traditions and conflated the sexual threat of the black transient with the political threat posed by the expansive New Deal state.

Published in 1935, Leyendecker's cover image was indeed intended as a racialized and sexualized critique of New Deal relief policy. Yet transiency had been a politically sensational topic since before Roosevelt came to office. Early in the 1930s, sensational reports had dramatized the growth of "an army of boys on the loose."[4] As one newspaper columnist put it in the summer of 1932, such boys, usually figured as white, were "swiftly becoming idle, shiftless, and dishonest. Appeal is made to organizations to help keep all boys at home and to undertake to save those who are on the move from becoming hardened hoboes."[5] In September of that year, the *New York Times* lamented that "a great army of young hoboes" was being "driven into gangs and cities of their own where, through panhandling and petty thievery, they eke out their existence."[6] Although such a state of affairs was alarming in itself, far greater alarm attended the alleged sexual encounters that took place between such "impressionable youth" and an older generation of seasoned tramps. As one sociologist alleged, "The older wanderer entices children away from home and teaches them to beg and steal. Homosexual practices are more common than not in this group."[7]

Throughout the Depression years, sensational accounts of transient "perversions"—particularly those involving the seduction of impressionable white youth by older, inveterate hoboes—pervaded American culture, infusing popular culture and political rhetoric and delimiting the sexual, racial, class, and generational contours of citizenship in the emergent welfare state.

One thing narratives of transient sex were *not* is an accurate depiction of lived experience in the Depression. Particularly florid in the early 1930s, such stories vastly overstated both the number of youthful wanderers *and* the extent of sexual intercourse between boys and men on the road.[8] Yet neither were such stories mere empty sensationalism intended to boost audiences or sagging circulations. Generated during a period of tremendous social and political uncertainty, such narratives deployed the familiar figure of the hobo—a figure that, Barbara Meil Hobson reminds us, had long been recognized as "the ultimate figure of male deviancy" in America—to contemplate the Depression's impact on institutions and concepts at the center of American civic life.[9]

Moreover, the popular discourse surrounding transiency, particularly in the early 1930s, had all the markings of a moral panic, and more specifically, a sex panic. At a time when Americans feared the social and sexual consequences of the Depression, contributors to the transient-perversion narrative helped to constitute a national public by focusing collective hostility on the "chronic" or "recidivistic" hobo who imperiled "wandering youth." In the language of moral panic theory, the chronic hobo was a compelling "folk devil" whose deviant and dangerous sexual behavior in transient-perversion narratives evoked collective feelings of sexual fear and repulsion. Those feelings, in turn, helped to naturalize conjugal heterosexuality as "normal" and the alternative sexual practices of "unattached" transients as threatening and disgusting, and thus urgently in need of state regulation.[10]

Moral panics, and particularly those that center on perceived sexual dangers, afford rich opportunities to contemplate the affective dimensions of national public life. As a sex panic, the perceived transient crisis of the early Depression drew on intense feelings, including fear and disgust, but also pleasure and titillation. Evoking such feelings collectively and discursively through repeated stories of intergenerational homosexual seduction, transient-perversion narratives helped to bring a national public into being.[11] For a time, transient-perversion narratives mobilized support for state intervention to save youthful wanderers from inveterate transients' sexual wiles.

Stories of transient perversion were highly conventionalized. Invariably, an older "wolf" corrupted an innocent boy, inducting him into the perverse-transient subculture and ruining him for an adulthood of conjugal-domestic intimacy and civic responsibility. The "chronic hobo" in such tales was never only a homosexual; he was also an opponent of productive labor, community settlement, and most other things civilized and domestic.[12] Hobo jungles were also "spaces where black, white, and Mexican tramps mixed freely."[13] The culture that chronic hoboes inhabited was thus threateningly at odds with established notions of order and hierarchy. Transients embraced a manly ethic of mutualism, bartering and sharing with each other, and showing relative disregard for social distinctions and private property.[14] In transient-perversion narratives, the impressionable youth who entered the transient subculture was thus exposed to a vast range of subversive practices, of which intergenerational sexual seduction was only the most disturbing and sensational.

Sociologists, welfare reformers, politicians, journalists, fiction writers, and New Deal administrators were prolific authors of transient-perversion narratives. According to Nels Anderson, the transient hysteria began in 1932 with a study by the Children's Bureau that vastly exaggerated the number of young wanderers who were taking to the road in response to the Depression. In an effort to claim a larger share of diminishing welfare resources, private welfare agencies stressed young migrants' vulnerability to sexual seduction as a means of legitimating their efforts to combat the transient problem. In response to growing public concern, the U.S. Congress convened highly publicized hearings on the problem of youthful transients in January 1933. And when the Roosevelt administration announced plans to establish a massive federal emergency relief apparatus in May 1933, officials attached this vast expansion of federal power to efforts to save wandering youth from a lifetime of transient perversion.

The Roosevelt administration established a Division of Transient Activities under the FERA in May 1933, setting aside $15 million specifically for transient relief. Yet this initiative was not the end of the transient-perversion narrative. As Leyendecker's cover illustration indicates, the figure of the degenerate hobo became ammunition in battles between New Deal critics and Roosevelt officials from the Transient Division's inception until its demise at the end of 1935. Reflecting the volatility and disproportionality that characterize all moral panics, the crisis of transient perversion abated as suddenly as it appeared, breathing its last sensational gasps in the context of the 1936 federal election.

As with other compelling stories of collective civic identity in the Depression, the transient-perversion narrative was widely contested. Although most versions of the narrative were highly sensationalized, working to constitute an affective public that might consent to one or another effort to "police the crisis" of intergenerational seduction, the authors often disagreed about which agencies or groups were authorized to effect the necessary changes.

In her work on New Deal transient relief, Margot Canaday states that "welfare has been incredibly under-studied in its relationship to sexuality."[15] She argues that the FTP was an unusual instance of federal relief provision because it targeted 'non-family' individuals and thus "opened up radical possibilities for the structuring of relief provision."[16] However, careful consideration of the Federal Transient Program's (FTP's) origins in transient-perversion narratives undercuts claims that the program "opened up radical possibilities" and helps to explain the program's inordinate preoccupation with youthful transients, as well as its unpopularity and rapid demise. Federal officials, like other contributors to the transient panic, were to some extent taken in by lurid stories of intergenerational transient perversion. Rather than intentionally accommodating sexual diversity, they sought to structure federal relief to combat homosexual contact between older and younger transient men. In other words, New Deal relief administrators' intent had always been to "police the crisis" of intergenerational transient perversion, thereby enlisting broad popular support for the New Deal state. Unfortunately, the transient-perversion crisis proved too volatile, and New Deal administrators quickly began to orchestrate the rhetorical disappearance of the transient, and with it federal aid to flesh-and-blood transients, before the 1936 election year.

✦ "Boys on the Loose"

Writing in December 1933, public health administrator Ellen C. Potter declared that "the freights have swarmed with adventurous young manhood."

Suggesting a distinct lack of numerical specificity, Potter estimated that "the numbers on the road" in the winter of 1932 might range anywhere "from 200,000 to 1,500,000."[17] Sociologist A. Wayne McMillen similarly acknowledged the unreliability of available statistics on what he termed the "army of boys on the loose"; however, he insisted that whatever the number, the problem was one of "alarming proportions." McMillen acknowledged that exaggerated statistics on transient youth had "electrified the country to writing and reading multiple pages about them." He added, "They have become the answer to the photographer's prayer and scarcely a magazine appears today without pictures of young fellows jumping freight trains, huddled in box cars, [and] cooking Mulligan stew in the jungle." Despite his own observation that available accounts of wandering youth were exaggerated and unreliable, McMillen concluded, "Whatever the number, none of the measures thus far advocated is too generous."[18]

In addition to magnifying the transient problem (acknowledging that his own estimates reflected not "recorded evidence" but hearsay and "first-hand observations"), McMillen also supplied readers with photographs to illustrate his commentary. The photographs portrayed transient youth as a fraternal body characterized by youthful vulnerability, interracial comradeship, and dangerous physical exposure. Not surprisingly, McMillen dwelled on "the moral hazards of the road," which he alleged to be "incalculable." Not only were youthful wanderers thrown into contact with professional thieves, but more importantly, they encountered "the infectious 'no-work' attitude of the seasoned hobo" and were "in danger of becoming the prey of degenerates." McMillen applauded police efforts to "curb perverted practices and to prevent young boys from solicitation." Unless more was done to fortify American homes and communities against jobless youth's "urge to wander," McMillen warned, "transients will continue to be passed on from one community to the next and demoralization—particularly of the young—will gain momentum."[19]

In a book-length account of transient youth, sociologist Thomas Minehan likewise raised the transient alarm. He predicted that if the problem of wandering youth was not soon checked, "Street beggars, hideous, deformed, and depressing, may swarm our land and deface our cities and . . . many of them will be graduate child tramps."[20] To Minehan's Depression-era audience, his claims about the "hideousness" and "deformity" of "graduate child tramps" had powerful sexual connotations. For in all likelihood, his readers would be thoroughly familiar with the narrative of wandering boys' sexual seduction by seasoned tramps.[21]

Minehan was an enthusiastic contributor to the transient-perversion narrative. He wrote suggestively, "One of the first lessons that a boy learns on the road is to beware of certain older men. These men become friendly with a lonely boy and attempt to seduce him."[22] Just as other transient storytellers preferred hyperbole to accuracy in their accounts of transient homosexuality, Minehan relied on hearsay and imagination. He stated, "It is impossible to estimate the extent of perversion among men on the road today. But, as one of the boy tramps told me, whenever you see a trainload of transients, there is always a wolf on the tender and a fruiter on the green light. Like the vultures following a caravan, the perverts trail boys, waiting with bribes and force to ensnare them."[23]

Claiming to have gone undercover as a participant-observer in the transient subculture, Minehan shared sensational stories that his subjects had allegedly shared with him. "Tales of wolves using wiles and force to gain the body of a boy are . . . common," he reported. He elaborated, "The older man befriends a boy, giving him food or clothing. He tries to gain his will by persuasion. When persuasion does not succeed, he attempts force. He lures the boy to a deserted corner of a freight yard where the boy's screams cannot be heard, or some night at a lonely water tower he induces him to drop from a train, or he gets the boy drunk and takes him into a thicket."

As if his evocation of "deserted corners," "thickets," and "screams" were not disturbing (or titillating) enough, Minehan carried the narrative still further, describing the fully realized intergenerational couplings that sometimes resulted from such seductions. He stated, "At times the wiles succeed. I have seen wolves and their little 'lambs' or 'fairies,' and their relationship seemed to be one of mutual satisfaction. . . . Far from being miserable, the boy did not want to be separated from his friend. He resented and refused all efforts at his 'rescue.'"[24]

Published in 1934, after the initial hysteria surrounding wandering youth had abated, Minehan's book came in for considerable professional criticism. Social-scientific reviewers lambasted Minehan for dispensing with responsible, quantitative analysis in favor of prurient reporting.[25] Yet Minehan was not alone in allowing the lurid details of the popular transient narrative to displace quantitive analysis. Another sociologist to be swept up in sexual sensationalism was Towne Nylander. Like Minehan, Nylander dwelled on the perils of transient homosociality confronting wandering youth. In a 1932 essay, he contrasted the figure of the innocent and impressionable wandering youth with that of the corrupt and calculating adult migrant. Nylander stated, "The adult migrant is homeless, jobless, and womanless. Being homeless he has no stake or interest in normal life. . . . Being jobless. . . . [h]e derides honesty, hard steady work, and sobriety. . . . Being womanless the adult migrant resorts to illicit relations and perversions."[26]

According to Nylander, those young men who stayed on the road for any length of time could look forward to becoming like "the unfortunate youngster who has come under the control of some pervert." In Nylander's account, as in others, homosexual perversion was the logical outcome of a life that began with the rejection of home and local community and with the simultaneous embrace of rootlessness, "getting-by," and civic irresponsibility. What was so alarming about the transient, Nylander informed his readers, was that "he [had] no stake or interest in normal life." Significantly, Nylander's definition of "normal" included having a home, being employed, and exercising authority within the private domain of marriage and family life.[27]

Reacting to the rising tide of transient sensationalism, the St. Louis Community Council created a Committee on Migrant Boys to study the problem. In its September 1933 report, the committee acknowledged that "much has been written about perversion and vice on the road."[28] Although their own investigation showed that the "wolf and the pansy" were indeed a part of the transient subculture, they concluded that "conditions in this respect do not differ greatly from conditions in any strictly masculine group." The Committee on Migrant Boys was one of many groups to discover that early Depression accounts of transient "perversion" had perhaps been overblown. Writing in 1939, New Deal analyst John N. Webb noted that prior to the inauguration of the transient program in July 1933, "estimates greatly overstated the size of the transient homeless population."[29] He added, "In the absence of any definite knowledge concerning the transient population, the exceptional case could be exploited and, by implication, exaggerated all out of proportion, without fear of contradiction."[30]

In the early Depression, the transient problem was indeed "exaggerated all out of proportion." In journalistic accounts, in congressional testimony, and in the discourses of social science and welfare reform, the transient epitomized both a crisis of American masculine citizenship and a crisis of national sexual continence. If the ideal citizen was a successful white family breadwinner who actively participated in local civic affairs, the transient was his diametrical opposite. The transient spurned economic and political obligations and inhabited a homosocial, rather than a heterosexual, world. Criminality, illicit sexuality, and particularly intergenerational sex between men came together in early Depression narratives of transient life. That New Deal administrators should be so responsive to such sensational narratives and that their program for dealing with transiency should engender heated political debate suggests that the transient, in all of his gender and sexual significance, was indeed central to the process of civic storytelling that took place throughout the Depression years.

← Federal Transient Relief

The Roosevelt administration responded to popular anxieties about transiency by setting up two relief programs to combat the problem. Their first response was the celebrated Civilian Conservation Corps (CCC), which sought to recuperate the "army of boys on the loose" who fell victim, in popular accounts, to inveterate transients' homosexual wiles.[31] Also intended primarily to save transient youth from becoming chronic wanderers, the FTP was established under the auspices of the Federal Emergency Relief Administration in May 1933.[32]

The transient and homeless populations had been a liability to the Hoover administration, which had had to contend with "Hoovervilles" and the politically costly Bonus march. Eager to avert similar trouble in 1933, Roosevelt took a proactive approach to the transient crisis. At a time when transient-perversion narratives proliferated, his administration worked to position the New Deal as that narrative's savior, restoring young wanderers to useful citizenship and protecting them from the menacing "transient horde." By claiming authorship of the transient narrative through the rhetoric and practices of transient relief, New Deal officials also sought to present the administration as a conservator of traditional gender and sexual roles. Accentuating the administration's *sexual* conservatism was a means of combating popular anxieties about the transformative and expansive nature of the emergent welfare state.

Containing the disruptive potential of chronic hoboes while protecting younger wanderers was always the central purpose of the FTP. According to FTP officials, the transient program served to stop "aimless and unnecessary wandering," and to reestablish "in as many cases as possible normal economic, social, and home ties of transients." By this means, the FTP protected "society from vagrancy and crime." The program also provided "a constructive and educational experience for the younger and more hopeful members of the transient group, so that . . . they may become useful citizens, instead of the vagrants and hoboes so typical of the older transients under the old system of neglect."[33] According to an FERA press release dated June 6, 1935, "The educational work is designed . . . to make clear the futility of aimless 'floating' about the country, with attendant dangers to the individuals and communities, and to encourage 'anchoring' somewhere."[34] In all aspects of the FTP, administrators stressed proper age segregation of the transient group.[35] Particularly with regard to sleeping arrangements, the "younger and more hopeful" transients were to be separated from the "vagrants and hoboes" who seduced youthful wanderers in popular transient narratives. The FTP also pledged to provide "appropriate care and treatment for the aged, sick, incompetent, and vagrant groups among the transients," but its major interest was in salvaging youthful male transients for useful citizenship.[36]

Outside observers also emphasized that federal transient relief should prevent the intermingling of inveterate transients and wandering youth. Echoing earlier narratives of transient perversion, sociologist George Outland wrote, "The warped social outlook which frequently results when transient boys and men are mingled over a long period, is often accompanied by definite physical dangers. Sex perversion is the worst of these, with cases frequently found where a boy has been bought, or forced, or led into degeneracy. All possible steps should be taken to prevent the spread of such perversion, and the initial and most important step is the complete segregation of the two groups in the Federal Transient Program."[37]

Not only was the FTP the first federal agency to address the needs of transients; it was also unique among New Deal agencies in that it was funded wholly by the federal government. In setting up the FTP, relief officials stressed that the problem of transiency was one of *interstate* migrations and was therefore a *federal* responsibility. Not to be confused with the state and local homeless populations, the transient was defined as "a person who has been within a given state less than twelve months."[38] The federal nature of the FTP differed from traditional methods of relief-giving and from the general practice of New Deal relief, which tended to rely on cooperation between federal, state, and local relief administrations. Webb noted that, prior to the New Deal, "each locality [was] only responsible for the care of its own needy citizens." Poor laws excluded "all needy nonresidents," thus forcing the wanderer to continue his travels from one community to the next.[39] By such methods, transients had historically been kept at the periphery of American communities. In setting up the FTP and thereby making transiency a federal issue, New Deal administrators temporarily disrupted the transient's peripheral relation to American civic life. As one welfare official observed, "Mr. and Mrs. Citizen . . . must shake off that provincialism which catalogues the needy stranger as an 'undesirable citizen,' and begin to think in terms of national responsibility for all our fellows, giving our law-making bodies time to crystallize in the statutes our broader concept of national life."[40] Indeed, transient relief was exceptional in the context of the broader emergency relief, insofar as its structure was *strictly* federal. State and local relief administrators played a relatively minor role in federal transient relief, which is one of the reasons that the agency came to be seen by administration critics as the worst example of New Deal–style "bureaucratic centralism."

Administration of the FTP varied by region, state, and location. As Ellen C. Potter observed, "Great latitude was granted the states in the development of plans."[41] Large cities had transient centers, short-term holding facilities from which transients were moved to rural camps. Many smaller communities contracted FTP services through local private agencies, lodging houses, and restaurants. FTP camps were large-scale, single-sex communities that challenged all of the long-standing approaches to transients in favor of congregate care and professional casework. Most communities resisted the establishment of FTP camps in their vicinity.

Throughout its brief tenure, the FTP lacked unity and consistency and suffered from weak federal leadership. Administrative discontinuity characterized the agency, which was directed first by Morris Lewis, who was perceived to be "too friendly" to transients, then briefly by William J. Plunkert, Lewis's assistant, and finally by Elizabeth Wickenden, who was only twenty-four years old when she assumed the directorship in 1934.[42] In addition to inconsistent federal oversight, critics complained that the unevenness of transient provisions actually promoted migration as transients moved from one shelter or camp to the next in search of better provisions. Turnover among FTP camp residents was high in any case; measured weekly, it ranged from 100 to 142 percent.[43] Writing in 1934, Plunkert acknowledged that "lack of coordination between the transient division and the state administration" was a major problem for the agency. He complained that, too often, transient directors "turned directly to the Washington office for instruction."[44] Recognizing mounting tensions between the FTP and local communities, an FTP circular dated December 20, 1934, stated, "Further decentralization of the transient program is necessary. State transient departments shall function as all other departments of the [state emergency relief administrations]."[45]

Despite their mission to serve a group whom most Americans considered undeserving of federal relief, FTP officials initially did their best to cast the FTP as a positive, nation-saving program. In public speeches and official publications, they attempted to generate sympathy for "the suffering and neglect of this large body of American citizens" by stressing its relative youth and high civic potential. Rather than extend the bounds of civic community to *include* older, inveterate transients, officials sought to distance Depression wanderers from stereotypical hoboes and bums. Proponents of the transient program were quick to point out that most individuals served by the FTP were not "the chronic hobo type." Gertrude Springer differentiated the "1933 model" of the transient from the "chronic hobo" class. Potter estimated that 90 percent of them were "average normal citizens with at least a common school to a high school education," who possessed "good work habits."[46] According to such New Deal sympathizers, the new transients of the Depression were motivated not by a desire to *avoid* work, but to find it.[47] Others likened the Depression transient to an earlier generation of American pioneers whose initiative and pride prevented them from waiting in their home communities for jobs to appear. As Webb wrote, "In not a few instances, a search for work in some other place was the only alternative to 'going on relief.'"[48] According to the December 1934 report of the FTP, "Transients are the people who have clung most tenaciously during the depression to the American tradition that somewhere there exists an opportunity for the man willing and able to work. Refusal to accept unemployment passively and subsequent movement from industrial center to harvest field to construction project springs from the same enterprising spirit that motivated the pioneers of an earlier day."[49]

In a document titled "The Transient Program," Plunkert maintained that the transients constituted "a large body of American citizens" who "represent a cross-section of American life." He added, "I believe that the public is beginning to realize that our job is not with professional hoboes and bums, but with a group of men and families with something very real to sell in the line of skilled trades and professions, but for which there is no market available."[50] In this way, Plunkert and other transient officials sought to identify the depression transient *with*, rather than *against*, the social and civic conventions of masculine adulthood.

Although some rural transient camps, such as Camp Frontier in upstate New York, were open to all racial groups, racial segregation was the norm in the FTP, particularly in urban transient centers and throughout the South. Ellery Reed noted that African American transient facilities were often inferior to those provided for whites. Even so, racial conflict was negligible in the FTP. In 1935, African American transients numbered 12 percent of the total population, whereas blacks were only about 10 percent of the overall population in 1930 census.[51]

Evidence of the FTP's conservative gender and sexual politics can be found in the agency's approach to female transients. To begin with, unattached female transients were few in number, though their numbers (and startling sexual proclivities) had been exaggerated in early Depression accounts of transient life. Regardless of whether female transients traveled as individuals, with other women, or as members of family groups, they were always treated as members of family groups and sent back to their place of origin. As "Boxcar Bertha" Thompson observed, female transients were generally motivated by the same factors as male transients: financial distress and a search for economic opportunity. Thompson recalled that officials were always willing to pay a woman's fare to anyplace where she might reunite with family; many female transients invented family ties in order to advance their travels in this way. Ben Reitman obtained FERA figures that placed the number of female transients under care nationwide at only 5 percent.[52]

The FTP ran up against many problems. As one historian observes, "State indifference and local hostility delayed development of the transient program and influenced the form it took."[53] Many urban communities objected when transient shelters were placed within their limits. As one FTP official remarked, such communities were unwilling "to permit a large group of transient men to be concentrated in their midst indefinitely." Beginning in April 1934, the FTP devised a system of rural camps to replace the unpopular city shelters.[54] Yet in emphasizing the rural camp program, FTP officials alienated younger transients—the very population it was most eager to engage. According to Webb, transients under twenty-five years of age stayed an average of less than three days in transient camps, while older transients often remained indefinitely.[55]

In an effort to deflect criticism of the FTP, officials created a situation in which most of the men under their care were mature transients, for whom little popular sympathy and much popular revulsion existed. As Wickenden later lamented, "The camps . . . removed the transient from all possible contact with private employment, from normal society, from contact with women, and normal family relationships." She added, "Most serious of all was the way in which the camp tended to brand men once and for all as 'transients,' a breed apart."[56]

Despite their clients' unpopularity, FTP officials did their best to return them to productive citizenship. Camp residents were expected to put in a few hours' work each day for their room, board, and minimal cash allowance. The program furnished residents with clothing and limited medical care and offered a variety of other services. Classes in reading, writing, and elementary arithmetic were offered at some camps, while others fielded softball and volleyball teams during the summer months. Bands, glee clubs, and amateur shows were also common. Many camps operated canteens, libraries, and even camp or center newspapers. Internal camp governance was often fairly democratic, and camp residents often policed the camps themselves.[57]

Yet it would be a mistake to assume that New Deal administrators were ever enthusiastic about extending relief benefits to needy transients, particularly those among the FTP's clients whom agency officials classed as "hoboes and vagrants." As many officials would later suggest, the FTP had been an ill-conceived reaction to overblown accounts of older transients' seduction of "an army of boys on the loose."

☛ "Uncle Sam's Wayside Inns"

Just as the transient had been a sensational figure in the early 1930s, the federal transient camp became focal to national political debate *after* 1933, and especially in 1935 and 1936, when Republicans attacked it as a particularly disastrous example of federal disrespect for local civic autonomy and of emasculating government paternalism. At a time when both New Dealers and their critics increasingly identified their programs with a family-based model of collective civic identity, the transient program stood as the worst example of misplaced generosity on the part of "an indulgent paternal Government."[58] Under the auspices of the FTP, critics claimed, the New Deal was promoting, rather than correcting, a whole host of social, sexual, and civic misbehaviors. "The strongest condemnation of the relief program concerns federal relief for transients," sociologist Ernest Groves commented in 1935. He noted that the FTP "is even charged with seeming to entice men and boys to leave home."[59] J. O. Reade, a defender of the federal transient relief, nevertheless acknowledged that "unquestionably, the transient service has been taken by some as an invitation to tour the country."[60] Likewise, Evelyn Harvey stated, "The Transient Bureaus . . . have had a tendency to increase the wanderings of the foot-loose traveler." She added,

> Now a tramp can go comfortably from coast to coast. In a string of camps and shelters stretched from Maine to California, he is well-fed, clothed, treated free of charge by doctors. . . . He is well-treated, entertained by radio and moving pictures. A barber cuts his hair and shaves him; a shower bath makes him clean before he dons the new suit which, if it does not suit his fancy, he generally can manage to exchange for another at a different shelter . . . When he tires of one shelter, he moves at will to the next.[61]

Some critics referred to the transient camps as "Uncle Sam's Wayside Inns." While providing residents with luxury accommodations, critics alleged, FTP administrators expected little in return. In this way, the camps fostered an unhealthy sense of entitlement in their clients. Critics stressed the high turnover rate in the transient camps. Most were unimpressed with FTP director Plunkert's statement that "there is no compulsion in the whole transient program. The idea behind the camps is to make them so attractive that the transients will stay."[62] One critic commented that residents' civic consciousness revealed "little evidence of their responsibility as social beings; little idea that they have any obligation toward the Government that is taking care of them."[63] According to another critic, camp residents were generally unworthy of the federal consideration they received. Although claiming to be searching for work, many were fugitives or family deserters, and some would be better served by residence in "a psychopathic ward" than in a federal transient camp.[64] Critics alleged that younger transients often took to the road for no better reason than that they disliked "family-imposed discipline." According to one writer, most were motivated by "a desire to ramble, a hunger for something, excitement perhaps, which they could not or dared not gratify in their home communities."[65]

Sensational accounts of life in the transient camps detailed plenty of excitement that could not be gratified in residents' "home communities." Stories of criminality, drunkenness, and general "hell-raising" commonly appeared in the local and national media. According to one account, "Police in the towns neighboring the camps are inclined to class them all as 'hell raisers.' Liquor shops near the camps flourish. Ostensibly the purpose of the undertaking is rehabilitation, but reports indicate that the actual effect is often further demoralization."[66] This same report contrasted "the homes of hardworking citizens" to the transient camps, which it characterized as "institutions of questionable social value." As described in the foregoing excerpts, the tension between the traditional, male-headed home and the transient camp arose repeatedly in politically motivated criticisms of the FTP.

The tension between transient camps and family-based local communities was at issue in Pender County, North Carolina, where transient camp residents helped to build a colony of subsistence homes. The colony's developer, Hugh MacRae, told a reporter that "I decided to ask for the removal of the transients' camp from the project when we began bringing in picked families who were to settle on the land." He explained, "I felt that it would be unfair to those families to have that camp located in their neighborhood. The concentration of a large body of men close to a settlement of families has recognized dangers."[67] MacRae assumed that the newspaper-reading public would know what those "dangers" were—among them, the threat of homosexual perversion.

Danger and excitement mingled in accounts of sexual perversion in the camps. Just as illicit sexuality had been a central feature of earlier transient narratives, accounts of the transient camps often detailed homosexual incidents. Joseph Cartier, a disgruntled resident of a New York transient camp, made reference to such accounts in a letter to WPA officials. "Articles have appeared in the local papers condemning the morals and discipline of this camp," Cartier wrote. Such articles owed much to the camp's location "about 150 feet from a thru highway" and the lack of "shades or curtains on the windows." Cartier alleged that it was "not an uncommon sight, especially these warm nights, for men to be seen running around and getting into their double bunks, naked."⁶⁸ Cartier noted the national political significance of such incidents, warning relief officials that Republican groups would use such stories to their advantage in the 1936 election. Invoking a fear of homosociality that ran deep in Depression-era culture, he added, "Now anyone with an ounce of common sense must know, that after a period of two years there is an accumulation of middle aged and young men . . . [who] through lack of money, and time hanging heavy . . . turn to their own sex."⁶⁹

Cartier was not the only camp resident to allege improper fraternization in the camps. In a similar report, Howard Thomas of Syracuse wrote, "The degeneracy that has been allowed to run rampant here includes such boldness as kissing each other good night, powdering their nose and calling endearing names, even so bold as to offer money for those they are passionate toward." Affirming his own proper masculinity, Thomas added, "There are quite a few real men here now who are willing to tell and prove the truth of what I have briefly outlined."⁷⁰

Such allegations were sufficiently concerning to FERA administrators in Washington that a new set of guidelines was established to discourage improper fraternization among camp residents. In a memo "To All State Relief Administrators," Hopkins wrote,

> You are instructed to put into effect immediately the following regulations in all transient centers and camps:
>
> 1. No double-decker beds are to be used.
> 2. There shall be at least two feet between edges of adjoining mattresses.
> 3. No two men shall sleep with their heads at the same ends of the beds.
> 4. So far as possible, not more than 20 men will sleep in one room.

Reflecting persisting anxieties about intergenerational sexual contact, Hopkins further stipulated that, in cases where younger transients were present, "the space between edges of adjoining mattresses shall not be less than *three* feet [emphasis added]."⁷¹

✐ Erasing the Transient

Throughout the brief history of the FTP, relief officials did their best to combat popular criticisms of their efforts. Not only did they police residents' sleeping arrangements; they placed transient camps as far as possible from population centers and rural family settlements, and they tried to separate older transients from younger ones. Initially, they worked to build a program around the needs of transient youth, only to find that the youngest transients were neither sufficient in number nor particularly interested in a system of rural camps. Contrary to the intentions of federal relief administrators, transient camps thus became havens for older "hoboes and vagrants" whose regular unemployment, seasonal migrations, and homosocial lifestyle were vastly at odds with the masculine and family-based ideals that increasingly defined civic membership in the emergent welfare state.

Looking back on the transient program in *Spending to Save*, FERA administrator Harry Hopkins lamented that "the more enterprising [transients] remained in camp only a short time," whereas other less employable individuals stayed on indefinitely. In describing the older transient group, Hopkins used what by 1936 had become a somewhat worn military metaphor. He wrote, "It was the men who became so well adjusted to the secure, if limited, life of a transient camp who hoped, like certain soldiers, that the war would never end."[72] By 1936, New Deal relief officials had determined that transient relief was a distinct political liability. As relief officials turned their attention to creating public work for the nation's jobless breadwinners, transients went the way of other "unemployables" who did not conform to the masculine breadwinning ideal. As Franklin Roosevelt informed a correspondent after the closure of transient camps, "The Federal Government has definitely withdrawn from the field of direct relief and cannot accept this responsibility." Ignoring the residence requirement often stipulated by local certification boards for WPA eligibility, Roosevelt disingenuously added, "On the other hand, employment on our present Work Program is open to transients on the same basis as other persons."[73]

In 1936, Hopkins stated with evident satisfaction that "there are, at the present time, no statistics available to prove how many transients are engaged on the work program; they have lost their identity as transients."[74] New Deal officials worked hard to orchestrate the transients' rhetorical disappearance, in part by disbanding the infamous FTP, and in part by inventing a new category of late Depression wanderers called "migrants."[75] Migrants differed from their early Depression transient counterparts, officials maintained, because they moved as members of family groups and not as individuals. Thus, although they defied the civic ideal of stable community residence and responsible civic participation, they did not represent the same profound threat to America's family-based way of life as the age-differentiated, homosocial "transient army" had.

New Deal officials maintained, late in the decade, that Depression migrants represented the best characteristics of male American citizenship. According to David Cushman Coyle, "Migration is a valuable part of our American tradition," and those who migrated were "Americans in the old tradition, doing their best to fend for themselves."[76] In terms that accentuated the migrant's youthfulness, rugged individualism, and family orientation, he added, "Most of these people are on the road for the same reasons that kept the covered wagons rumbling across the prairies for the better part of a century.... That is who the penniless migrants are—young men 'going West' with wife and child, taking the risks of pioneering and some of them losing their last nickel in the gamble."[77]

Not only did the image of the migrant family recall the idealized pioneer family spreading white civilization westward across the continent; that same family embodied principles of civic individualism and family-based political authority in contrast to the centralized bureaucracy and questionable paternalism that were so often alleged by anti–New Deal forces. If the federal government had sponsored "resort hotels" for homosexual transients and imperiled the independence and integrity of the local civic community in the early New Deal years, its late Depression praise for the migrant family had altogether different rhetorical implications.

At a time when traditional concepts of U.S. civic identity were undercut first by the Depression and then by the New Deal itself, the transient's indeterminate status as social and sexual outlier reflected a broader national context of social, sexual, and civic uncertainty. Transient perversion narratives also reflect the importance of kinship metaphors in defining—and *re*defining— U.S. national community. As a metaphor for national community, the family form serves to naturalize gender and racial inequalities and restricts sexual expression to the private, conjugal realm.[78]

During the 1930s, New Deal officials and their political opponents sought to align their political agendas with the familiar ideal of the heterosexual white-male-headed home. The largely homosocial, racially promiscuous, and allegedly homosexual transient community represented the antithesis of that home. It was the impetus for what Janice Irvine calls a "sex panic"—expressed through affectively dense narratives of intergenerational sexual seduction that mobilized public support for the efforts of New Dealers and their political opponents to "police the crisis." After first attempting to recuperate the "transient horde," and particularly its youngest, most "salvageable" members, federal relief officials came to regard the transient as a symbolic liability—one that, as Republican critics were quick to point out, increased the Roosevelt administration's vulnerability to criticisms of indulgent federal paternalism and bureaucratic interference with local civic and familial ideals. In the face of stinging transient counternarratives that maligned relief officials for setting up a system of "Uncle Sam's Wayside Inns," New Deal officials beat a rapid practical and rhetorical retreat. They abandoned the transient program—and with it, the transient—in favor of the new, family-based figure of the migrant.

Despite the sensationalism and political expediency that characterize transient-perversion narratives, such stories and the civic hierarchies they motivated had meaningful consequences for flesh-and-blood transients, many of whom did engage in sexual liaisons with other men. Such individuals were not only homeless and jobless; they were sexually stigmatized and deprived of both the material resources and civic status to freely exercise their intimate sexual desires.

CHAPTER 3

"Builder of Men"
Homosociality and the Nationalist Accents of the Civilian Conservation Corps

In 1933, Warner Brothers released *Wild Boys of the Road*, William Wellman's social drama of homeless youth in the Depression.[1] The film's protagonists, Eddie (Frankie Darro) and Tommy (Edwin Phillips), are working-class youth who take to the road to relieve the financial pressure on their families. The audience first encounters the pair at a high school dance, where Eddie dresses Tommy as a girl to avoid paying admission. Once on the road, the teenagers steal, panhandle, elude law enforcement, and take the law into their own hands, as when an older transient molests a female companion and they throw him from the car. The boys also risk physical injury each time they hop on or off a moving train. In one scene that shocked depression audiences, Tommy jumps from one train, falling across the path of another and seriously injuring his leg. The resulting amputation reinforces Tommy's dependence on Eddie, the dominant partner in their relationship. Together with Sally (Dorothy Coonan), who dresses like a boy to avoid sexual conflict, Eddie and Tommy make a life for themselves in dumps and shantytowns until the law catches up with them. Their fortunes improve when their case is assigned to a benevolent judge who bears a striking resemblance to President Roosevelt. In a somewhat implausible ending, given the overall bleakness of the film, the judge promises to help them find jobs so that they can resume living decently. In the final scene, Eddie, Tommy, and Sally leave the courthouse together, eager to begin their new lives as reputable citizens.[2]

With its optimistic New Deal ending, *Wild Boys of the Road* was somewhat more hopeful than most accounts of wandering youth in the Depression. Not only does the film end on a positive note, but Eddie, Tommy, and Sally survive their brush with crime and homelessness without undergoing significant character degeneration. Although the film plays with themes of youthful criminality, cross-dressing, and transgressive sexuality, the protagonists' deviant behavior is situationally justified, and Sally's presence helps to normalize what might otherwise appear to be a marriage-like relationship between Eddie and Tommy. Although the film depicts older transients as sexually threatening, it dramatizes that threat in heterosexual terms.

In contrast to *Wild Boys*, Norman Taurog's *Boys Town* (1938) offered a more mixed portrayal of homeless youth. Claiming to "hold up a mirror to life," the film opens at a high-security prison, where Dan Farrow (Leslie Fenton) is about to be executed for murder. Unrepentant until moments before his death, Farrow at last expresses remorse to his priest, Father Flanagan (Spencer Tracy).[3] Although he confesses his crime, Farrow balks when the judge asks him to admit his debt to the State. "*My* debt to the State?," he replies incredulously. "Where was the State when a lonely, crying kid cried himself to sleep in a flophouse with a bunch of drunks, tramps, and hoboes?" Farrow's retort implies that, had he not been forced to share sleeping quarters with "drunks, tramps, and hoboes," he might have lived out his life as an honorable citizen. Grasping this, Father Flanagan resolves to leave his city mission, where he serves primarily older vagrants, and create a home for boys. Modeled on the real Father Flanagan's home for boys in rural Nebraska, the filmic Boys Town offers refuge to homeless youth who might otherwise commingle with degenerate hoboes and tramps.

Dedicating *Somebody in Boots* to "the homeless boys of America," novelist Nelson Algren similarly connected homosexual perversion, crime, and incarceration in his portrayal of wandering youth. When Cass McCay, the young drifter at the heart of the novel, is jailed for vagrancy, not only does he rub shoulders with other vagrants and criminals; he also bears witness to their violent homosexual practices: "On such nights Cass sweated in terror, remembering a man in a park in Chicago. . . . The man had given Cass . . . a long brown cigarette to smoke, and they had sat on a bench together. After a while the man said something to Cass, and touched Cass's thigh as he said it, and Cass had tried to run away. But the long brown cigarette was half smoked away, and he had been unable to go; he had been unable to walk, far less run, without leaning upon the man's shoulder."[4]

Like the opening of *Boys Town*, the jailhouse chapter in *Somebody in Boots* links vagrant homosexuality with criminality, degradation, and violence. Such linkages were also evident in newspaper accounts of "the army of boys on the loose." "Away from home, fireside and friends," the *Atlanta Constitution* editorialized, homeless youth fell "into bad companionship, then into trouble." Their encounters with older hoboes and vagrants were "making public enemies of them."[5] In a published interview, Judge Samuel Blake of the Los Angeles Juvenile Court lamented, "the chronic vagrant, the hobo, the bum and the panhandlers" had become "glorified leaders of the homeless children." The result, he stated, was a "widespread degeneration of morals which those contacts must produce and only can produce."[6]

☛ "Boys on the Loose"

In addition to being the New Deal's most popular relief agency, the Civilian Conservation Corps (CCC) served as a staging ground for broader anxieties about working-class bachelor society and intergenerational male intimacy that animated many facets of U.S. national culture in the Depression.[7] The CCC removed impressionable, working-class youth from the urban flophouses and hobo jungles where they risked moral and physical degradation. It placed them in racially segregated wilderness camps far removed from tantalizing urban vices, where they performed hard manual labor while conforming to strict standards of physical hygiene. Thus disciplined away from urban vices, their physical hardihood assured, they underwent a remarkable transformation from "public enemies" to exemplars of privileged national values.

Certainly, the CCC seemed to dispel anxieties about the improper socialization of white working-class youth in the Depression. But to see the agency's success only in these terms is to miss its most compelling sexual accents.[8] It fails to account for the intensely pleasurable portrayals of "loosely-clad" male bodies and intimate male friendships that animated popular and official representations of the CCC. Indeed, throughout the narrative and iconography of CCC life, stories about relations between seasoned Army officers and callow young recruits recalled more troubling associations between transient "wolves" and "lambs." Detailed descriptions of enrollees' heavily muscled yet compliant bodies carried at least as much erotic charge as descriptions of homeless boys' scrawnier physiques. If there was so much concern about the improper homosociality of the working-class bachelor subculture in the 1930s, then why were erotically charged representations of CCC youth so popular?

Looking at how New Deal officials appropriated the narrative of wandering youth, harnessing its pleasures and dangers to the CCC, illuminates the relation of gender and sexuality to the unequal terms of citizenship and nationality in the emergent welfare state. It also allows sheds light on the racial dimensions of New Deal social citizenship. Saving impressionable youth and containing its erotic potential meant, among other things, purifying it racially. CCC administrator James J. McEntee referred to the CCC as "a great white chain of camps," and the racial characteristics of the "loosely-clad forester"—his "deeply tanned" but essentially white physique—were central to the agency's tremendous popularity.

If images of "wild boys" and impressionable youth loomed large in early depression accounts of gender and national crisis, one possible response to that crisis was the careful containment of unemployed white youth within military bounds. Republican senator James Couzens made such a proposal in the spring of 1933, when he put forward legislation authorizing the Army to house, feed, and clothe unemployed young men between the ages of seventeen and twenty-four on centralized military reservations, which he called "concentration camps," for the duration of the depression. In this way, the senator suggested, the collective activities of masculine youth could be monitored; their exposure to criminal and immoral elements prevented; and their potential threat to national stability forestalled.[9]

The Couzens proposal generated considerable discussion, but it was finally shelved, in part because of opposition from military authorities.[10] The concept of using Army personnel and facilities to intervene in the youth crisis persisted, however, finding its way into the Roosevelt campaign to establish the Civilian Conservation Corps. Like the Couzens bill, Roosevelt's plan for emergency conservation work would place a portion of America's unemployed manhood in Army-administered work camps, remote from circumstances of "enforced idleness," poverty, and urban vice.[11] There they would form "an army with shovels," working to conserve the natural resources of the nation.

Proposed on March 27, 1933, and put to a vote on March 31, the legislation to establish the CCC went forward with a quickness that made some members of Congress and many relief activists uneasy. Some objected that proposed legislation gave too much discretion to the president. Others, including U.S. congressman William P. Connery and William Green of the American Federation of Labor, objected to the military accents of the bill. Connery argued that the proposed CCC sounded too much like a military draft. Although he managed to get some of the offending language removed, he, Green, and others continued to object to the low, dollar-a-day wage and "regimentation of labor" included in the CCC proposal.[12]

Roosevelt worked to garner labor leaders' approval by appointing Robert H. Fechner, a labor leader and vice president of the International Association of Machinists, to head the agency. Fechner's background as a union leader, along with his Southern roots (he was born in Tennessee and grew up in Georgia) helped to rally two crucial Democratic constituencies behind the CCC: organized labor and white Southern Democrats.

If Fechner's appointment reassured Southern Democrats that the CCC would preserve racial segregation, an amendment inserted into CCC legislation by African American congressman Oscar De Priest (Rep.-IL) did the opposite. De Priest's amendment prohibited the CCC from discriminating on the basis of race, creed, or color. Thus the CCC became the only New Deal relief agency explicitly to prohibit race discrimination at its inception. As a result, African American civil rights leaders and journalists celebrated the CCC for its equalitarian potential, even as they criticized the agency for failing to realize that potential.

The first New Deal agency legally committed to racial nondiscrimination, the CCC was rife with discrimination in practice. Moreover, CCC rhetoric and imagery was dedicated to the recuperation of white male bodies through rigorous conservation work. When prominent African Americans criticized the agency, CCC officials used the agency's complex administrative structure, which divided authority among several federal departments, to deflect blame for CCC racism away from their own administrative domain and onto another administering department.

For his part, Director Fechner remained steadfast in his commitment to Jim Crow segregation within the agency. He did everything he could to ensure that the CCC would emerge as the "great white chain of camps" that so captivated the American imagination throughout the New Deal years.

When it was first proposed in March 1933, the Civilian Conservation Corps was not age-specific. Roosevelt had imagined that the CCC would be open to men of all ages, and that all men would benefit from the agency's conservation work in field and forest. Yet as the proposed agency underwent congressional consideration, many politicians, welfare reformers, and labor leaders objected to the agency's application to mature male breadwinners.[13] They made their objections on several grounds. First, they objected to breadwinners' removal from the family circle and placement in remote wilderness camps. Second, they objected to the imposition of army-style regimentation on mature American men. And third, they objected to the low, dollar-a-day wage and compulsory family allotments that were part of the proposed CCC. Such provisions, they argued, constituted a threat to the American family and to basic American liberties such as freedom of contract and the right to a living wage.[14]

As it evolved, the CCC fulfilled some of labor organizers' worst fears. Unions were banned from CCC camps, wages were kept unnaturally low, and Army control resulted in antidemocratic responses to many worker complaints. Yet as the decade proceeded, labor leaders embraced the CCC along with most other Americans.

By restricting eligibility to young unemployed men between the ages of eighteen and twenty-five, formulators of CCC legislation overcame reservations of labor leaders, welfare reformers, and others who saw in the proposed CCC an abridgment of basic American liberties. Applied to young American men, such provisions as the dollar-a-day wage, military supervision, and removal from the family circle seemed acceptable and even praiseworthy, as the near-universal acclaim that the CCC enjoyed throughout the 1930s attests.

Establishing the CCC

Roosevelt took office on March 4, 1933; on March 31, he signed legislation authorizing the establishment of the CCC. Throughout the month of March, the process of formulating and promoting the conservation plan had proceeded with remarkable expediency. As James J. McEntee would later recall, "Speed was the President's keynote." The hurry to set the CCC in motion influenced its administrative structure. As McEntee explained, "Instead of setting up a great and cumbersome administrative organ, the President utilized old-line existing departments to carry on this enterprise."[15]

Appropriate to the perceived breadth and immediacy of the crisis it was designed to combat, CCC administration was a genuinely collaborative, urgently national project. Top administrators from the departments of War, Labor, and the Interior were brought together with representatives from a handful of other agencies under Fechner's directorship. The tasks of initial mobilization and ongoing administration were divided up among the departments, with the Army and technical services doing the largest part of the work, and the Office of the Director coordinating the overall program. A committee with representatives from each agency, known as the Advisory Council, was also set up to facilitate interagency collaboration. Initial funding was to be drawn from existing relief allocations, meaning that money would be taken away from other public works projects to fund the CCC.[16]

Significantly, the Army was to play the largest role in day-to-day camp administration. According to an early administrative report, the Department of War was instructed "to physically examine those selected, to enroll those physically fit, to feed, clothe, house, and condition those enrolled, [and] to operate and administer all work camps." In addition, it was directed "to provide educational, recreational, and religious facilities" for the enrollees.[17] In contrast to the Army's considerable workload, Labor Department responsibility was limited to enrollee selection, and the Forestry Service and other technical services were assigned the singular task of administering enrollee work projects. Finally, the Office of Education offered a limited academic curriculum during enrollees' nonwork hours.[18]

In addition to the several federal departments involved, the CCC was divided between federal, state, and local administrative units. State and local officials oversaw selection of enrollees and approved the establishment of CCC projects in each state. In their capacity as selection agents, local relief administrators wielded considerable control over who could, and who could not, participate in the CCC. In spite of the agency's legal policy of nondiscrimination, local selection boards often severely restricted the participation of African Americans and other nonwhite youth. In the state of Georgia, not a single African American had been enrolled as of June 1933 because "most of the local recruiting committees had never been impressed with the fact that the government really meant them to recruit Negroes, as well as whites, for forestry work."[19] Similar situations prevailed in other states. African Americans' exclusion from initial CCC enrollments made it harder for them to be assigned during subsequent enrollment periods, since most of the camps were originally set up for whites only. According to Garth Akridge of the Julius Rosenwald Fund, "the plain facts indicate beyond the remotest possibility of a doubt that in many, yes in practically all sections of the south Negroes are not being placed in Civilian Conservation Corps on anything like an equitable basis."[20] In some instances, the Labor Department, which was charged with overseeing the selection process, interceded to enforce at least limited enrollment of African Americans. In general, though, black youth's efforts to enroll in the CCC met with a number of obstacles, particularly in the South. Southern selection boards argued that the families of African American youth did not need $25 monthly for subsistence, that black enrollees were mentally and physically unfit, that blacks were inherently unambitious and *preferred* to stay in their home communities in contrast to whites, and that black youth in rural areas did not need CCC relief because they could always work for white farmers.

By mid-April, 1933, the first CCC camp, dubbed "Camp Roosevelt," began operation in Virginia; by midsummer, approximately 250,000 young men were working in 1,300 camps across the country.[21] The efficiency with which

CCC units were mobilized was favorably compared to U.S. mobilization in the opening months of World War I. Moreover, although only about 250,000 young, unemployed males were at work on CCC projects, the agency was credited with revolutionizing the situation of America's masculine youth. "The most astounding fact shown up glaringly by the 3-C campaign," one journalist commented, "was the physical, mental, and spiritual flabbiness of much of the youth of the country."[22] According to Fechner, once America's "flabby" youth entered the CCC, "The combination of good food, suitable clothing, a useful occupation and healthful exercise . . . quickly put [them] in a cheerful frame of mind, increased their weight, and changed their entire outlook on life."[23]

Typifying public opinion, the superintendent of a Florida penal farm claimed to see immediate and positive results. Within months of the agency's inception, he published statistics showing that because of the CCC, there had been "an amazing falling off of the number of young men committed to his care." He added, "So long as the camps are maintained, very few of these young men will get into trouble with the law."[24]

Vast claims about youthful regeneration quickly translated into claims about *national* regeneration. As early as July 1933, Fechner wrote to Roosevelt, "The reports reaching my office make it evident that the mobilization of this quarter of a million men for forestry duty has gone a long way toward breaking the back of the depression." He elaborated: "Business conditions throughout the whole country have been tremendously stimulated through the expenditure of funds needed for feeding, housing, and working such a large number of men."[25]

In addition to its material effects, administrators claimed, the CCC was also "morally and spiritually" beneficial to the nation. Fechner declared that the CCC program "would prove of great moral and spiritual value not only to the young men," but by extension, "to the whole country."[26] This boost to national morale derived in part from the representative character of the enrollee group. According to Labor Secretary Frances Perkins, "They are looked upon in each community from which they came as representative of that community. So long as they are in the service their welfare will be the subject of community interest and discussion." In the spring of 1934, Perkins stated that "it is clear that no single attack upon unemployment of similar magnitude could have accomplished more good socially or economically or aroused more widespread or deeply felt approval."[27]

Initially, the CCC left the matter of assigning enrollees to camps up to the states; consequently, some states established racially integrated camps, although these generally had segregated facilities for blacks and whites, while other states segregated whole camps from the beginning. Fechner established the rule that African Americans could not leave their home states to attend a CCC camp, unless their state of origin did not have an African American camp, in which case they were prohibited from traveling beyond their own Corps area. In this way, blacks and whites were prevented from commingling. Equally important, Southern blacks were prevented from migrating out of the Jim Crow South or mingling with Northern blacks.

CCC enrollment peaked in 1935. In 1937, the CCC failed to garner congressional approval for its bid to become a permanent agency, and enrollments never again surged as they had in the period 1933–35, but the agency remained popular. When budgetary austerity required periodic cuts after 1937, African American camps were often the first eliminated, even as the proportion of blacks on the relief rolls continued to climb. At the same time, under the reassuring supervision of U.S. Army personnel, the CCC continued to burnish its reputation as a "great white chain of camps," peopled by white male youth whose bodies and minds were vastly improved through hard work, military-style discipline, and exposure to the elements.

✑ CCC Storytelling

In its most basic outlines, the story of the CCC youth began with the removal of jobless white youth from broken homes, hobo jungles, and other unsavory environs and their placement in the healthful surrounds of a militarized wilderness camp. Once enrolled, the CCC youth learned the principles of personal sacrifice and obedience at the hands of Army officers and other mature male role models in charge of the camps. The fraternal experience of military-style camp life taught them the virtues of selflessness, group spiritedness, and respect for others, and they received a vocational training on work projects supervised by the personnel of the Forestry Service and other technical services. Although literacy training and other educational courses were available to enrollees in their nonwork hours, most popular and official stories of CCC youth focused on "the scholarship in work experience" that enrollees received on the job. The CCC was thus a race- and class-appropriate coming-of-age experience wherein white working-class youth learned to do a hard day's work and like it; it taught the young "army with shovels" endurance and obedience that would stand both them and their prospective employers in good stead in the private labor market.

Representations of CCC youth as poorly educated, working-class, and destined for a life of hard manual labor competed with other narratives that depicted the CCC youth as a more broadly representative figure—not strictly working-class, but "the hope and the cream" of young American manhood. Situated in the midst of the nation's magnificent natural landscape, CCC youth stood as a link to the nation's rugged pioneer past and its compelling national resource. In such narratives, the CCC prevented not only soil erosion, but "human erosion"; young white men who entered the camps "pasty-faced" and "slack-fibered" were transformed through healthful outdoor work into veritable supermen; and a potent, racialized metaphor of U.S. national community emerged.

Part of what explains the diversity of stories about the CCC—some emphasizing military socialization, others emphasizing its approximation of normal American civic life, still others emphasizing its sexual and racial contours—is the diversity of professionals involved in CCC camp administration. Labor activists, foresters, educators, and army officers all produced narratives of CCC life consistent with their respective professional priorities. In addition, the CCC had a division of public relations that produced pamphlets and press releases, commissioned artworks and photographs, and compiled files of "success stories" and "benefit letters" submitted by CCC enrollees. Given the popularity and symbolic centrality of the CCC in Depression-era public discourse, politicians, civic leaders, and welfare reformers also made praise for the CCC a staple of public discourse. And finally, camp newspapers produced in every camp under the supervision of the Office of Education and *Happy Days*, an independent national newspaper published in Washington, DC, extolled the virtues of CCC life and set a model emulated by other CCC storytellers.

The story of Tony, an enrollee "from the slums of one of our large midwestern cities," is an exemplary account of CCC-style Americanization. According to the Wisconsin forester who authored Tony's narrative, Tony entered to the CCC as a "shrimp of a kid" who could not even wield an ax. Over the course of his enrollment, the author notes, Tony underwent a remarkable transformation. No longer destined to follow in the footsteps of "a shiftless father who died and left a poverty-stricken mother with a family of hungry and growing kids," Tony developed work skills and a sense of family responsibility necessary to succeed as a family provider. He told the narrator "of his pride in being able to help 'ma and the kids.'" In entering the CCC, Tony also left behind a past "of bad companions, of hookey from school, petty thievery, juvenile court, [and] probation." He emerged from the agency an upstanding citizen whose great ambition was "to work for the very construction company he had snitched lumber and coal from a little more than a year ago."[28]

Not only had Tony developed a valuable work ethic and sense of family obligation; he had also "found a new life . . . close to the heart of nature" as a member of "Uncle Sam's great army of woodsmen."[29] He had blended into the fraternity of the CCC camp, forming friendships and sharing confidences with other CCC men. As a result of hard work and healthful outdoor surroundings, Tony also emerged from the CCC camp "heavier and hard-muscled." Thus fortified in mind and body, he was no longer recognizable as an ethnic child of the slums. Once a civic liability, he was now an asset to family and nation.

Not surprisingly, this story by "A Wisconsin Forestry Foreman" emphasized the CCC's work program over other aspects of the agency. Because the Forestry Service supervised CCC work projects, foresters tended to highlight the importance of rugged outdoor work among the many benefits of enrollment. Likewise, educators emphasized educational work, chaplains emphasized moral uplift, and Army officers stressed the lessons in discipline, regularity, and patriotism that enrollees learned from military officers. For their part, high-ranking CCC officials and publicists took a broader view of the agency's national benefits. This variety of authorial perspectives adds to the complexity of the CCC narrative, particularly when enrollees' own prolific storytelling practices are added to the mix.

Yet for all of their variety, most stories of CCC life bore similarities to Tony's narrative. As a whole, they detailed a positive process of "Americanization" that began when enrollees left behind urban vices, negative social and familial influences, and destitution to enter the healthful environs of the CCC camp. They emphasized the self-discipline, obedience, and national pride that enrollees learned from military officers; the hard work, physical endurance, and love of nature that they learned from forestry foremen; and the wholesome friendships that they formed with supervisors and with other CCC youth.

Stories also dwelled on the agency's immense physical benefits. Just as Tony became "heavier and hard-muscled," enrollees in countless CCC stories became stronger and more physically appealing. Their increased strength and virility, combined with self-discipline, willingness to work, and positive national outlook, made them compelling figures of national recovery throughout the New Deal years.

Stories authored by African Americans pose an exception to these narrative conventions. Accounts of CCC life published in the black press detailed the racism that black enrollees encountered from Army officers, white CCC youth, and whites in nearby communities.[30] But African Americans also authored racially specific success stories. One black enrollee who served in an integrated camp prior to the blanket segregation policy titled his story, "Why I Am Glad to be a Negro in the CCC." The author derived inspiration from following in the footsteps of great African Americans who had overcome adversity to do great things. Although white CCC narratives emphasized physical development, African American CCC narratives stressed the value of education, whether it meant overcoming illiteracy or, in exceptional circumstances, receiving instruction from a black educational adviser. For black youth, the CCC represented a chance—albeit a small one—for educational and occupational mobility that redounded not just to the individual but to the entire black community. Black CCC enrollments were announced in the society pages of some black newspapers, and considerable fanfare attended black appointments to CCC professional posts.[31] Throughout the period 1933–42, African American leaders pressed for more black professional postings in segregated CCC camps. All-black camps often had a handful of African American educational advisers, chaplains, or medical personnel, but only two camps in the history of the CCC—one at Gettysburg National Park, Pennsylvania, and the other at Fisher's Landing, New York—had all-black staffs, including black commanding officers.[32]

Part of the satisfaction of the CCC story had to do with its responsiveness to class-based anxieties. The average CCC enrollee was represented as an urban white working-class youth from a questionable home. "In the main," McEntee wrote, "the men who served . . . came from economically insecure homes. They were drawn almost entirely from that third of the population which President Roosevelt had described as 'ill fed, ill housed, and ill clothed.'"[33] The *Nation* praised the CCC for bringing "town and city boys into the forests" where it built up "their undernourished bodies and strengthened their characters."[34] Similarly, McEntee wrote, "Boys from New York's teeming East Side found themselves . . . in the high meadows of Glacier National Park" and "the pallid battalions of Chicago waded through the Spring thaw in Mount Hood National Forest in Oregon."[35]

Confronted with "the majesty of nature," white working-class enrollees forgot about urban vices and embraced healthful outdoor pursuits. Blazing mountain trails, fighting forest fires, and taking all-day hikes with their fellows replaced loitering on street corners and languishing in enforced idleness. In the process, as one CCC forester observed, enrollees "learned about America." As John Dennett Guthrie wrote, they witnessed "her vastness, her beauty, her grandeur, her nakedness, / her raped forests and soils and wildlife and waters."[36] And, acting as good "husbands" to the "naked" feminized landscape, they "helped to build America" through reforestation, flood control, and other conservation work.[37]

The CCC invoked not only the land itself, but white American men's historical relationship to the land. As CCC enrollees combated fires, floods, erosion, and other natural threats, they became a symbolic link to the nation's pioneer past of racial conquest and empire building. Accounts likened enrollees to wilderness adventurers such as "Kit Carson, Daniel Boone, Lewis and Clark, Marquette, Sera and all the rest of that vast legion of honor."[38] From the encounter with nature, a new generation of white American manhood—one that had more in common with the nation's forebears—was being forged. Describing CCC youth in terms that recalled earlier wilderness adventurers, one educational adviser wrote, "Tall and sun-crowned, our faces blessed by summer rains, and our weather-beaten hands evidencing tasks conquered, snows endured, we are walking into the morning."[39] Thus transformed by their encounter with nature into upstanding American citizens, enrollees could look forward to a wholesome and promising future—one removed from the negative influences of their Depression-mired pasts.

❧ Regulating Youth

If recapitulating the pioneer experience helped enrollees to overcome their troubled pasts, so too did the routines of living in a carefully administered camp. Popular and official accounts highlighted the emphasis on health, sanitation, and "orderly living." In the CCC, sleeping hours, dress, and personal cleanliness were strictly regimented. According to one report, "Regularity replaced irregularity. Food three times a day . . . appeared instead of irregular meals. . . . Neatness and personal cleanliness were stressed and many thousands were acquainted with the shower bath and the toothbrush for the first time in the CCC."[40]

The very regularity of camp life was reputed to foster a process of "Americanization." Although enrollees might come from a range of backgrounds, the common issue of uniforms, work shoes, and toilet kits, together with the shared experience of rigorous work and leisure activities, was alleged to have an equalizing influence. As one forester remarked, "This has been a great leveling process as well as a genuine educational force for good." Overcoming the provincialism of individual backgrounds to find a higher, national consciousness was one features of CCC life that supporters often praised.[41]

African Americans were categorically excluded from the education in Americanization and idealized fraternal living that came from living with a diverse group of others in a CCC camp. Placed in segregated camps and prevented from leaving their home Corps areas, African American enrollees were disallowed the opportunity explore new American vistas and mingle with different kinds of people, as white enrollees were encouraged to do.[42]

Fraternal living was a salient feature of CCC camp life. McEntee stated that living with "199 other boys" instilled an ethic of civic accountability, requiring enrollees to "acquire a give-and-take attitude, make concessions, govern [their] temper."[43] In the process, they gave up negative behaviors learned in destitute working-class homes. They also left behind negative maternal influences. According to McEntee, those "who had been 'mama's boys' quickly found that the 199 other boys in a camp would not defer to them or coddle them as a mother used to do."[44] One enrollee who described himself as "just a kid whose mother would not push him out into the world to fight for himself" learned to be selfless and courageous in the CCC.[45] At a time when widespread joblessness seemed to imperil American fatherhood, such stories stressed masculine youth's protection from mothers' corrupting influence.[46]

In removing youth from their homes, the CCC also implicitly criticized the broader effects of government relief on American family life. In particular, it criticized fathers who failed to provide adequately for their families and succumbed to welfare dependency. One Missouri relief administrator characterized enrollees' parents as "careless and indifferent," and another stated, "These boys are all of humble parentage and the environment at home may not be such that they would profit by precept or example in their daily lives."[47] An Illinois relief administrator told the story of one youth "who had never had a job of any kind. The family was a chronic welfare case. The father was very shiftless."[48]

If relief-dependent parents were not competent to socialize masculine youth, then who was? Many accounts of CCC life stressed the role of military officers in reshaping the character and outlook of idle youth. "No group of men understands youth so well or holds it in greater affection than does the commissioned personnel of the Army," declared Secretary of War George H. Dern. He continued, "The understanding leadership of the Army has lifted the head, quickened the pace, given assurance to the approach of practically every member of the Corps." A CCC educational adviser agreed, stating that Army officers "have done more to strengthen the good character of the men in our camp than anything else." They did this through "proper discipline, discouragement of bad habits, and the examples set the enrollees."[49] According to McEntee, the commanding officer's significance was inestimable; he stated, "the whole camp revolved around the C.O."[50]

Accounts of CCC militarism thus accentuated positive intergenerational relations between white officers and enrollees. Yet such accounts also addressed widespread public ambivalence toward "wild boys" and delinquent youth. Like the more explicitly militarized "concentration camps" that Senator Couzens had proposed, CCC militarism punished idle youth's transgressions by subjecting enrollees to rigorous physical and mental discipline. Observance of military hierarchy and ritual was important to this process. As John Dennett Guthrie described, "There were Reveille and Mess Call and Taps, / And the Flag went up, all over America."[51] Enrollees followed a fast-paced routine punctuated by military rituals. Every aspect of their lives was carried out under the watchful eye of military officers and other supervisory personnel.

Accounts of CCC militarism stressed the self-sacrifice and cooperation required of enrollees. Stories emphasized the lessons in endurance that CCC enrollees learned on the job and in the performance of camp duties. Although CCC work projects were not subject to military supervision, widely circulating images of white CCC youth, laboring in unison with their peers, suggested youth's containment within military bounds.

Military supervision also ensured that enrollees would engage in wholesome leisure pursuits. Criminality and illicit sexuality, which had been central to accounts of homeless and delinquent youth, were almost entirely absent from narratives of CCC life. Careful guidance, positive role modeling, and strict supervision by military officers helped to contain the threat of subversive homosociality. As in the U.S. military, the CCC enforced heteronormativity by subjecting nonconforming individuals to emasculating taunts. Young men who failed to conform to the model of masculinity privileged in the CCC were called "gold brickers" and "pansies." According to camp newspapers, effeminate enrollees quickly realized that they had no place in the agency and "went over the hill." Allegedly, only "men who could take it" remained in the CCC for any length of time. The hypermasculine expression, "We can take it," was a nationally approved CCC motto throughout its years of operation.[52]

Overall, jobless white youth who entered into the military context of the CCC camp were forced to undergo a physical and mental transformation. They learned lessons of obedience and endurance. From their origins as a national threat, they became a national resource conceived in military terms. Journalists, civic leaders, and a range of professionals associated with the camps praised the agency for transforming what had been a menacing "army of boys on the loose" into a young white "army with shovels," sometimes called "Roosevelt's tree army" or "Roosevelt's Green Guard."

Some accounts of CCC militarism were taken to extremes. Assistant Secretary of War Henry Woodring stirred up trouble in March 1934 when he characterized the CCC as "a dress rehearsal of the Army's ability to intervene, under Constitutional authority, in combating the Depression." Woodring positioned enrollees within a broader network of "economic storm troops that could support the government's efforts to smash the depression."[53] In another controversial account, Major General Johnson Hagood of the Eighth Corps Army described the CCC group as "[m]en that can take care of themselves in the woods, hands hardened to the pick and shovel, feet hardened to the road, nerves and muscles that respond to the word of command."[54] As this account suggests, the CCC youth was at once physically strong—an exemplar of powerful white working-class manhood—and carefully contained, occupied with the physically taxing responsibilities of CCC life.

Such accounts elicited protests, particularly from labor groups that questioned the regimentation and antidemocratic implications of the CCC.[55] They also provoked the anger of CCC publicists who lamented that they could not censor the statements of military officers like Woodring and Hagood.[56]

Yet the same officials who lamented extreme representations of CCC militarism subtly accentuated the military accents of white CCC youth. Officials like Stephen Early and McEntee emphasized the benefits of military guidance, regularity, and discipline for idle unemployed youth. Sometimes, a high-ranking CCC official would even suggest the possibility of incorporating military exercises into the CCC, as Fechner did in 1939.[57] CCC officials were careful to keep their representations of CCC militarism within carefully defined limits. Subtly portrayed, CCC militarism was politically popular, whereas too much emphasis on the military's role might have made the New Deal administration seem power hungry and antidemocratic.

In his final report as CCC director, McEntee described the ritual of "Retreat," during which "the men show respect for the flag when it is lowered." He wrote, "They like it. . . . During the moments while they stand at attention, they know that they are more than individuals; they are a part of that camp, they are a part of a big organization working to preserve the health and wealth of America; they are citizens of the United States."[58] In numerous accounts of camp life, military rituals impressed on enrollees that they were more than individuals—that they were members of an organization that embodied national community. As one enrollee explained, "I have learned the value of . . . brotherhood. I know that I am not individually important but am only one of millions and that success is nothing much except collectively speaking." For this essayist, the fraternal bonds formed through service in the CCC translated into a deep love of country. He added, "I have become more patriotic than I ever dreamed I could be and have confidence in the future America. . . . I have been made to feel the value of comradeship and, somehow, I feel lately that I am a definite part of society, that I am a part of America, with my part to be done."[59]

Participation in the CCC distinguished enrollees as *more* virtuous, *more* manly, and *more* patriotic than their civilian counterparts. In the narrative of distinguished military service and privileged fraternal membership, the class accents of the enrollee group fell away. In such narratives, white youth enrolled in the CCC were less often depicted as idle, working-class delinquents and were instead represented as exemplary American boys—as the "hope" and the "cream" of America.

As in more punitive accounts, the work activities of youth were imbued with military accents, this time emphasizing enrollees' glory and sacrifice. Representations of CCC youth who battled forest fires offered particularly compelling versions of the youthful soldier ideal. Guthrie writes, "The CCC came in long truck caravans . . . / With ready arms and legs and backs. / They fought on a thousand fire fronts."[60] One enrollee described, "Heroes of the night . . . to the rescue . . . while the populace sleeps. . . . Silhouette of trucks with denim-clad men against looming timber ahead . . . symbolic of the Nation's youth."[61] Another enrollee wrote, "I've thrilled to the wonderful courage and valor of these kids as they battled against forest fires and have reveled in this young American manhood that never winced even in the midst of a raging inferno, but carried on without complaint, followed orders without hesitancy, and exhibited a bravery that even the most highly-rated shock troops might well envy."[62]

One source for such positive accounts of CCC militarism was the newspaper *Happy Days*, whose editors had previously contributed to the *Stars and Stripes* during World War I.[63] But CCC officials also promoted the martial idealism of the agency, issuing letters of commendation and merit to young enrollees who demonstrated unusual heroism or sacrifice. Reflecting the racial limits of the CCC's idealized military fraternity, the first and possibly only citation for valor awarded to an African American enrollee was given to H. Mears in 1940. Mears's valor could hardly be discounted; while enrolled in a Louisiana camp, he risked his life to save two children who had been swept away in a river flood. With the exception of Mears, African Americans were generally overlooked in rituals that highlighted the CCC's martial idealism. Certainly, images of CCC military fraternity excluded African Americans, who were likelier to be represented as singers or minstrel performers than as valiant and resolute defenders of American honor.

Although some accounts of CCC militarism described a threat contained, and others described a more ideal, fraternal model of citizenship embodied, the military framework of the CCC also licensed more positive accounts of homosociality. Whereas the subversive homosociality of the transient community had been among its most alarming characteristics, the carefully ordered military-style fraternity of the CCC posed a reassuring and appealing alternative. Accounts of CCC life were often effusive in their descriptions of male bonding that took place in the camps. Both relationships between peers and between enrollees and officers were described in terms that could only be characterized as passionate.

One source for such stories was an essay contest on "What the CCC Has Done for Me," sponsored by the agency's public relations division in 1933. In a prize-winning essay, enrollee Allen Cook presents a very sentimental portrait of his CCC experience. He begins by describing how, at a moment when he is pondering his past as a "boy who wearily tramped the streets," he is discovered by his commanding officer:

> "Mooning?" A pleasant voice breaks in upon the sad retrospect. I look up and behold the smiling face of my beloved captain.
>
> "N-no, sir," I stammer, wiping the back of my hand across the eyes that I know are suspiciously moist. "I-I'm just thinking—how good and how wonderful this all is," sweeping out my hand to include the camp, the hills, the trees, the stars, the flowers. "After some things this is like—Heaven."

Cook continues,

> And it is, too. I know the heavenly exhilaration that comes from good clothes, good food, and clean hard muscle; from dawn on the hills and a flaming sunset. I know the divine serenity of soul that comes from a quiet well-ordered life; from the silence of night, the whisper of wind, and the perfume of dew-drenched flowers.
>
> Peace? Ah, I have found it at last. And happiness . . . it's here, right here.

Cook's apparent love for his captain and his description of "the heavenly exhilaration that comes from . . . clean hard muscle" was sufficiently compelling that CCC publicists arranged for its publication in *American Forests*.[64] Other accounts gave a more general impression of the fraternal camaraderie of the CCC camps. The CCC "gave me the opportunity to make friendships that will live forever," enrollee Robert Miller wrote. He elaborated, "Days of work in the woods, nights around the fire in the barracks, a trick played on an innocent chap, an all day hike with some of my friends, a fishing trip with one of my pals, the rush for the mess hall when the gong sounds, all of these thoughts are dear to me."[65] Suggesting the deep emotional bond that many in the CCC shared, former enrollee Keith Hufford wrote, "And now, I often become homesick for the noise and clamor of the mess hall where 150 ravenous boys troop in three times a day, the twang of guitars as a soft-voiced enrollee sings a plaintive mountain melody on the steps of the barrack in the soft, summer twilight, the smell of clean steaming bodies and the stinging crack of a turkish towel in the bathhouse after the day's work is done. All of these things, and many more, I long for, but I must make way for some other young fellow."[66]

Hufford's description of "clean steaming bodies and the stinging crack of a turkish towel," like Cook's reference to his "beloved captain" and the "heavenly feel of . . . clean, hard muscle," were not explicitly sexualized. Nevertheless, within their Depression context, such narratives played on the public preoccupation with the sexuality of masculine youth. CCC publicists' enthusiasm for such stories suggests that they were interested not in *dispelling* improper homosociality, but in harnessing its power to the nation-building project of the New Deal state.

Moreover, other authors seemed deliberate in queering the CCC narrative. Ray Hoyt, the editor of *Happy Days*, generally accentuated the wholesome homosociality of camp life in his paper and in a booklet titled *"We Can Take It": A Short Story of the C.C.C.* In both texts, Hoyt describes plenty of conventionally masculine activities such as baseball, wrestling, and playing pool in the camp canteen. But he also highlights more transgressive moments, as when participants in CCC theatricals masqueraded as women. "Camps are taking drama seriously," he wrote. He added that although the actors usually choose "plays which have a minimum of female characters," they do take over "the female . . . parts when necessary." Hoyt's description of CCC dance classes is similarly provocative. Noting that CCC camps sometimes held dances to which girls from nearby communities were invited, he stated, "Many of the men had to learn the art of dancing after getting to camp. Afternoon classes in dancing frequently are held by the men, and it is common to see one man instructing another in the steps of a waltz in the barracks, their heavy Army shoes notwithstanding."[67]

Whether the subject was the emotional bond formed between a callow enrollee and his "beloved captain," or an account of recreational activities like swimming or acting, representations of camp life described the intimacy of male bonding in rich detail.[68] Visual imagery within the CCC likewise emphasized the fraternal dimension of camp life. Although images showing physical contact between two enrollees were generally absent, physical gestures of friendship and horseplay between three or more enrollees commonly appeared.

Figure 5. Kenneth Baker, Swimming and Boating on Lake McDonald, Glacier Park, MN, June 25, 1939. Civilian Conservation Corps, B&W photograph, National Archives and Records Administration, Still Pictures Branch.

Far from undermining the national objectives of the CCC, such male bonding took place within properly militarized bounds and so contributed to their success. CCC enrollees were, after all, men who could "take it"; in popular rhetoric, they were contrasted with the "pansies" and "cream puffs" who could not.[69] The exemplary enrollee was both morally and physically irreproachable. "You can build a new state out of men like these," remarked one journalist. He declared, "They are the Green Guard of the Roosevelt Revolution."[70]

❧ Embodied Youth

According to media accounts, after six months or a year of service, the CCC enrollee underwent a transformation that was at once physical, mental, and spiritual. Mentally, the CCC enrollee had learned the value of "a good day's work." From one who was in danger of becoming a habitual loafer, he had become a productive citizen. Spiritually, the enrollee had learned the value of self-discipline, cooperative effort, and national service. From one who had endured "poverty and wretchedness . . . and the manifold temptations that attach themselves to idleness," he found new hope in the fraternity of camp life and embraced a fervent patriotism.[71]

But even more than mental or spiritual improvements, it was the *physical* regeneration of masculine youth that functioned as a metaphor for national recovery. Claims of CCC success invariably emphasized the physical transformation of youth. One CCC enthusiast described the transformation wrought by CCC service as follows: "Into the camps," he began, "the relief organizations . . . fed . . . hordes of pasty-faced, slack-fibered youngsters. . . . Out of the camps came at least 200,000 sun-tanned, clear-eyed young *men*."[72] Another CCC enthusiast gave a similar account. He remarked, "There was certainly a great contrast between the thin, white, anemic-looking faces of last spring and the brown and bronzed faces and bulging muscles of late summer."[73]

Success was routinely measured in pounds gained and inches grown. In the fall of 1933, administrators proudly reported that the average weight gain for the first six-month term had exceeded ten pounds. Camp administrators kept careful records on each enrollee's weight and height, and enrollees self-consciously identified themselves in these terms as well. In a personal letter to Fechner requesting an extension of his service, one enrollee seemed defensive that his in-service weight gain had been below average. While he had gained fewer than five pounds, he anxiously explained, he had benefited from the CCC in many other ways.[74] Popular accounts of CCC life dwelled on enrollees' lusty appetites and on the bountiful, heavy meals that enrollees consumed between the hours of rugged outdoor work (see Figure 2). If the rest of America could be said to be "pasty-faced" and "slack-fibered," such criticisms could no longer be applied to the typical CCC enrollee. Instead, "The boys developed the muscles and chests of football players. They began to take pride in their bodies. They became as brown as Indians."[75]

In a typical account, one military officer observed, "Pale skins are bronzed; chests deepen; shoulders long sagged with the burden of idleness straighten; muscles once again become firm; bodily vigor and strength increase."[76] Ray Hoyt, editor of *Happy Days*, described the physical regeneration that enrollees underwent as a result of hard outdoor work: "They soon bared their backs to the sun and worked without shirts. Many of them wore nothing but shoes, socks, and G.I. 'shorts.' Bodies gradually became tanned, and the muscles tough."[77] Guthrie elaborated,

> The boys went to work,
> Stripped to the waist, soon became
> Brown-armed, brown-shouldered, chests, backs, and legs –
> Like Indians, modern American Redmen.
> The boys set the stripped style,
> CCC boys-stripped-to-the waist-style, all over America.

Best way to work, clean, healthy,—
All in CCC camps.[78]

As Guthrie's account suggests, the "CCC boy-stripped-to-the-waist" was a popular racialized icon of the New Deal. Feature articles in magazines typically contained photographs of half-clothed enrollees engaged in rugged outdoor work, and government civilian recruitment pamphlets deployed such images as well. Recognizing the appeal of the "loosely-clad forestry worker," top CCC officials commissioned WPA artists to immortalize the figure in 1935. Official publicity pamphlets featured photographs and drawings of white CCC youth stripped to the waist and hard at work.

Figure 6. Cover Detail. U.S. Civilian Conservation Corps, *Woodsmanship for the Civilian Conservation Corps* (Washington, DC: U.S. Government Printing Office, 1936). Illustrator: Rudy Wendelin.

In his final report in 1942, Director McEntee revealed much of what was at stake in the physical program of the CCC. McEntee bemoaned the "scrawny, underweight" condition that most youth manifested on entering the CCC, and he praised the CCC's record in "building up" enrollees. He thus drew a link between enrollees' physical health and their mental and psychological capacities. "That a man should weigh 130 pounds or 150 pounds, so far as sheer poundage is concerned, is not particularly important," he stated. "But," he added, "the all-around physical, mental, and psychical differences which . . . are tangibly exemplified by those twenty pounds . . . are important to the individual, to the community, and to the Nation." According to McEntee, the underweight youth lost "economic productivity . . . capacity for citizenship, and . . . usefulness as parents." Yet even more alarmingly, he underwent a "more subtle and more dangerous character-degeneration."[79]

McEntee's account raised the specter of a nation of "light-weights"—men who, like the "wild boys" of early Depression popular narratives, were physically damaged, politically and economically useless, and sexually deviant, incapable of fathering the children on whose shoulders the nation's future would rest. He argued that "this country cannot afford to allow young people to grow up underweight and with correctable defects when a few months in an outdoor camp like the CCC can build [them] up." Having presented a bleak portrait of youthful degeneration, he went on to describe the positive effects of the CCC: "Flat chests assumed more normal contours. Droopy shoulders acquired a manlike square set. Dull eyes and pasty complexions took on a new brightness and sparkle. Flabby arms, legs, and torsos built up an armour of tough muscles—usually overlaid with deeply tanned young human hides."[80]

Although McEntee went on to state that "a mighty physique was never considered to be an end in itself" but was only "a very firm foundation for a great deal of other human development," his own account of CCC accomplishments dwelled primarily on the physical. Legs and torsos, strong bones, firm muscles, and "deeply-tanned human hides"—these were the most compelling images McEntee could find to prove that the CCC deserved a lasting place in postwar America. McEntee also claimed that the CCC had made vital contributions to national defense. The young man who served in the CCC, he contended, was "better soldier material" than the man who did not. Among other things, he argued, CCC "graduates" were immune to epidemic diseases like meningitis which struck individuals who lacked prior experience living in large groups of men.[81]

Although administrators claimed to transform the "lightweight" and "slack-fibered" into exemplary male citizens, they also insisted that requirements for entry into the CCC were highly selective. An early administrative bulletin declared, "The undertaking is one of the most significant experiments ever entered upon by the American government. Only the best men available are wanted."[82] To qualify as "best men," potential participants had to be "young men of *character*—men who are clean-cut, purposeful, and ambitious." All of these were traits that, like the capacity to "bronze" in the sun, were typically associated with whiteness. In visual terms, the "loosely-clad forestry worker" might become "brown as an Indian" through rugged outdoor labor, but he was invariably white to begin with.

The photographic record maintained by CCC officials throughout the agency's tenure is evidence of the lesser status given to African Americans in the program. By 1940, thousands of photographic portraits of enrollees had been collected in official files. Despite the participation of many thousands of African Americans in the CCC, an official noted that, "on checking up, I find that we have less than a dozen photos showing negro enrollees at work."[83] Additionally, African American enrollees received almost no coverage in white-controlled newspapers, and they escaped mention in every single one of the Director's ten annual reports. Native American and Mexican American enrollees were also largely excluded from official and popular imagery. Like African Americans, they escaped notice by the artists and photographers who preferred to "immortalize" young white "loosely-clad forestry workers." Far from exemplifying the model of young masculine citizenship so frequently celebrated in CCC accounts, their place within the organization, although officially sanctioned, was peripheral and threatened to undermine both that model of citizenship and the concept of nationality it supported.

➵ CCC Exclusiveness

According to an early administrative bulletin, the CCC was "a national project." "In accordance with the spirit of American government and American ideals of fair play," the bulletin continued, "there will be no discrimination on account of race, creed, color, or politics."[84] Reflected in this statement is a tension that was central to the constitution of the CCC, and to its idealized imagery of youthful manhood. The CCC was a *national* project, and as such it was rhetorically bound to principles of "fair play" and nondiscrimination. Individuals of all races, creeds, colors, and politics were officially eligible for CCC enrollment. Moreover, the CCC reported that its camps were "small democracies in action," based on principles of fraternity and equality, where enrollees underwent "a leveling process" and came to exemplify "a finer, better type of citizen."

With regard to race, practice deviated significantly from policy, as the experience of African American enrollees suggests. Consistent with the rhetoric of democracy and fair play, the CCC adopted an official policy of enrolling African Americans in direct proportion to their percentage in the general population. This objective, however, was never achieved. Local selection boards, particularly in the South, discriminated against African Americans, and officials claimed that African American enrollees were difficult to place. As Fechner explained, many communities resisted the establishment of all-black camps in their vicinities.[85] A Southerner himself, Fechner wholeheartedly embraced racial segregation, and he supported the Army's discriminatory policies.[86] Other CCC administrators were racist as well. Southern African Americans were under the authority of General George Van Horn Mosley, commander of the Army's Fourth Corps Division. According to historian George Rawick, Mosley "insisted that Negroes were inferiors both socially and biologically and he treated them accordingly."[87] In justifying the broader practice of racial discrimination in the CCC, Fechner remarked, "It is unfortunate that racial feeling prevails in this country but we have not yet reached that state of perfection where it can be totally avoided."[88]

Fechner's claim that CCC racism merely reflected the imperfection of the larger society does not adequately explain the coexistence of racism and nationalism within the CCC. The CCC was a national project. As such, it was rhetorically committed to a policy of inclusion. But because the CCC, as a national project, also served to model a particular vision of citizenship and national community—one that defined equality in terms of *sameness* and national community in terms of *brotherhood*—it was also committed to a practice of racial exclusion.

When enrollees entered the "model communities" of the CCC to partake of "democracy in action," they entered a society characterized by homogeneity. The CCC was purported to strip America's unemployed youth down to their "essential similarity." Out of that similarity would come mutual understanding, group loyalty, and collective commitments that no other institution of American social life could provide.

In the rhetoric of the CCC, perfect equality, in the sense of mutual respect for rights and privileges, came from recognition that one was neither better nor worse than—that one was essentially the same as—the "199 other fellows in camp."[89] Incoming enrollees were advised that their peers in the CCC "would not coddle them as a mother used to do." Indeed, such true equality could not coexist with gender or racial difference. The absence of women and segregation of African Americans in the CCC freed enrollees from the weighty gender and racial conflicts of the Depression decade, thus enabling their otherwise embattled white masculinity to flourish.

Women's absence from the camps might have prompted fears of sexual perversion, but it did not. Accounts of other all-male domains, such as prisons, flophouses, and even the Federal Transient Program raised the specter of improper homosociality in the 1930s. In contrast, Americans were exceptionally tolerant of CCC homosociality. As previously described, CCC storytellers did not eliminate same-sex attraction from their narratives. Erotically charged images of "loosely-clad forestry workers," together with romantic accounts of male friendships, animated representations of CCC life. Yet far from generating alarm, such representations generated vast approval.

A working-class bachelor subculture—heterogeneous, nonprocreative, and potentially anticapitalist—flourished at the start of the Depression.[90] It was the idle youth's exposure to that subculture that generated public alarm over the fate of the "army of boys on the loose." Whereas the bachelor subculture subverted class, racial, and generational divisions, the CCC fashioned a racially white working-class and generationally compliant group of enrollees. Consequently, the homoeroticism of CCC representations was not just less dangerous; it was positively pleasurable. At a time of national uncertainty, the enrollee's virile white masculinity stood as a metaphor for strong decisive nationhood. His appealing white body encouraged the identification of national community with racial community. As an object of sexual fantasy, it provided the ground on which a power-differentiated conception of nationhood could emerge.

In his final report, McEntee described the CCC as a "great white chain of camps." He also called it a "strange new army—different from anything the world had seen—an army with shovels."[91] In doing so, he drew a link between the nation's most vital human resource—its white masculine youth—and its most inspiring physical resources—its plains, mountains, streams, and lakes. In New Deal rhetoric, both the nation's physical and its human resources became metaphors for national crisis. Both had been sickened by the immense growth of urban communities, with their problems of congestion, poverty, racial commingling, and crime. Under the nation-saving rhetoric of the New Deal, the conservation of both human and physical resources became a potent metaphor for national recovery. Roosevelt's invocations of "America, the beautiful" restored to former greatness by the CCC's "loosely-clad foresters," helped a gendered and racialized New Deal public to cohere.

In a climate of intense economic and gender insecurity, the CCC intervened to safeguard white masculine youth against the potentially dire effects of prolonged social dislocation. It removed impressionable youth from "the distress of the family circle and the perils of the streetcorner" to the rugged, healthful surrounds of the Army-supervised work camp. There, in an environment of carefully monitored, partially militarized fraternal living, enrollees learned habits of discipline and regularity; they partook of "democracy in action"; and they internalized the social values of mutualism, cooperation, and compromise that membership in a fraternal community was uniquely suited to provide. The militarized fraternal accents of camp life were credited with instilling both patriotism and mature, masculine virtues in youthful enrollees. Participants were taught to make *personal* adjustments to Depression conditions rather than turning to "radical panaceas" or succumbing to chronic dependency. Enrollees who successfully completed their terms of service, official CCC rhetoric contended, were men who could "take it"; neither paupers nor "pansies," they represented a recuperated white masculinity that many viewed as a potent metaphor for national recovery in the Depression years.

Indeed, at a time when military metaphors were constantly being used to describe America's assault on the Depression, unemployed youth proved to be an invaluable symbolic resource. No other group was so precisely suited to representation in military terms. From "an army of boys on the loose" which many feared would wage war on settled society, unemployed youth were transformed into the much-admired "forest expeditionary force," exemplifying "a new order of service to the nation." In this way, a group that had symbolized social crisis was deployed as evidence of the palliative effects of the New Deal.[92]

For the bulk of Americans who praised the CCC, few things were as reassuring as the image of rejuvenated young men "knuckling down to hard work and liking it," far removed from the tantalizing social vices that had provoked widespread alarm in the early Depression years. This image of the hard-working enrollee reveals ambivalence about masculine youth that was crucial to the CCC's popularity. Praised as an exemplar of national service on the one hand, the CCC enrollee was also a threat that needed to be contained. An inmate in a sort of "concentration camp," his service had punitive implications; firm military guidance was deemed necessary to restore him to productive membership in society.

The CCC was an immensely popular New Deal program, and the rehabilitated CCC enrollee was an intensely pleasurable symbol of national recovery. The relationship between particular representations of masculine youth and much larger claims about national recovery merits close attention, for it reveals the extent to which political and specifically *national* problems are frequently worked out on the terrains of gender, race, and sexuality. As the next chapter on Depression womanhood reveals, the intersection of gender, race, and politics in the 1930s also resulted in official and popular practices of woman blaming, wherein wage-earning women were accused of stealing men's jobs, and nonwage-earning women were criticized for being punishingly frigid toward unemployed husbands.

CHAPTER 4

"To Wallop the Ladies"
Woman Blaming and Nation Saving in the Rhetoric of Emergency Relief

When Chicago's Century of Progress Exposition opened its gates for a second season on May 27, 1934, select visitors were invited to a gala performance of William Shakespeare's *The Taming of the Shrew*. The play took place in "Merrie England" on a stage modeled after Shakespeare's Globe Theater. One reviewer assured prospective audiences that far from being dry and out of date, this play about a husband who torments his unruly wife was "roaring fun." Writing for the *Chicago Tribune*, Charles Collins commended Carl Benton Reid's "burly, vigorous, red-blooded" portrayal of Petruchio, as well as actress Jackson Perkin's "shin-kicking . . . and haughty" performance as Petruchio's shrewish bride.[1]

Elizabethan theater might seem out of place in an exposition designed to showcase the nation's scientific and industrial progress. But as one reviewer wrote, *The Taming of the Shrew* possessed "a robust aliveness" found in few plays of any period.[2] Exemplifying what one critic terms "a tenacious popular tradition of depicting domestic violence as funny," the play enjoyed a vital existence in Depression America.[3] Early in the Depression, Douglas Fairbanks and Mary Pickford starred as Petruchio and Katherine in a film version of the play, in which Fairbanks's Petruchio roundly humiliates his on- and off-screen wife.[4] Beginning in 1936, Alfred Lunt and Lynn Fontanne, billed as "the First Married Couple of the American stage," starred in a long-running Broadway production that featured "plenty of bustle-smacking" on Petruchio's part.[5] *The Taming of the Shrew* was also a staple of the Federal Theatre Project (FTP), appearing in town halls and public schools throughout the country. Critics commended such performances as enjoyable and elevating for white working-class audiences who might otherwise never experience a live Shakespearean performance.

Americans who failed to see the play in its original could still find variations at their local movie theaters. In *Bluebeard's Eighth Wife* (Paramount, 1938), Michael Brandon (Gary Cooper) reads *The Taming of the Shrew* and decides to spank his insubordinate mate (Claudette Colbert). Although Brandon's wife remains defiant, physical correction proves more effective in other films of the decade, including *When Strangers Marry* (Columbia, 1933), *Hell Cat* (Columbia, 1933), and the wildly popular *It Happened One Night* (Columbia, 1934). In the last film, which won five Academy Awards including Best Picture in 1934, Peter Warne (Clark Gable) resolves a dispute with spoiled heiress Ellie Andrews (Claudette Colbert) by swatting her behind. Throughout the film, he addresses her as "brat," and when he finally meets Ellie's father (Walter Connolly), he heatedly informs him that "what she needs is a guy that'd take a sock at her once a day, whether it's coming to her or not." Apparently, this strikes both men as a prescription for domestic happiness, and Ellie's father helps to orchestrate Warne's marriage to his daughter.

If theater and film drew inspiration from *The Taming of the Shrew*, so too did advice columnists and domestic courts. Caroline Chatfield, columnist for the *Atlanta Constitution*, informed readers that "the classic for husbands who are afflicted with shrewish wives is Shakespeare's *The Taming of the Shrew*." She explained, "In this play Shakespeare told the world how a husband could put an obstreperous wife in her place" by "assert[ing] his manly prerogatives and tell[ing] her where to get off."[6] Similarly, in an article subtitled "Wielding Club of Authority May Cure the Shrew," syndicated columnist Doris Blake wrote, "There are some women . . . who need the club of authority wielded over them. They need a man who'll tell them to behave."[7] In yet another Shakespearean flourish, a court reporter titled his account of Chicago's domestic court, "To Slap Wife or Not—That's the Question." The article features one judge's affirmative response. Citing common law, he stated, "A man may slap his wife as hard as he wants to if he doesn't kill her." He added, "If more wives were slapped there would be fewer divorces."[8]

The same sentiment was echoed by the Wives of Spanking Husbands' Club, established in Sioux Falls, North Dakota, in 1937. The organization, whose slogan was "Spare the hairbrush and spoil the wife," sponsored fifty-nine chapters nationwide and even organized a daughters' auxiliary (predictably called the "Daughters of Spanking Fathers' Club"). The club's spokeswoman explained that "spanking makes home life happy and saves a lot of homes from the divorce courts."[9]

Certainly, while many people feared that hard times would compromise American marriages, not everyone agreed that corporal punishment of wives was an appropriate solution to domestic discord. Observing the vogue in wife spanking that seemed to be sweeping the nation, one Los Angeleno advised American men to travel to Europe, where "men are men and don't need a rod to prove it."[10] Some wives who brought charges of domestic abuse against husbands who spanked had their complaints sustained in court. But others who sought legal recourse were not so fortunate.

The apparent pleasure that Depression Americans took in enacting, viewing, or reading about wife spanking reflects a general climate of woman blaming in the Great Depression. Writing in 1931, Gail Laughlin of the National Woman's Party observed, "One of the first impulses in these times of depression is to wallop the ladies."[11] Laughlin was not suggesting that men literally "walloped" women when confronted with financial hardship (though some apparently did); rather, she was describing a tendency to scapegoat women for the economic crisis and to curtail their civic and economic opportunities. In 1939, Norman Cousins lent credence to Laughlin's perspective when he stated, "There are approximately ten million people out of work in the United States today. There are also ten million or more women, married or single, who are jobholders. Simply fire the women, who shouldn't be working anyway, and hire the men. Presto! No unemployment. No relief roles. No Depression."[12]

The sentiment that "women . . . shouldn't be working anyway" belied wage-earning women's crucial contributions to household subsistence. It was also racially specific. Just as the forgotten man was a nationally central figure for white breadwinning manhood, the shrewish wife and the job-stealing woman worker were figures of disorderly white womanhood. White Americans generally did not object when African American women and other women of color were employed as field hands and domestic servants. Popular literature, film, and consumer culture idealized the figure of the black "mammy," as evident in the highly successful book and film versions of Fannie Hurst's *Imitation of Life* and Margaret Mitchell's *Gone with the Wind*.[13] Indeed, if African American and Mexican American domestics and field workers were perceived as problematic in the thirties, it was generally because there were *not enough* women of color who were willing to serve in those arduous and low-paid occupations. White householders frequently bemoaned the scarcity of competent black maids in the 1930s, and white landowners in the South and Southwest complained that women of color preferred "loafing" on federal relief projects to the backbreaking and poorly paid work of fruit, cotton, and tobacco harvesting. Insofar as women of color provoked ire by refusing traditional, poorly paid work when they could access federal unemployment relief, they, too, were subject to woman blaming, but of a racially specific kind.

Always attentive to the racial specificity of popular woman-blaming narratives, this chapter moves between such narratives, the broader public climate of hostility toward women, and the distinctly punitive features of federal relief policy in the Depression. As it attends to the interrelationships between these three dimensions of national public discourse, it contemplates the following question: Why was punishing women so cathartic in the 1930s, and how was that catharsis harnessed to the nation-building project of the emergent welfare state?

Holly A. Crocker asserts that "male control depends on sustaining the myth of female subordination."[14] In the 1930s, woman-blaming narratives focused on the specter of transgressive femininity, thereby justifying white men's righteous anger toward women and fortifying their collective power and identity. Depicted as shrewish, selfish, and sexually dangerous, popular figurations of white womanhood could not simply be expunged; rather, they were integral to a national public culture that valorized traditional white male authority in its many public and private forms.

Like narratives of forgotten manhood, inveterate transients, and wandering youth, stories of insubordinate, blameworthy womanhood formed a distinct civic genre in the Depression years. Some woman-blaming narratives featured unruly wives, others prostitutes, and still others professional women. Occasional narratives featured lazy and insubordinate women of color who shirked their obligation to serve white households. But regardless of such differences, all woman-blaming narratives remained intelligible in the opportunities they provided for exercising white male control amidst the economic and political uncertainties of the Depression.

ᛋ Woman-Blaming Narratives

Three negative figures of white womanhood predominate in Depression-era woman-blaming narratives: (1) the married woman worker, (2) the nagging wife, and (3) the sexually promiscuous woman alone. Each figure embodies negative traits that, particularly in the early Depression years, Americans were eager to distance from the privileged category of white forgotten manhood. Each also embodies traits that, as feminist political critics suggest, have long been feminized in U.S. political culture. The married woman worker's selfishness, the nagging wife's disrespect, and the woman alone's moral weakness all had precedents in American social and political thought.[15] Yet their incarnations in the 1930s also served decade-specific functions. Specifically, they provided familiar gendered and racialized terrain on which the nation's new and perplexing economic and political troubles could be worked out. Moreover, they provided scapegoats for Americans' collective anxiety and frustration, while encouraging particular restrictions on white women's economic and political roles.

No figure of white womanhood was more reviled in Depression-era public culture than the married woman worker, who allegedly turned her back on domestic responsibilities in order to vie for employment with men.[16] The decade witnessed a rash of legal restrictions on married women's work, including Section 213 of the 1932 Federal Economy Act, which effectively barred women from the civil service if their husbands were also federal employees.[17] Married-women schoolteachers, librarians, and other state and municipal employees were removed from their jobs in many localities. Private corporations restricted married women's work, and professional women in fields such as social work and nursing were increasingly displaced by men. Even as women's occupational choices diminished, financial necessity forced more and more women into the workforce. Thus regardless of marital status, white women who worked were "punished" for the Depression through their increasing concentration in menial and poorly paid service occupations.[18]

Although white married women suffered from the tangible effects of job discrimination, they were also victimized by a rhetorical climate that cast them as perpetrators of economic crisis. The campaign against married women's work reveals that many Americans attributed increasing joblessness among men to white women's workforce participation. In a typical account of married women's employment, one newspaper informed its readers that "housewives were 'deserting the kitchens' of the country to take jobs when millions of men were out of work."[19] Another carried the sensational headline, "Women Glut Labor Field."[20] Demonstrating the hostility with which many regarded white married women's work, a dean at Mount Holyoke College predicted that weak-willed white women would leave the workforce once they discovered that "competition with men in this world was not as easy as they thought it was."[21] Critics of married women's work also routinely alleged that white working women usurped men's jobs for the trivial purpose of earning "pin money." Rarely did popular accounts acknowledge that the majority of working wives, regardless of race, earned vital subsistence dollars.

During the 1930s, new methods for documenting unemployment emerged. The first national unemployment census, conducted in 1937, fed popular hostility toward white married women workers when its director, John Biggers, proclaimed that "the influx of women workers was a central factor" in persisting male unemployment.[22] Public opinion polls, which also had their beginning in the mid-1930s, likewise indicated widespread disapproval of the wage-earning wife. The rhetorical positions staked out by a 1938 Gallup Poll are revealing. When asked whether married women should work if their husbands could support the household, 78 percent of respondents indicated that they should not, on the grounds that to do so would restrict the employment field for needy men. Respondents' most frequent comments were the following: "There aren't enough jobs for married men" and "Married women who work when they don't have to are just taking bread out of the mouths of others." Only a small percentage of those surveyed affirmed married women's right to meaningful employment, regardless of gender and family circumstance. A 1936 survey yielded similar results, finding that 82 percent of respondents disapproved of married women jobholders.[23]

In Depression-era public discourse, married women's workforce participation came to be seen as a catalyst for white male unemployment and a contributing factor in the hardship that many Americans faced. The married woman who worked was said to be "taking bread out of the mouths of others." Accordingly, restoring women to their proper domestic sphere came to be seen as a partial solution to Depression hardship. The supporting logic clarifies white men's and women's different civic roles. In economic terms at least, white women's public claims were contingent on those of their husbands. Moreover, all white women, regardless of marital status, were regarded as a disruptive presence in the economic sphere.

Attacks on white married women's work also served as an outlet for Americans' collective anxiety and frustration. At a time when so much was changing and beyond ordinary Americans' control, the vast majority of Americans took a firm stand on married women's work. Even if few actually believed that wage-earning wives had *caused* the Depression, married women's financial sacrifice in giving up their jobs was considered restorative in itself. The married woman worker's centrality as an object of public hostility suggests that, like Petruchio's taming of the shrew, redomesticating white working wives served to fortify white male agency by warranting its angry and authoritative affect.[24]

Women of color were also subject to laws and general disapprobation affecting married women's work, but in different ways. African American and Mexican American women were generally excluded from civil service jobs and other occupations affected by married worker legislation. Moreover, it was the jobless white breadwinner, and not his African American or Mexican American counterpart, whose wage-earning prerogative was being usurped by the married woman who labored for "pin money." To be sure, married women of color sometimes rankled at federal relief policies that privileged male householders, regardless of race, over their female counterparts. But women of color were not figured as trivial and selfish job-stealing wives in the way that white women were; in a culture that assumed their lowly economic and occupational status, their earnings were not seen as trivial, nor were their jobs seen as desirable for white men. Finally, it was not *their* families, but those headed by white men, that were the primary concern in narratives about job-stealing wives.

The widespread outcry against the married woman worker in the 1930s can be partially attributed to actual increases in married women's workforce participation. The wife who nagged relentlessly or emasculated her husband by withholding sex, on the other hand, is a figure whose alleged misconduct was much less obvious or quantifiable. Neither statistics nor legislation substantiated the existence of harassing wives. Yet in Depression-era public discourse, they played a prominent role.

"Blame the Wives!" the *Chicago Daily Tribune* titled its August 5, 1938, editorial, which commented on a psychological study linking traffic accidents to "nagging wives." "Less nagging at home ... [would] cut traffic mishaps better than do fines and jail sentences," the study's authors asserted. Nagging wives had already been identified as a traffic hazard in the 1936 report of the National Safety Conference. "A husband who has dodged a milk bottle only a few hours previously is less apt to be alert" while driving, the Conference reported. Taking this idea to heart, a Florida man cited his nagging wife's negative impact on his driving in petitioning for divorce.

When they were not being blamed for traffic accidents, nagging wives were held to account for other social problems, ranging from simply making their husbands miserable, to causing marital infidelity and divorce, and even to prompting serious crimes. According to one account, embezzlers were often basically honest men who had been driven to criminality by their voracious and nagging wives.[25] Devoted fathers neglected their children because they could not face their wives' "fiendish dispositions." Advice columnist Doris Blake of the *Chicago Daily Tribune* described one father who longed to be with his child, "but that nagging, nagging, sour disposition of his wife is more than he can stand." In this case, the nagging wife compounded anxieties brought on the economic crisis: "His father had been out of work for a couple of years; his own income was not what it used to be, and the nagging wife, who nags for no reason at all, is a combination of troubles that is getting the man." Blake continued, "There are plenty of . . . these women who cannot see beyond their own noses, grouching, whining, working themselves up into a lather of discontent . . . venting their spleen on the poor devil of a husband immediately he hoves in sight at night, though his main concern is how to please the abominable creature."[26]

Throughout the 1930s, the popular press reported all sorts of havoc caused by nagging wives. An Associated Press report told the story of one man who, despite being a conscientious objector, pleaded to be admitted to the Army because "he would rather spend the rest of his life in the army than another week with his nagging wife."[27] His petition was granted, as was the petition of a Florida man who sought to divorce his wife without paying alimony on the grounds that she had nagged him. When the case came before the Florida Supreme Court, the justices ruled that there is "probably no greater cruelty which may be inflicted upon a man" than "that which is inflicted by a contentious, unreasonable, and fault-finding woman."[28]

Some wives were even blamed for their own murders, as in the case of Meri Kolb, who was beaten to death by her husband, Andy Kolb, in the couple's Dayton, Ohio, home. In Kolb's trial for first-degree murder, the defense team launched what might be called the "nagging wife" defense. They characterized Kolb as "a man of good repute, successful in business, who had been nagged into a state of perilous emotional reactions." Despite gruesome evidence of premeditation, the defense characterized Mrs. Kolb's murder as "inspired by pressure so provocative as to prove ultimately irresistible."[29] Whereas Kolb was convicted, another man who used the "nagging wife defense" had his sentence reduced to manslaughter, which carried a minimum sentence of three years. Steve Mattosh, who slashed his wife Anna's throat with a razor, garnered considerable sympathy from the court psychiatrist, Dr. L. Selling. Speaking to reporters, the doctor stated, "I can well imagine jail will be a relief for this man. His wife was a nagger, difficult to get along with. . . . It is surprising he lived with her as long as he did." Selling stopped just short of endorsing Mattosh's crime, stating that "we must discourage wife murder even when it is emotionally justified."[30]

If advice columns, editorials, and Associated Press reports propagated the figure of the nagging wife, so, too, did popular radio, fiction, and film. "The Home Port," an NBC radio play that aired on September 28, 1938, was the "tragic tale of a sea captain who goes insane while on a sea voyage after murdering his nagging wife." James Ronald's 1940 novel, *This Way Out*, offered an even more sympathetic portrayal of a man who kills his "his selfish, lazy, nagging wife." According to one reviewer, Ronald's novel "might better be called the tragedy of a fundamentally good man who kills in order to escape from an intolerable situation which affects not only himself but others." Thus the murder is not only emotionally justified; it is downright public-spirited as the hero kills to protect others from the nagging wife's "fiendish disposition." Finally, in the film *We Are Not Alone* (Warner Brothers, 1939), a hateful woman bullies her young son and relentlessly nags her husband, binding him to her and preventing him from finding happiness with another woman. Her accidental death late in the film seems to promise long-deferred happiness to the other principal characters until the authorities wrongfully arrest, convict, and execute her husband and his lover for allegedly murdering the wife. Significantly, the film's title, "We Are Not Alone," connects the fate of the wronged husband to the victims of totalitarian aggression in Europe. In this way, the film links nagging wives to the rise of unjust political regimes, just as other popular texts depicted nagging and emasculating wives as catalysts for economic crisis.[31]

The emasculating wife was also a stock figure in social scientific accounts of the Depression. Frequently, in cataloguing the hardships of unemployed men, social scientists gave a prominent place to the overly critical conduct of unemployed men's wives. Within such accounts, emasculating wives took pleasure in shaming their husbands and defying their household authority. Many seized the opportunity of their husbands' joblessness to enter the workforce themselves, reversing domestic **arrangements**.[32] In a 1933 account, one sociologist described a group of wives who "constantly nagged their husbands over not finding work, asserted to all and sundry that their husbands did not want to work, when extremely irritated called them 'no good.'"[33] In addition to berating their husbands, emasculating wives typically added to their husbands' demoralization by refusing sexual relations. In one such account, psychiatrist Nelson Ackerman reported, "The women punished the men for not bringing home the bacon by withholding themselves sexually. By belittling and emasculating the men, undermining their paternal authority, turning to the eldest son." Ackerman commented, "These men suffered from depression. They felt despised, they were ashamed of themselves . . . They avoided home."[34]

At a time when many commentators emphasized the need to boost jobless white men's morale, the emasculating wife willfully demoralized her husband. In drawing attention to his failings as a protector and provider, she contributed to a crisis of masculine citizenship. Motivated by selfishness and spite, she confused the lines of authority and deference within the home and fomented sexual disorder by refusing her husband's conjugal rights. Like the married woman worker, she—and not her demoralized husband, nor the economic crisis itself—was to blame for national instability. Proposals to restore jobless white breadwinners' authority had the added benefit of returning unruly wives to their proper, subordinate place.

Even more so than the married woman worker, the emasculating wife was a racially specific figure. The gender and sexual disorder that she embodied threatened to undermine not only her immediate white husband's household authority, but the collective authority of white male householders throughout the nation. Hypothetically, a married woman of color *could* impinge on the economic prerogatives of a jobless white man because her disorderly conduct would take place in the public sphere. But the drama of the emasculating wife, although it had dire public consequences, took place within the private, racially endogamous space of marriage.

Figures like the married woman worker and the emasculating wife helped give meaning to the white masculine ideals of public-spiritedness and moral fortitude by their own contrasting conduct. Narratives that represented both figures as treacherous and selfishly motivated also promoted affective bonds among members of a white male public defined in part by its hostility to such women. The same is true of two other figures of white womanhood who stood at the center of woman-blaming narratives: the prostitute and the female hobo. Located on the periphery of American society, both figures were nevertheless symbolically central to Depression-era public discourse. Through their alleged sexual misconduct, they posed a threat to national stability. Yet because of their peripheral location, the prostitute and female hobo also served as compelling scapegoats for negative characteristics that Americans were eager to disassociate from more privileged social groups, including unemployed white men.

One historian has noted that, in the Progressive era, prostitution served as "a master symbol, a code word, for a wide range of anxieties."[35] Although Americans' preoccupation with prostitution diminished after World War I, it resurfaced in the early years of the Great Depression. In 1931, a committee of prominent New Yorkers known as the Seabury Commission found that vice was on the increase in that city. The committee alleged, "Conditions in New York are drifting back to a plane which we left twenty years ago. . . . Street solicitation is again becoming an open sore."[36] Among the factors contributing to this change, its members contended, was the increase in female unemployment. The committee found that "the desperation of young women who cannot find work in this time of protracted depression is forcing many of them either directly into prostitution or at least into borderline occupations from which the ranks of prostitution are most generally recruited."[37]

Writing about Chicago in the early thirties, sociologist Walter Reckless documented a similar rise in organized vice. Like the Seabury Commission, he attributed the rise in prostitution to women's changing social roles. Not only financial conditions, but the breakdown of traditional family constraints and the allure of an urban leisure sphere were leading more women into "casual prostitution," from which the ranks of professional prostitutes were drawn. Reckless downplayed women's financial motives for becoming prostitutes, arguing instead that sexual commerce afforded prostitutes excitement, glamour, and independence, thus appealing to their self-indulgent dispositions and modern, materialistic sensibilities.[38]

Within Depression-era public discourse, the prostitute embodied uncontrolled sexuality and moral weakness, and she posed a threat to the moral and physical health of the nation. She shared these characteristics with another figure of lone womanhood, the female hobo. Stephanie Golden notes that "whereas a homeless man can be assigned comfortably to a variety of categories . . . a homeless woman creates discomfort because she cannot be categorized. Women are so entirely defined in terms of whom they belong to that no category exists for a woman without family or home."[39] While homeless women did indeed defy categorization in the Depression, woman-blaming narratives attached definite political meaning to their existence.

At hearings on relief for unemployed transients convened by the Senate in January 1933, many witnesses attested that female transiency had risen dramatically in recent years. A representative of one welfare agency characterized the number of female transients as "really surprisingly large," and another claimed that "four times the . . . women and girls [were homeless] in the year 1932 as in the year 1931."[40] Writing in 1934, Reckless predicted that "one of the many social pathologies that will result from the present depression is a growth of a chronic female hobo class."[41]

Accounts of female transiency in the Depression focused almost exclusively on the female transient's large and deviant sexual appetites. In his book-length study of the transient problem, Thomas Minehan restricted his consideration of female transients to a chapter titled "Sex Life." Estimating that about one in twenty transients was a woman, Minehan stated, "They go from jungle to jungle and from box car to box car without discrimination. Any place where there are men and boys, they know they will be welcome. They enter a box car or a jungle, and without more ado the line forms to the right."[42] In hearings on the transient problem, Senator Edward Costigian alleged that "[transient] girls are available to any and all boys in the camp including adults and late arrivals."[43] Similarly, a travelling correspondent for the *New Republic* wrote, "Heard many tales of women hoboes. One hobo told me how two women had lightened the journey of some twenty hoboes one night."⁴⁴

Sexualizing the female transient enabled commentators to separate female homelessness from the allegedly more pressing issue of youthful male transiency. As a representative of the Travelers Aid Society commented, "The women we get are, as a rule, not quite the same type as the men. I mean, they are not as independent and I think most would be social problems almost anywhere."⁴⁵ Thus if public discussions of transiency represented the young male transient as a victim of economic crisis, they depicted the female transient as motivated by an inborn propensity for moral weakness that was only exacerbated by the Depression.

Some commentators on transiency also lamented the female hobo's invasion of a formerly all-male domain. As Reckless observed, "There is no reason to assume . . . that the migratory homeless woman will not invade hobohemia and the jungles just as women generally have encroached upon all the other original provinces of men." He added, "The indication is that women are making pretty good hoboes as hoboes go."⁴⁶

At a time when many Americans feared a simultaneous breakdown of the gender and political orders, the prostitute and the female hobo were at once threatening harbingers of national collapse and useful scapegoats onto which more widely circulating fears could be displaced. Their unruly examples accentuated the dangers of women in public and the virtues of female confinement to the domestic sphere. Representations of the sexually promiscuous woman alone that emphasized her incursion on formerly all-male domains suggest her significance as a figure for all women whose economic and political activities had increased in recent years. Accounts that sensationalized her sexual activity and denied financial necessity as a motivation for her conduct reflected a broader tendency to trivialize women's public claims by sexualizing them.

As with narratives of married women workers and emasculating wives, stories about the sexually promiscuous woman alone dramatized the threat she posed to the white male-headed home. Although Depression-era commentators sometimes depicted male transients in mixed-race settings, female transients were invariably depicted as white women and girls who defied the gender and sexual authority of white male family members. Likewise, stories of prostitutes in the 1930s centered on white women whose attraction to a wanton and materialistic urban culture had led them into a life of sin.

Within a gender-differentiated scheme of citizenship and national belonging, figures such as wage-earning and emasculating wives, prostitutes, and female hoboes, drew attention away from the apparent shortcomings of white

Depression manhood. Scapegoating such female figures reinforced a gender division of political labor in which white men were protectors and providers and white women were their economic and political dependents.[47] By sexualizing so many of white women's struggles in the Depression, commentators trivialized their plight in comparison with men's, thereby justifying welfare responses that largely ignored women's problems and focused on the needs of white unemployed men.

Women of color figured differently in woman-blaming narratives than did white women. Certain negative stereotypes, such as the married woman worker and the nagging wife, were racialized as white. Long figured as Jezebels, black women occasionally appeared as prostitutes and loose women who exchanged sex for upward mobility. But the most central Depression-era stereotype of black womanhood was the desexualized figure of the mammy, which dovetailed well with relief policies that channeled women of color into domestic service projects. In the realm of popular culture, the character of Mammy in *Gone with the Wind* exemplifies this stereotype. Alternately grave and comical, physically massive, and committed to preserving the gender and racial orders, Mammy embraces her servitude and tries to temper her mistress's insubordinate behavior. It is Scarlett O'Hara, Mammy's white female employer, who poses the larger threat to family, race, and nation in the novel and the film. Throughout the narrative, Scarlett uses her sexuality to advance her fortune at the expense of her family. She is conventionally treacherous, small-minded, and lacking in maternal devotion. She is the married woman worker, the emasculating wife, and the sexually promiscuous independent woman all rolled into one. It is noteworthy that Hattie McDaniel and Vivien Leigh both won Academy Awards for their performances in the film version of *Gone with the Wind* (MGM, 1939). Just as the film's portrayal of the wartorn South resonated with contemporary anxieties about the Depression-torn United States, Mammy and Scarlett spoke to racially specific dimensions of woman blaming in the 1930s.

Prissy, the young slave woman in *Gone with the Wind*, also deserves mention. In contrast to Mammy, Prissy is an empty-headed malingerer who requires constant threats of punishment to stay on task; even under such threats, she is semicompetent at best. As the embodiment of an alternative black stereotype, Prissy indicates that black women were certainly subject to misogyny in the Great Depression. Her indolence and irresponsibility make her a liability to the white household. Had she not been a slave, she would have deserved the paltriest of wages, and she was not competent to perform any but the most menial, unskilled tasks under strict white supervision. This stereotype of black womanhood also played a role in Depression-era public culture, including the rhetoric and practice of federal emergency relief.

The relationship between representation and reality is by no means direct and is always difficult to distinguish. During the 1930s, women suffered from a range of negative figurations of Depression womanhood. The image of the white married woman who selfishly pursued employment in order to increase her "pin money" affected all women, as states and localities across the nation curtailed married women's employment. Nostalgic images of African American house servants legitimated employment discrimination against women of color, many of whom found their opportunities even more than usually restricted to agricultural and domestic work. And images of sexually punishing wives and sexually available female hoboes and prostitutes compromised the dignity and legitimacy of all women's public claims by placing the spotlight on their alleged sexual misconduct.

In her objection to such representations, one woman likely spoke for many others. Writing to the editors of the *New Republic* in 1931, Marian Clark sought to correct the impression that all jobless women became prostitutes. She stated, "Women out of jobs do need help, but not to keep them from prostitution." Instead of focusing on their supposed sexual exploits, she suggested, journalists and others would do well to consider women's real relief needs. Clark pointed out that "in the provisions for unemployment assistance [women] have been considered less than men; fewer relief agencies are open to them." She added, "The need is for agencies to which women of pride and independence—not potential prostitutes—can turn, and in which they will receive aid uninjurious to their self-respect."[48]

As this young woman's plea suggests, even as public commentators struggled to restore dignity to unemployed white men, they heaped indignity on unemployed women. The tendency to characterize women in public as sexually or selfishly motivated obscured women's real relief needs and disadvantaged them relative to men. It also left them vulnerable to considerable public hostility—hostility that quickly became harnessed to the nation-building project of the New Deal state.

➤ Early Relief for Women

It is one thing to identify the pervasiveness of woman blaming in the wide-ranging public discourse of the early Depression years. It is quite another to locate that same strategy in the official, nation-saving rhetoric of the New

Deal state. Yet a survey of New Deal relief policy suggests that Roosevelt officials contributed to the vast storehouse of negative female images in the Depression, embellishing such figures as the married woman worker and the sexually promiscuous woman alone and adding others like the "pantry-snooping" social worker and the chronically dependent older woman. Moreover, like the broader public culture that surrounded it, the thrust of New Deal relief policy toward women was punitive. Not only were women's relief benefits more miserly and difficult to procure, but many were designed to redomesticate needy women. Women's relief options were contingent on their family status, and female relief projects accentuated women's traditional household skills.

The Roosevelt administration thus participated in the frenzy of woman blaming that animated public discourse in the Depression. From the belated inception of the Women's Division in 1933, through sustained attacks on female relief projects in the final years of the Depression, the New Deal invoked the specter of transgressive femininity, appealing to men's righteous anger toward women and mobilizing their collective power and identity on behalf of the New Deal state. Within the evolving system of federal relief, many female administrators and clients came to understand that the nation-saving rhetoric and nation-building practices of federal emergency relief were not intended for them.

When the Federal Emergency Relief Administration (FERA) was established in May 1933 to fund and coordinate unemployment relief throughout the United States, women's relief needs were not an immediate priority, even though women represented 12 percent of all relief recipients under FERA. Initially, federal relief administrators were concerned with converting various state and local relief practices over to a more uniform, federal basis. Throughout its tenure from 1933 to 1935, FERA sponsored a variety of relief methods, ranging from "direct relief" in the forms of grocery orders and cash allotments, to state and local "work relief," which included various kinds of goods production (sewing, mattress-making, and canning) for women. As with the larger FERA setup, state and local relief offices exercised considerable discretion over how FERA women's relief would be administered. The ratio of direct relief to work relief varied from state to state and from region to region. In the South and Southwest, sewing rooms and other goods projects were usually segregated, and women of color were disproportionately assigned to custodial and outdoor manual labor projects.

Initially, New Deal relief administrators largely ignored the plight of needy women. Many women found themselves entirely without options in 1933 as the Depression continued to worsen. Commenting on the situation in New

York City, one relief official informed FERA director Harry Hopkins that it was "just plain fierce the way women are being passed around in this town."[49] After some months of being told that women's relief needs were not being met, Hopkins finally established the FERA Women's Division in August 1933. He appointed Ellen S. Woodward, a little-known dignitary of the Mississippi Democratic Party and member of the Mississippi State Welfare Board, to direct it. Appointed in August, Woodward began her work as director of the Women's Division under less than ideal circumstances. With two secretaries, a run-down office shared by administrators for the Federal Transient Program, and a loosely defined mandate, she set about to devise a place for women within the burgeoning system of federal relief.[50]

Woodward was not prominent in welfare reform circles. Instead, she had strong ties to the residual charity establishment and had been influenced by its punitive approach to the poor. At a time when other New Deal administrators proclaimed the need to separate old-style poor relief from the New Deal's more enlightened approach to relief provision, Woodward seemed fairly oblivious to such distinctions. Particularly early in her administrative tenure, she relied on members of the residual charity establishment in devising strategies for women's relief. As a consequence, traditionally punitive relief practices, such as requiring sewing or other make-work in return for relief benefits, remained characteristic of the Women's Division throughout the Depression years.[51]

Woodward was also a white Southerner. Although she was not as strident in her support for segregation as Robert Fechner, director of the Civilian Conservation Corps (CCC), neither was she a proponent of racial justice. As director of the Women's Division, Woodward condoned segregation of women's projects and helped to devise relief options for women of color, such as domestic service training projects, that would reinforce their low occupational status.

In contrast to the tremendous outpouring of human and material resources that characterized male relief programs in the first one hundred days, it would be several weeks before Woodward's efforts yielded tangible results. Not until mid-November, when Woodward convened a Conference on the Emergency Needs of Women, would the Women's Division gain any public exposure at all. Held at the White House with the participation and support of Eleanor Roosevelt, the conference gathered together representatives of white women's charities and professional organizations. Woodward excluded prominent African American women from the conference on the grounds that their presence might offend some white participants. Although some other prominent female reformers were absent because of last-minute planning, the conference nevertheless received ample publicity and helped to establish the long-term objectives of the Women's Division.[52]

The Conference on Emergency Needs illustrates the relative insignificance of the Women's Division within the larger relief system. Other than Eleanor Roosevelt and Woodward herself, official New Deal representation at the conference was limited to Hopkins, who gave a brief keynote address. That the conference was out of sync with the larger relief system is reflected in its timing. Intended as an inaugural event for the FERA Women's Division, the conference took place just as the FERA was being scaled back to make way for the Civil Works Administration (CWA). How the Women's Division would fare in the new administrative framework was by no means clear to conference participants.

The absence of a well-defined agenda and the odd assortment of participants also reflected the lack of a clear administrative mandate. Participants represented groups ranging from women's professional organizations, to private charities, to public welfare agencies. The strategies they proposed for meeting women's relief needs reflected their diverse organizational backgrounds. When asked what kinds of programs would most benefit women in need, representatives of women's professional organizations suggested specific programs for female nurses, librarians, and other professional groupings. Participants with ties to the charity establishment suggested traditional strategies such as sewing and other domestic work in return for relief allotments. Woodward revealed her own privileged background when she made a plea for well-to-do women who could no longer maintain the semblance of independent wealth. As such diverse responses suggest, conference participants generated neither a coherent picture of women's economic need nor a coherent strategy for women's betterment. Yet all agreed that women were underrepresented in the existing relief setup and needed better support.[53]

Most striking, perhaps, is conference participants' general agreement that the neediest example of Depression womanhood was the "woman alone." In terms that reflected early Depression anxieties about prostitution and female transiency, participants like Rose Schneidermann of the Women's Trade Union League dwelled on the plight of needy single women who lacked legitimate means of self-support. Schneidermann argued that many jobless single women spent days and nights riding the subway trains of large cities like New York for lack of better shelter. She stated that many were turning to prostitution in order to survive. By invoking the figure of the sexually promiscuous woman alone, Schneidermann sought to generate sympathy and material support for needy single women. In contrast to many of her contemporaries, Schneidermann characterized this figure as motivated by financial need, not by moral weakness or irresponsibility.[54]

Other conference participants reiterated Schneidermann's concern for needy single womanhood, including Eleanor Roosevelt. In a national press release announcing the conference, Roosevelt stated that "the needs of single women, in particular, call for action, because this group has been the most difficult to care for under ordinary relief and employment measures." Thus from the inception of New Deal efforts to address the relief needs of women, the woman alone was a central figure.[55]

Yet even as conferees dedicated themselves to the plight of needy single women, they expressed considerable ambivalence about them. Several participants were emphatic that programs for needy single women should not be fashioned after existing programs for needy men. In particular, conferencees agreed that "congregate care" was inappropriate for needy single women. They argued that while men might be suitably housed in large shelters, or else put to work on massive public works projects, women's relief needs were more individual and local. Participants insisted that women's desire for privacy and propriety was greater than men's and relief strategies should reflect their particular sensibilities.[56]

If female participants in the conference were willing at least to acknowledge the plight of the woman alone, even if they objected to congregate care, keynote speaker Hopkins was more cautious. He claimed that "unattached women" was a misnomer for this group, since most single women had been married at one time and continued to have at least some family ties. Hopkins favored policies that would accentuate the unattached woman's family orientation. Like other conference participants, he objected to congregate care in favor of more discreet, local, and small-scale projects for needy women.[57]

Thus New Deal administrators appropriated the figure of the woman alone, while at the same time working to contain her within family bonds. The refusal to institute congregate care for women, like the insistence on her family orientation, contrasts strikingly with policies for men. Large-scale projects for needy men, especially the popular CCC, were central to New Deal rhetoric and practice. Yet no such program was deemed appropriate for needy women. Instead, projects for women were small, local, and more firmly tied to the residual charity establishment.

Convened late in 1933, with relatively few white women and no women of color in attendance, the Conference on the Emergency Needs of Women was a somewhat inauspicious beginning to the work of the Women's Division.

Yet discussions among the conferees helped to shape women's place in the nation-saving rhetoric and practice of New Deal relief. Just as conferees would have it, female relief clients faced an altogether different set of relief options from their male counterparts. As the wives of needy men, female relief applicants had relatively little recourse in a system that privileged white male providers. As single needy women, their needs were met inadequately, on terms that were different from and less generous than those designed for single white men. At no point did the image of needy womanhood, restored to self-sufficiency through emergency relief, come to stand for national recovery. Single needy women who had augured national crisis in the opening years of the Depression were quickly contained and rhetorically and practically reinserted into traditional gender roles.

If white women's relief prospects looked bleak coming out of the Emergency Conference on Women's Needs, the needs of women of color appeared all the more so. Not surprisingly, the all-white conferees did not address such women's specific relief needs. They did not discuss the higher jobless rates that African Americans and Mexican Americans suffered compared to whites; initial federal relief practices, particularly in the South and Southwest, that were rife with racial discrimination; or the results of a 1933 relief census that indicated African American women comprised the majority of black relief applicants under the age of 45.[58] Instead, conference participants focused primarily on the relief needs of the jobless white "woman alone." Although symbolically central to Depression-era public culture, that figure distorted both the family obligations and racial diversity of actual female relief applicants.

The appropriation and containment of the white woman alone reflects how New Deal publicists and administrators drew from stock gender images in American political culture to make emergent concepts of citizenship and national community more palatable. It also shows how federal relief administrators sought to manage and contain pervasive gender and sexual anxieties in gathering support for the New Deal. Capitalizing on Americans' anxieties about the white woman alone, administrators for the Women's Division both deployed and contained this figure. Their strategies for addressing the plight of single needy womanhood reflect the centrality of family and domesticity in defining white women's citizenship. Moreover, by restricting women's relief claims as much as possible, federal relief administrators participated in the punitive approach to Depression womanhood that was already well established prior to the New Deal.

Even as the Conference on the Emergency Needs of Women was taking place, the FERA was being suspended to make way for the Civil Works Administration. More so than the FERA, the CWA was a male-biased relief agency that reinforced the connection between white masculine providership and national well-being. CWA workers performed highly visible, manly work that demonstrated their value to the nation. Officials touted the CWA as proof that the government could combat the economic crisis without compromising principles such as masculine self-respect and male authority within the home. Although the FERA had discriminated against female relief clients in practice, the CWA formalized that discrimination through its creation of a separate and less-well-funded agency, the Civil Works Service (CWS). Women, who had constituted 12 percent of FERA workers, dropped to 7 percent of relief workers on CWA. They were categorically excluded from most CWA projects on the grounds that they lacked the manly vigor necessary to perform heavy outdoor work. A few women were fortunate enough to obtain auxiliary work on CWA and benefited from the agency's minimum wage of a dollar an hour. Most female relief clients, however, had to make do with the much smaller CWS minimum of thirty cents an hour.[59]

As CWS workers, female relief clients continued to perform the same kinds of work that they had done under the FERA. A majority of women worked in sewing rooms and other goods production projects. Thus occupied, their activities remained largely invisible in contrast to male CWA work. If New Deal officials touted the national benefits of CWA, particularly its restoration of health and vigor to the nation's white forgotten men, they were largely silent about women's CWS activities.

CWA and CWS approaches to means-testing were also very different. Hopkins and other relief officials made much of CWA's policy to eliminate "pantry-snooping" social workers, who would no longer dictate the financial needs of jobless breadwinners and their families. In an effort to restore dignity to the unemployed, Hopkins announced that such meddlesome professional women and their means-testing ways would be eliminated from the relief setup. Yet if New Deal relief officials saw means-testing as too demeaning to male relief clients, they endorsed its use on needy women. Women could not be certified for CWS assignments without first undergoing a means test.

Within the Women's Division, female administrators fought against the double standard that was so apparent in the shift to CWA. They challenged state and local relief officials who barred unemployed women from CWA rolls, and they worked to devise projects for women that would qualify for CWA funds. Yet for the most part, their efforts were unsuccessful. Earmarked for public works, CWA funds were hard for Women's Division administrators to obtain. National CWA administrators placed a higher priority on projects that would forge links between jobless men, their immediate communities, and the nation. Local sponsors, who footed part of every project bill, likewise favored projects that, in their estimation, had tangible community value—projects such as road building and airport construction that were monumental in scope and masculine in design.[60]

Yet if the CWA highlighted the strength and vigor of America's white forgotten men, New Deal publicists and administrators did not simply ignore women. Instead, many administrators regarded women's exclusion from CWA as necessary to the agency's rhetorical and practical accomplishment. Relief officials announced the shift to CWA amidst allegations that federal emergency relief "unmanned" jobless breadwinners, turning them into chronic dependents. In the face of such criticism, administrators excluded women from CWA in order to accentuate the agency's association with masculine productivity, strength, and self-reliance. Both needy women and female relief administrators were affected by this policy of exclusion. While female relief clients found themselves barred from CWA payrolls, female administrators encountered hostility and resistance from many male colleagues. When one Women's Division administrator had difficulty obtaining space in her state's CWA office, she commented that male relief officials seemed to think it was "dangerous for a woman to be [found] around CWA headquarters."[61]

CWA gender politics exemplify the New Deal practice of using residual woman-blaming concepts to make new forms of state policy and action more palatable. At a time when many Americans were ambivalent about the New Deal's expanded role in the lives of relief-dependent citizens, CWA officials sought to dispel that ambivalence by demonstrating the national vitality of unemployed white men. Even if such men were forced to rely on the government for subsistence, officials maintained, they could still perform rugged outdoor work, in the company of their countrymen, and receive pay sufficient to provide for their families. Moreover, they could derive collective satisfaction from New Deal policies that sought to redomesticate needy women.

CWA administrators punished female relief applicants by largely restricting them to the miserly, means-tested CWS. There they continued to work on the same goods and service projects to which they had been assigned under FERA. Significantly, not only women, but men of color as well, generally found themselves restricted to CWS assignments—if they were fortunate enough to obtain even those.

An important sacrificial figure in the transition to CWA had been the "pantry-snooping" social worker.[62] Represented as meddlesome, self-important, and demeaning to white male relief clients, the "pantry-snooper" represented yet another variation on the woman-blaming narrative—one that originated with New Deal officials. As a figure for single, professional womanhood, she provoked hostility by usurping masculine prerogatives.[63] One white male relief client spoke for many when he complained that "too many young girls [are] trying to tell families how to get along on nothin'." Such women had no right to tell families how to run their finances, he maintained, since generally speaking, they were single professionals who had rejected traditional feminine roles. As he put it, "what the hell do *they* know about taking care of a family?"[64]

Writing in 1937, Maxine Davis agreed that social workers had been "far too dominant a factor" in the relief program. Davis described one social worker who offered child-rearing advice to her clients, even though she herself was a "poor dried-up little thing" who knew "nothing of children." Worse still, "case workers meddled in intimate family relationships," offering birth control advice to relief-dependent wives and mothers even though they lacked relevant sexual experience. Worst of all, the social worker wielded undue economic power over the jobless male breadwinner, who was "wholly dependent on her for his relief job." Social workers' power even extended to reviewing "the kind, character, and location of relief projects." According to Davis, "They had a loud voice in the approval of projects when they were actually wholly unqualified to form any opinion whatsoever."[65]

Commenting on the pantry-snooper in a letter to Hopkins, Lorena Hickok asked, "How would you like it if some smooth-faced young girl, nicely dressed, all made up, with powder and lipstick, and pink fingernails, sat down on the edge of a chair and began to ask you a lot of personal questions? You'd want to throw something at her, wouldn't you?" Hickok suggested that the typically young female social workers be replaced with "middle-aged men."[66] Stated another critic of the pantry-snooper, "power in small hands is a very dangerous thing." With only "a smattering of Freud to recommend [her]," the "Visitor talks to the neighbors, listens to back-fence gossip, returns to the office and records every minute bit of scandal she has been able to gather. She draws her clients out and inveigles them into discussing their affairs, even their most intimate marital relations, matters that decent people as a rule do not discuss promiscuously. Then the Visitor gives advice. Always, you understand, with the grocery order in her hand."[67]

As a figure for working womanhood in the Depression, the pantry-snooper was a close relative of the married woman worker. Unfeminine, meddlesome, and sexually disruptive, she abused the authority vested in her by the federal relief administration. And, as Hickok observed, she prompted everyone she met to "want to throw something at her." Like other blameworthy white women, the pantry-snooper elicited strongly negative emotions. Federal officials sought to mobilize those feelings in support of a gendered New Deal public by pledging to eradicate the obnoxious pantry-snooper from the CWA setup.

The CWA was a nationally celebrated relief experiment, but it was also extremely costly, frequently mismanaged, and therefore short-lived. Initiated in November 1933, the agency was phased out in March of the following year, as administrators reverted to FERA-style relief. Under the new title of the Emergency Work Relief Program, federal relief continued in a holding pattern until the summer of 1935, when top-level administrators announced the next great departure in emergency relief, the Works Progress Administration.

✦ WPA and Women

Just as the CWA had relied on a gendered politics of exclusion to mark its difference from earlier relief experiments, so did the WPA. Introduced at a time when public attitudes toward the New Deal were increasingly ambivalent, the WPA accentuated masculine ideals of productivity and providership as well as stereotypically feminine traits of dependency, treachery, and moral weakness.[68] Proclaiming their commitment to restoring dignity and independence to the forgotten man, WPA officials argued that earlier relief experiments had been fettered by a misplaced sense of obligation to the chronically dependent unemployed, particularly mothers of small children and "unemployable" women, as well as elderly and infirm individuals. In what administrators characterized as a genuinely "American" departure in relief, the WPA would provide work relief to the "employables" (predominantly white male breadwinners) and would return care of the "unemployables" (including a disproportionate number of white women and nonwhite women and men) to local and private relief.

In explaining eligibility guidelines under WPA, Hopkins carefully accentuated the independence and ability of the average WPA worker. Describing members of the "employable" group, he stated, "The unemployed to whom the Federal program applies are those who are able-bodied but who can not find private jobs and are dependent on a helping hand because of the failure of the economic system." He added, "Jobs are ALL the WPA gives. It gives no direct relief, all of which is handled by the States and localities. Every WPA check is in return for work done."[69]

In *Spending to Save*, Hopkins noted that although earlier relief programs had sometimes employed married women and other questionable applicants, the WPA restricted eligibility as much as possible to jobless white breadwinning men. "The typical unemployed . . . worker on relief [is] a white man, thirty-eight years of age and the head of a household," he stated. Far from disrupting the gender order, he claimed, the WPA restored dignity to unemployed white men and enforced women's respect for their husbands. In Hopkins's account, the statement of one WPA worker's wife stood for many others: she "tossed her head and said, 'We aren't on relief any more, my husband is working for the Government.'"[70]

If the WPA celebrated the recuperation of "employable" breadwinning men, as well as the renewed admiration and respect of properly submissive wives, its consequences for other relief-dependent women were less positive. Women were disproportionately represented in the "unemployable" group whom Hopkins defined as beyond the purview of federal unemployment relief. Women's greater concentration in the "unemployable" category clearly had punitive implications. In WPA rhetoric, "employables" were jobless because of economic forces beyond their control and were therefore entitled to national emergency relief. "Unemployables," on the other hand, were jobless because of personal deficiencies that made them incompetent to work. Characterized as individuals who would be out of work regardless of economic conditions, unemployables were properly the responsibility of local and private relief. Compared to WPA work relief, such old-style poor relief was not only stigmatizing and miserly, but also difficult to obtain after years of Depression had depleted local welfare resources. Local relief was especially hard to obtain for women and men of color because many forms of private and local relief were reserved for whites.

In elaborating on the unemployable group, WPA officials frequently described two, rather pitiful, female figures. On the one hand, they described the white mother whom need had propelled into the workforce against the interests of her children. By removing such mothers from work relief, administrators reinforced the primacy of maternity in white women's lives. With the advent of Aid to Dependent Children in 1936, soon after the shift to WPA, such women had a new resource—once again, poorly compensated, punitive, and often slow to be implemented—that would meet their economic needs while affirming their family responsibilities. The establishment of specific protections for mothers with minor children was another means by which New Deal administrators aligned themselves *with* traditional gender concepts, even as they otherwise transformed the contours of the U.S. nation-state.

CHAPTER 4

A second figure that administrators used to illustrate the unemployable category was the chronically dependent older woman. This figure had never worked before the Depression but had somehow managed to obtain work relief and would once again be returned to local and private charity under WPA. Inefficient, slow, and not particularly task-oriented, such women impeded the effectiveness of federal relief and claimed benefits that would be better spent elsewhere. Getting rid of the chronically dependent older woman was a way to fortify the new WPA against allegations of waste and inefficiency that had plagued earlier federal relief programs.[71]

As a woman without family ties, the chronically dependent older woman reflects Americans' growing smugness toward the woman alone in the middle Depression years. No longer as concerned after years of Depression with lone women's potential sexual disruptiveness, New Deal officials and others converted the lone woman into a pathetic and unattractive older figure.[72] That figure, WPA officials claimed, was certainly not the intended beneficiary of New Deal emergency relief. Albeit much less threatening than her younger early Depression counterpart, the unemployable older woman was still punished for the Depression through her nonproductive designation and relegation to old-style poor relief.

The WPA was by far the largest and costliest relief experiment yet introduced. Many more Americans would, for longer periods of time, find themselves dependent on WPA relief than on any previous program. Although it expanded federal authority into the households and communities of ordinary Americans, New Deal officials packaged the WPA as a defense of the white- male-headed home. Administrators privileged the figure of white breadwinning manhood and excluded women who deviated from conventional family life. In addition to the chronically dependent woman alone and the mother of small children, the married woman worker was largely excluded from WPA relief. Capitalizing on widespread animosity toward wage-earning wives, Hopkins and other relief officials pledged to stamp out the married woman relief worker—and in so doing, to implement a genuinely American approach to relief.

Yet if Hopkins and others worked assiduously to elevate the WPA above the controversies and concerns that preceded it, they were not always successful. After years of economic crisis, many Americans had grown skeptical of relief officials' nation-saving rhetoric, and they regarded the growing relief bureaucracy and its large body of relief-dependent citizens as evidence that American political culture was in crisis. Sociologist Nels Anderson commented that "charges of parasitism, shiftlessness, and lost morale" were on the rise by mid-decade, and white middle-class Americans increasingly regarded the unemployed as a separate and undesirable caste.[73] A newspaper editor in Muncie, Indiana, asserted that individuals who "pulled themselves up by their own bootstraps" were "the *real* forgotten men."[74] Without a doubt, federal relief officials confronted as much or more criticism of relief clients and relief projects after 1935 as they had in 1933 and 1934. Characteristically, they responded to that criticism in part by deflecting that criticism onto unemployed women on relief.

With the transition to WPA, Hopkins and others began referring to the relief setup as a business. Their use of the term "business" was deliberate and self-consciously masculine. Since unemployment figures remained high and an end to emergency relief was nowhere in sight, administrators sought to *simulate* relief workers' return to private employment by referring to relief as a "business" and by making relief jobs conform to the standards of private employment. Once again, women's presence on federal relief rolls compromised this rhetorical strategy. Business culture was characterized by efficiency, decisiveness, and male comradeship, and women had little place within it. Frustrated that women should compromise their efforts to build a positive public image for New Deal relief, some WPA administrators attacked women's relief projects and particularly the sewing rooms that employed a majority of female relief clients.

In his evaluation of the WPA for the Russell Sage Foundation, Donald S. Howard criticized WPA women's work for impeding "some of the most important objectives of a work program." According to Howard, standards of employment and production on male work projects were commensurate with those of private industry. Women's projects, he claimed, were another matter altogether. He stated, "projects on which women are employed fail to prepare them to find jobs open to women in private enterprise or fail (as the sewing projects are said to fail) to maintain normal standards of production."[75] As such, he claimed, projects for women marred the agency's reputation and effectiveness as a practical, work-giving enterprise.

Other analysts shared Howard's impression of what was necessary to improve the WPA. Writing in 1938, Marie Dresden Lane and Francis Steegmuller also criticized the sewing rooms, commenting that "more definite and more rigorous standards of employability must be established if the WPA is to continue in its present form as a works program."[76]

In a classified internal report completed in 1937, WPA policy analyst S. D. Ozer made sweeping recommendations for the transformation of WPA women's work. Ozer applauded Aid to Dependent Children, which took the mother of young children off public relief rolls. He expressed skepticism of all women who applied for relief, on the grounds that "custom compels an able-bodied man to work, [while] no such pressure applies to women." He recommended a contraction and reorientation of WPA women's work, reserving his most heated criticism for the sewing rooms. He stated, "early on in the WPA, these projects were considered wholesale 'dumping grounds' for needy women, regardless of skill and experience level." As such, he claimed, they did little to prepare women to move from WPA sewing projects to private employment.[77] Ozer advocated purging the sewing rooms of unemployable women, particularly older women whose workforce participation, in his view, represented a disturbing new trend. Those sewing projects that remained, he advised, should be run according to principles of scientific management.

Although Ozer recommended reforming the sewing rooms, the greatest hope for improvement, in his view, lay in developing other programs altogether. In particular, he proposed the expansion of three parts of WPA women's work: Household Workers Training, Hot School Lunches, and Housekeeping Aides. Of these programs, Ozer states, "Here are definite services rendered to the community which could be carried on as a function of government."

Woodward also recognized the need for community service projects that would neither detract from the attention given to male relief projects nor compete with private industry as women's sewing projects allegedly had done. By shifting more and more WPA women's work over to service projects, Woodward capitulated to hostile public opinion and attempted to minimize public objections to women's work relief.

The sewing-room debate that waged within WPA administrative circles reflects the agency's participation in a more general discourse of woman blaming. In the late 1930s as the sewing-room controversy unfolded, critics of the New Deal faulted the WPA for harboring "chronic relievers" who had lost all personal initiative and were now content to subsist on government handouts. Far from promoting the national welfare, critics contended, the growth of a complacent relief population posed a threat to basic American values such as economic self-sufficiency and political independence. Many relief clients had been on relief for years, critics alleged, and were no longer competent to engage in private employment.

WPA administrators' fixation on the sewing rooms as sites of inefficiency and chronic dependency reflects their desire to deflect criticism away from the broader relief administration and onto its already stigmatized, female component. In doing so, administrators capitalized on Americans' demonstrated willingness—one might even say eagerness—to scapegoat women for the problems of the Depression. Also, they mobilized negative feelings against relief-dependent women as a means of promoting white male identification with the New Deal state. Although the sewing rooms remained the primary form of WPA women's work throughout the 1930s, the frequent attacks they suffered translated into cutbacks, closures, and general instability—both for the projects themselves and for the needy women who depended on them.

If the sewing-room controversy had one set of meanings for white women on relief, it had other meanings for women of color, and particularly African American women. First of all, black women's work on sewing projects differed from white women's work. Sewing projects were often segregated by race. Although finding local sponsors for any sewing projects was difficult, it was particularly challenging when black women were to be employed. As Jacqueline Jones notes, throughout the history of the post–Civil War South, blacks had been excluded from textile mills and other forms of industrial employment. Jones argues that this exclusionary practice helped to foster a racialized sense of community among white millworkers and white employers in Southern mill towns. For their part, white Southern mill owners propagated the myth that blacks were incapable of operating industrial equipment such as sewing machines.[78] The longstanding myth of black industrial incompetence ran up against the federal practice of placing large numbers of female relief clients, regardless of race, on sewing projects. African American community leaders heralded black women's employment on sewing projects as breaking a long-standing racial barrier. As one black newspaper editorialized, "Many of the group have been trained . . . in cutting, sewing, and making all kinds of garments . . . This has made it possible for them to apply for a position in shirt factories, women's and men's wear factories, because they have had the experience which is necessary in asking for a position, thus opening up a new avenue of employment that the race has not been accustomed to securing in many places."[79]

Linda Gordon and Jones observe that African American communities, like black women themselves, were generally more accepting of the idea that black wives and mothers would earn wages.[80] And they lauded black women's sewing work both for breaking the racial barrier against black industrial employment and for providing black women with jobs, generally classified as semiskilled, that elevated them above the occupations of field labor and domestic service.

African American women had their own complaints about the sewing rooms. Those who worked on mixed-race projects sometimes complained about unfair treatment. One African American woman in San Marco, Texas, wrote to Washington to ask, "Do these poor Negro women have to get out and mow the grass and pull weeds from the lawn around the sewing room while white and Mexican women sit in the sewing room and do nothing?"[81] On another project, black women complained that they were required to complete custodial work like sweeping floors and cleaning washrooms, which required them to arrive earlier and stay later than other project workers. Throughout the South, the practice of forcing black women to split shifts—and thus to earn half as much as white women—was common.[82] All of these local practices were noncompliant with federal nondiscrimination policies. But state and local administrators disregarded federal mandates or found ways around them, and federal administrators were unwilling to push too hard against Southern white racial practices.

Mexican American women also encountered segregation and discrimination on WPA women's projects. Obtaining WPA work assignments was difficult for Mexican American women, many of whom, like their male counterparts, were wrongfully categorized as "undeserving" aliens. Like black women, Mexican American women also found local relief boards reluctant to assign them WPA work that might "spoil" them for their poorly paid agricultural and domestic occupations. WPA sewing projects were typically segregated and local communities were expected to furnish sewing machines and other necessary materials. Impoverished Mexican American communities often lacked the resources required to start up a sewing project.

Throughout the South and Southwest, state and local relief administrators often forced women of color out of the sewing rooms during the harvest seasons for berries, cotton, tobacco, and other crops. As one African American woman from Georgia wrote to President Roosevelt, "Mr. Roosevelt this is what I want you to understand. We all spell off relief roll until we get through picking beans for some other man farm. This is how they take advantage of us poor colored folks in Georgia. They did not call one white woman to pick beans."[83] Black women frequently expressed such complaints to federal administrators in Washington. When queried about this racist practice, local relief administrators in states like Georgia, North Carolina, and Texas patiently explained that women of color were fitted for arduous field work whereas white women were not.

Whites did object not in principle to African American and Mexican American women's waged work, as they did to white women's employment. However, many did object to the new opportunities that work relief, and particularly sewing work, afforded women of color to escape from domestic and agricultural labor. Throughout the United States, many whites wrote to local papers or to the federal relief administration complaining that African American and Mexican American women's work relief had led to a serious shortage of domestic servants. This was as true in New York and Chicago as it was in Birmingham and San Antonio. White critics alleged that the decent pay and short hours afforded sewing room workers ruined women of color for domestic work. As a Dayton, Ohio woman wrote to her congressman in April 1937, "We find it almost impossible here in the city of Dayton to get a colored or white domestic, and particularly a colored domestic, because a majority of them can get on these WPA projects at $15 per week." She asked, "In all fairness, is this giving the taxpayer a square deal to have to support these loafers who will not work?"[84]

Since a majority of black women had been employed in domestic service prior to the Depression, many whites regarded black women's access to work relief as a major crisis. Critics complained that black women chose to "loaf" on sewing projects at taxpayers' expense when many domestic service positions went unfilled. When the federal administration responded to the unpopularity of sewing rooms by encouraging diversification of women's relief jobs, black sewing projects were disproportionately closed and replaced with cleaning and rehabilitation, rat-catching, and beautification projects.

Such practices led to considerable outcry from African Americans. As one African American businessman wrote to Smith in 1936, "I made a trip to Georgetown, South Carolina, and saw Negro women on the streets digging ditches."[85] Another South Carolina observer wrote to Washington to report, "The negro women of the beautification project have been treated disgraceful. They have been compelled to use picks, shovels, and wheel-barrows. They also are expected to dig holes from three to four feet deep and set out water oaks in the streets. They also load trucks with dirt."[86]

Southern African American women sometimes had to leave not only the sewing rooms, but also their homes, in order to perform seasonal agricultural work. As one Portsmouth, Virginia, resident wrote to Smith, "They would have to leave their babes, afflicted husbands, dependent mothers, and other beloved ones behind, while they would have been relegated to housing quarters worse that those provided for dumb animals, strange men and women all living, cooking, and sleeping together."[87] Thus, in many parts of the country, white concerns about removing women from the workforce and redomesticating them did not apply to black women on relief.

If the sewing rooms were at the heart of WPA gender scapegoating, other activities of what by then had become the Division of Women's and Professional Projects (WPP) also came in for political and administrative scrutiny. It is not surprising that in addition to WPA sewing rooms, the other major target of criticism in the WPA was the Federal Arts, Theater and Writing Projects. A subdivision of the Women's and Professional Projects Division, the Federal Arts Projects were headed by a woman, Hallie Flanagan, who became a favorite target of congressional scrutiny. Between the sewing rooms and the federal arts, Ellen Woodward notes, her division "took about 90 percent of the heat for what amounted to about 10 per cent of WPA projects."[88]

Women were at the center of much of the controversy that circulated within and around the WPA. Yet within the relatively small and embattled space that female administrators carved out for themselves and their clients, they sought to promote a positive national image and role for the nation's needy women. After 1936, when the Aid to Dependent Children clause of Social Security legislation went into effect, one controversial category of needy womanhood—jobless single mothers with children aged sixteen and under—was removed from their purview. Yet they remained responsible for devising and administering appropriate and acceptable projects for other women who were certifiable as economic heads of households, including needy single women and women married to men with disabilities.

The officials who administered the Division of Women's and Professional Projects were largely the same ones who had administered the earlier Women's Division, although its inclusion of professional projects entailed the addition of some male administrators. With Woodward at the head and many of the same state-level officials, relief options for women remained largely unchanged. As with earlier programs, the scope of women's relief was limited by administrators' desire to avoid infringing on the domain of male work relief. Thus since male relief projects were calculated to stress tangible productivity, women's work projects aside from goods production stressed training and community service.

If sewing rooms were the most controversial aspect of women's work relief, the most valued were its Housekeeping Aides, Household Workers Training, and Hot School Lunch programs. In addition to being noncompetitive with male work programs, these programs reinforced residual gender and racial concepts, particularly the association of female citizenship with domesticity and servility. If the sewing rooms were regarded as "female ditch-digging projects" and as "an unfruitful and blind alley," projects like Household Workers Training and Hot School Lunches were said to have "real community value," precisely because they reinforced women's domestic skills.[89] As publicists for the New York City Housekeeping Aides program stated, "The value of the instruction is not limited to the improvement of the housekeeper's efficiency on her job. . . . She carries her training back to her own home. . . . Neighbors learn and are benefited in turn; and gradually better standards spread through the whole community."[90]

In promoting the work of the women's program, Woodward likewise drew attention to the agency's emphasis on women's traditional domestic skills. In

1938, Woodward stated, "Enrollees in WPA centers are instructed in the various intricacies of childcare, the preparation of food, and the serving of meals. They are taught the proper method for making a bed, cleaning wood floors and carpets, airing a room, arranging a linen closet, and laundering. . . ."[91] Yet if such programs earned praise from the same quarters that criticized the sewing rooms, it is worth pondering their appeal more fully. For indeed, not only did programs like Household Workers Training and Hot School Lunches reinforce women's traditional domestic skills at a time when many considered women's redomestication necessary to national recovery, they also had punitive implications at a time when many found woman blaming a satisfying outlet for deeply felt national anxieties. For example, Household Workers Training—easily the most highly touted aspect of WPA women's work—punished relief clients by preparing them for work that was poorly paid and had been declining in occupational status for over a century.[92] Nevertheless, Woodward herself publicly celebrated Household Workers Training as often as possible, encouraging state and local administrators to do the same. Hot School Lunch programs—another project of "definite community value" that many found preferable to the sewing rooms—was inherently part-time and reinforced women's nurturing relationship with children.

That Woodward placed so much public emphasis on Household Workers Training and similar WPP activities suggests her awareness of the national political significance of emergency relief. Herself a veteran of Democratic Party politics and a strong Roosevelt supporter, Woodward was always conscious of the political implications of women's relief work. In her administrative capacity, she promoted the fortunes of the Roosevelt administration at every opportunity.[93] She also established a publicity arm within her division, doing her best to promote the national political benefits of women's relief work, particularly work of a traditionally feminine nature. In addition to applauding Household Workers Training and other domesticating projects, publicists for the Division of Women's and Professional Projects also promoted traditional female crafts such as quilting and basket weaving. WPP fairs regularly showcased women's crafts in every region and in Washington, DC. The emphasis on traditional feminine skills within the women's division received support from Hopkins. In *Spending to Save*, he wrote, "The bulk of the women's program . . . has been built around their traditional skills, and has taught thousands of women to make clothes, to can and to cook with knowledge of food values."[94]

Yet if Woodward and possibly even Hopkins believed that women's relief projects had some positive publicity value insofar as they reinforced traditional feminine skills, Woodward was not so convinced of her division's popularity to trumpet its accomplishments in an election year. Instead, during the 1936 campaign, Woodward discouraged the Women's Division of the Democratic Party from highlighting WPA women's work. In her own political remarks, she chose instead to speak of the virility and vigor of male workers on relief. In terms that resonate with the masculine orientation of so much New Deal rhetoric, she told a Florida women's group, "The Administration is not willing to accept the implication that millions of American workers have suddenly lost all virility, all backbone, and all capacity."[95] Thus even Woodward, dubbed "New Deal advocate for women" by biographer Martha Swain, knew when to stop advocating and start backpedaling on women's relief entitlements.

Resistance by state and local relief officials, as well as by local sponsorship boards, was a major obstacle to the success of WPA women's work. Even when national administrators were willing to advocate equitable relief policies, state and local officials frequently opposed their implementation. When the Women's Division was expanded to include professional projects, many state WPA directors took the opportunity to replace state-level Women's Division directors with male administrators. Only when Hopkins insisted that state heads of the Women's and Professional Projects be women were the female directors reinstated. Local resistance to WPA women's work also took the form of a refusal to sponsor women's projects. Under WPA, local sponsorship made up part of the funding for every relief project, and many communities refused public support for women's projects. This lack of local support was particularly true for African American and Mexican American women's projects; organizers of those projects often had to appeal to the cash-strapped communities of color for materials and financial support. Finally, local certification boards that determined relief eligibility formed a considerable obstacle to women's relief work. Composed of white civic leaders and businessmen, such local boards frequently refused to certify women for WPA relief, even if they had legitimate claims as primary breadwinners for their families. In her travels around the country, Hickok commented, "Your average businessmen just won't believe that there are any women who are absolutely self-supporting."[96] Howard attributed such resistance to local officials' desire to avoid criticism for employing "too many women" and their desire to "put some check on . . . women's eagerness to be the family breadwinner, wage recipient, and controller of the family pocketbook."[97]

Some Roosevelt officials, along with some New Deal scholars, have attributed the remarkable discrimination against women to state and local forces, rather than to national policy or practice.[98] Certainly, state and local relief officials and certification boards were frequently prejudiced against female relief clients and regarded them as interlopers in a relief system intended to serve the needs of white men. Yet to overemphasize local forces is to fundamentally misread one of the ways in which the New Deal functioned as a nation-saving project. Roosevelt administrators imbued emergency relief with national significance. By investing responsibility for the administration of emergency relief in states and localities, they sought to engage state and local actors in a nation-building project. Insofar as the investment of authority at state and local levels was intentional, meant to place a widely dispersed citizenry in dialogue with the nation, New Deal administrators were complicit in gender and racial discrimination that took place at the local level.

Once again, the shifting gender anxieties that animated developments in welfare policy at mid-decade did not affect women of color and white women in the same way. The reconstruction of white manhood was a primary preoccupation of 1930s political culture, and the reconstruction of white womanhood was closely related to it. The reconstruction of other racial categories of womanhood, on the other hand, followed a somewhat different, though no less punitive trajectory. In a White House Conference on the Participation of Negro Women and Children in Federal Welfare Programs, organized by Mary McLeod Bethune and convened in April 1938, members of the National Council of Negro Women lamented African American women's marginal status within the structure of federal relief. "As good Americans," the conference report stated, "we should aspire to make our rightful contribution to the social advancement of the nation. We do not feel this can be accomplished as long as so large a sector as we represent is so largely excluded from the full benefits of social welfare legislation." Conferees recommended that more African American women be placed in administrative posts "strategic to the full participation of Negro women and children in several government programs."[99] Besides Bethune herself, federal relief administrators were generally unenthusiastic about the conference, and most of its findings were never carried out.[100]

In the South, African American newspapers charged that when African American women applied for work relief, administrators often disregarded their status as *women*. "It has been charged that Negro women have been compelled to work at 'men's jobs' in all kinds of weather," a WPA field investigator reported. He cited a newspaper account that alleged that African American women were made to wear a "uniform stamping them as some sort of convicts."[101] As these statements suggest, while administrators maintained white women on conventionally feminine assignments such as sewing projects, the same administrators often made little effort to provide gender-appropriate tasks to women of color. And when sewing rooms were downsized throughout the country, African American and Mexican American women were the first to be removed from project payrolls.

That concerns about white womanhood did not extend to women of color, and in fact were often defined *against* the latter group, can also be seen in publicity surrounding the WPA's Housekeeping Aides Projects, established in 1938. These projects employed needy women to provide temporary help to distressed families. Housekeeping aides performed vital household services such as cleaning, cooking, and childcare during the absence or illness of a wife or mother.

Publicists for the Housekeeping Aides Project asserted that not all women were equally suited for this type of employment. In contrast to those who expected their work to follow a clearly defined schedule, a publicity bulletin advised, "housekeeping aides must not be clock-watchers." Moreover, candidates should not be sexually provocative. The person most suited to these qualifications, publicists decided, was a middle-aged African American woman. "Negro women are more efficient, adaptable, and interested in this type of work than white women," one press report suggested. Not only was African American women's "experience in taking responsibility valuable," the report continued, but "they are less likely to encounter difficulties with the men of the families for whom they work while the wife or mother is ill or absent."[102]

Indeed, if the unemployed white woman was of questionable usefulness in the Depression-era workforce, the African American Housekeeping Aide was not. Within the logic of WPA politics, her function as domestic servant reinforced traditional gender and racial expectations. Throughout the 1930s, African American women's workforce participation was not imbued with the same sexual accents that characterized representations of the white working woman. Instead, their status as particular *kinds* of workers was readily accepted within the gender and racial conventions of Depression-era society.

Well before Roosevelt's "forgotten-man" speech, Americans were using conventional gender images to make sense of the nation's economic and political troubles. The figure of the white unemployed man, reduced to apple-selling or standing in breadlines, appeared everywhere, eliciting Americans' sympathy and concern. Also quite pervasive were distinctly negative images of white womanhood, such as the married woman worker, the emasculating wife, and the sexually promiscuous woman alone. At the intersection of gender, race, and politics in the Great Depression, such negative female imagery also had its place. An analysis of Depression-era public discourse reveals that women functioned as scapegoats for the economic crisis and attendant political problems. Imbued with negative characteristics such as selfishness and volatility, figures like the married woman worker and the female hobo helped to establish men's political independence and moral fortitude by their own contrasting conduct. Their position as scapegoats made them satisfying targets for male frustrations that might otherwise have been channeled elsewhere. Finally, translating the nation's economic crisis into a crisis of unruly womanhood gave some Depression Americans a sense of positive forward movement. Even if they could not solve the nation's complex economic problems, they could restrict the economic activities of "bad" women such as the wage-earning wife and the "woman adrift." Stories, images, and even New Deal policies that punished women for the Depression helped to constitute a gendered civic community whose members derived emotional sustenance from their shared hostility to women.

It is one thing to identify the pervasiveness of woman blaming in the wide-ranging public discourse of the early Depression years. It is quite another to locate that same imagery in the official, nation-saving rhetoric and practices of the New Deal state. Historians have long touted the New Deal years as a transformative moment in American political life. They credit the Roosevelt administration with challenging conventions ranging from the role of the presidency to the place of government in American economic life. Perhaps the largest change attributed to the New Deal is its transformation of the reciprocal rights and obligations binding citizens to the state. In its implementation of the modern U.S. welfare state, the New Deal established the principle of government responsibility for the poor, thus compromising the long-standing ideal of self-sufficient citizenship. Introducing such vast political changes prompted widespread political anxieties, and at no point in its history was New Deal relief policy uncontested. Confronted with frequent criticism and eager to garner popular support, Roosevelt officials aligned state policy and action with residual gender concepts such as the forgotten man, the militarized youth, and the disorderly woman.

By looking at the interplay of residual gender imagery and emergent welfare politics, we learn much about the politics of state and nation formation in the New Deal years. Specifically, we learn how emotionally charged woman-blaming practices were incorporated in order to make new forms of state policy and action more palatable.

132   CHAPTER 4

✑ Final Shrew-Taming Episode

Having explored New Deal complicity in the popular practice of woman blaming, this chapter concludes by offering one final, late Depression scene of woman spanking. The scene takes place in Frank Capra's critically acclaimed film, *Meet John Doe* (Warner Brothers, 1941). Although primarily a story about mass media and the contest between democracy and fascism, the film also centers on the shrew-taming romance of Long John Willoughby (Gary Cooper) and Anne Mitchell (Barbara Stanwyck). Initially a jobless outcast, John is recruited by Anne Mitchell, an unethical newspaperwoman, to assume the persona of John Doe, a character Anne has invented in order to save her job. As John grows into his assumed role, he gradually gains power over Anne, until finally the dynamics of their relationship are reversed, and she is thoroughly punished for her transgressions. Significantly, Anne's humble submission coincides with John's ascendance to a position of authentic civic authority. This crucial turning point in their relationship is anticipated when John tells Anne about a dream he has had in which he thoroughly spanks her:

> But here's the funniest part of it all. I was the fellow up there doing the marrying, you know, the justice of the peace?
>
> You? I thought you were chasing me.
>
> Well, yes, I was, but I was your father then, see? But the real me, John Doe or, that is, Long John Willoughby, I was the fellow up there with the book, you know what I mean?
>
> I guess so. Then what happened?
>
> Well, I took you across my knee and I started spanking you. That is, *I* didn't do it, I mean, I *did* do it, it wasn't me you see, I was your father then.

As Anne listens in astonishment, John describes how, as the father continues to spank her, the justice of the peace encourages him, saying, "Go to it, pop, whack her one for me because that's just the way I feel about it too." The father invites the judge to join him in the spanking. John, who identifies with both male figures, continues, "So I came down and whacked you a good one, see? And then he whacked you. And I whacked you another one and we both started whacking you."

"Dreams are sure crazy, aren't they?" John says to Anne. However "crazy" dreams may be, as Fredric Jameson observes, the utopian longings that they and other narrative forms express also enable complex collective identities to form and change.[103] In dialogue with popular woman-blaming narratives,

New Deal officials wove their own dreamlike web of "affective intensities and assurances" that centered on negative figurations of Depression womanhood.[104] In the process, they engaged the utopian longings of a gendered American public beset by a broad range of material and ideological conflicts. And in so doing, they enabled that public to bracket its many differences in pursuit of a shared, emotionally and materially satisfying woman-blaming ideal.

CHAPTER 5

Civilian Protectors and Meddlesome Women

Gendering the War Effort through the Office of Civilian Defense

On June 13, 1942, New Yorkers witnessed what one promoter described as "the greatest parade the United States has ever seen." The eleven-hour spectacle featured "300 floats, scores of bands, and thousands of flags and banners." The parade's prologue, "America Mobilizes," told the story of the Second World War in a series of spectacular floats. Six marching divisions followed, divided equally between military and civilian units. The parade ended at dusk with a small torchlight procession. At scheduled intervals, fighter planes flew overhead, and an air-raid drill briefly halted festivities in the middle of the day.[1]

The parade was indeed spectacular, even circuslike at times. The *New York Times* characterized it as "a bit of the World's Fair come back for a day." Air-raid wardens wore gaudy blue and orange uniforms and carried large fiberboard swords painted red, white, and blue. Teenage "emergency couriers" paraded on bicycles and roller skates, and a fifteen-foot-tall minuteman, "the largest ever constructed," symbolized the launch of the summer's Liberty Bond campaign. The Axis powers were depicted as a huge dragon, fifty-five-feet long and three stories tall, which emitted real smoke from its nostrils and sides. A tribute to the Filipino troops featured Igorot natives, replete with loincloths and spears, riding atop American-built tanks. A float dedicated to the United States' Good Neighbor Policy carried beautiful Latinas in evening gowns, each wearing a sash inscribed with her nation of origin. Representatives of the various nations, many in traditional ethnic costume, participated along with "loyal" German and Italian aliens. Although people of color figured more as categorical referents than as full-fledged participants, Japanese Americans were the only group to be wholly excluded from the parade. The people of Japan, by contrast, were depicted as rats on a float bearing the banner, "Tokyo, We Are Coming!" The float also featured a large, mechanized American eagle, which scattered the rats into the sea.

Although the parade was widely hailed as a success, some observers questioned its appropriateness in wartime. At a time of austerity and sacrifice, critics queried, was such a carnival-like event really the best use of national resources?

The Committee on Mobilization for New York at War—a group of fourteen civic leaders charged with the task of planning the parade—rankled at suggestions that the event was frivolous and ill-timed. Speaking for the committee, Dr. Frank Monaghan called the parade "a somber, grim representation of the city's grim resolve to destroy what the Axis stands for."[2] Mayor Fiorello La Guardia insisted that the parade was a crucial, morale-building event through which millions of New Yorkers would experience the city's will to victory.

La Guardia used the parade to promote the U.S. Office of Civilian Defense (OCD), declaring the week leading up to the parade "Civilian Defense Week" for the nation.[3] As the OCD's national director from June 1940 until January 1942, La Guardia firmly believed in the value of parades and pageantry. In addition to parades, he promoted frequent blackouts and emergency drills. Like parades, such drills enabled U.S. civilians to don uniforms and engage their neighbors in a role-oriented, difference-based drama of wartime civic preparedness.

The OCD was a remarkably inclusive wartime agency that helped U.S. civilians to span the difficult transition from an isolationist to an interventionist nation-state. It helped them to cope with sexual anxieties borne of the divergent wartime experiences of soldiers and civilians and of settled and migratory civilian populations. It alleviated gender anxieties caused by women's increasing workforce participation and civilian men's compromised status relative to young male soldiers. Finally, the OCD managed racial anxieties prompted by African American civil rights activism; by the inconsistency of fighting racial intolerance abroad while maintaining Jim Crow segregation at home; and by the demographic pressures of a highly mobile, racially diverse civilian population. Through parades and through other public rituals and narratives of civic obligation, the OCD enlisted civilians in defending their communities and securing a wide range of social and civic meanings rendered unstable by the war.

Not every aspect of the OCD was devoted to enacting a role-oriented, difference-based script of national loyalty through parades, emergency drills, and other civic rituals. That was the province of the Civilian Protection Branch. The agency's other division, the Civilian Defense Volunteer Office, was charged with the very different task of carrying on normal civic and welfare tasks that had been necessary in peacetime, but that its participants regarded as even more vital in wartime. Such tasks included child care, housing assistance, and other family and community support services. The officials who administered this division tended to be liberal New Dealers who had long advocated welfare and social work. The volunteers whom they enlisted tended to be white civilian women, African Americans, and other people of color who were looking for gender- and race-appropriate ways to contribute to the war effort at a time when the most dramatic defense roles were reserved for white civilian men.

Both divisions—the dramatic Civilian Protection Branch and the service-oriented Civilian Defense Volunteer Office—worked to fulfill the OCD's mandate, which was to "sustain national morale."[4] Yet their efforts were often at cross-purposes, perhaps because "national morale," although widely discussed, had no precise or obvious meanings. To some Americans, it meant "having useful work to do," living normally in spite of wartime conditions, and preserving civilians' "homes as their castles."[5] But others noted that national morale was rife with "danger spots"; some associated it with Nazi-style propaganda; and its instrumentality was widely debated.[6]

In a radio address marking the opening of the 1940 Mobilization for Human Needs, President Roosevelt offered his own, highly influential definition of national morale. While "events abroad have warned us . . . of the need of planes and tanks, of ships and guns," Roosevelt began, "they have also warned us of the need of grit and sacrifice, of daring and devotion, and all those intangible things which go to make up a nation's morale."[7] Roosevelt's emphasis on the affective features of national morale, including "grit and sacrifice," "daring and devotion," and other emotional "intangibles," raises the following questions: What are the emotional valences of wartime narratives and rituals of civic preparedness, and how did they map onto a diverse civilian population? To what extent did OCD narratives and rituals of civic preparedness "sustain national morale" by evoking white male civilians' hostility not only toward Axis aggressors, but also toward unpatriotic women and other home-front enemies? Finally, in cultivating the affect of grimness and determination among white civilian men, how did narratives and rituals of civic preparedness constitute a racialized and gendered American public that was willing to support the interventionist policies and actions of the wartime state?

How New Deal social policy fared in the transition to war illuminates the changing gender, racial, and sexual dimensions of civic storytelling and national belonging throughout the Roosevelt years. During the Depression, New Deal officials worked assiduously to masculinize federal relief. But as the Roosevelt administration mobilized for war, federal officials and other aspirants to political power began to feminize New Deal social policy, casting it as frivolous social experimentation during a time that called for decisive, masculine leadership.[8] As New Deal relief agencies made way for wartime agencies like the OCD, a new affective politics of scapegoating emerged—one that continued to constitute a white masculine public at the expense of women and people of color, but that also cast a hostile eye on feminized New Deal bureaucrats.

Total War

The OCD successfully engaged so many civilians in part because it drew on a broader discourse of total war. That discourse, which sought to convince civilians that the "home front" was as vital to winning the war as the "military front," invoked traditional gender, racial, and family ideals.[9] In particular, stories and images of white men who used their strength and authority as family breadwinners to fashion a new, hands-on approach to national defense proliferated in the popular iconography of the war period.

In December 1941, a Hearst editorial cartoon showed Uncle Sam kneeling in anguish over the body of America's fallen son. Signifying the nation's response to Pearl Harbor, the cartoon cast America's declaration of war in familial terms (in this case, focusing on the bond between father and son), and it proposed a central role for the mature family patriarch in the war. The cartoon implied that the nation's mature family heads must avenge the treacherous attack on Pearl Harbor and prevent future assaults on America's families and communities.

Such images of Uncle Sam—no longer avuncular but grim and determined—appeared countless times during the war. A 1942 war bonds poster featured a husky and resolute Uncle Sam looming over America's forward-marching troops. And a December 1941 pamphlet, *What to Do in an Air Raid*, featured the same grim and determined Uncle Sam, sleeves

138   CHAPTER 5

FIGURE 7. Cartoon by Burris Jenkins Jr. of the *New-York Journal-American*, "Hearst Sports Cartoonist Jenkins Denounced Foul Play," *Life*, December 22, 1941, 7. Rightsholder: T. Hans Groenhoff.

rolled up to expose muscular forearms, this time looming not over soldiers but over the civilian OCD membership. In this image, Uncle Sam's grim countenance is mirrored in the expressions of the white, predominantly male group of civilian defenders beneath him.

If a grim and determined Uncle Sam served as one role model for mature civilian men, advertisements that focused on the vigilance and moral authority of the white family breadwinner offered another. As companies converted to war production, many began advertising patriotism and postwar prosperity instead of consumer goods.[10] Throughout the war, ad campaigns often focused on the valor of the war worker, figured as a white man beyond service-eligible age, and on the exemplary moral and civic leadership of America's family breadwinners. "There are men in war plants who have worked at top speed seven days a week since long before Pearl Harbor," a 1942 ad for machine tools reported.[11] At the center of the ad stands a middle-aged factory worker absorbed in his work. By putting in long hours at the factory, the ad suggests, America's breadwinners performed a civic duty comparable to that of the nation's soldiers. They worked hard

FIGURE 8. Pamphlet illustration featuring grim and determined Uncle Sam. U.S. Office of Civilian Defense, *What to Do in an Air Raid* (Washington, DC: U.S. Government Printing Office, 1942).

because they "believe that this—and fighting—are the ways to be true Americans."

Yet seasoned war workers did not cease their exemplary Americanism at the factory gates. In addition to performing vital war work, the ad continues, "These are the men who are the good Americans in all other ways, too." Suggesting their important leadership role in the *family* war effort, the ad states, "Tired as they are, they somehow find time to be the first in scrap drives. It is their wives who save every tin can, every ounce of fats. It is their families who buy the most in War Bonds." The ad concludes, "Thank God there are many such men and such homes. They are the only hope of a free, strong America."[12]

A United States Rubber Company advertisement depicts a white civilian breadwinner, not at his job, but standing next to his wife and daughter in a family pew at church.[13] Suggesting his moral authority within the family group, the breadwinner declares, "I want to preach a sermon." His words appear in large, bold print. In the ensuing sermon, he invokes his own experience of struggle. Recalling the hardships of the Depression, he comments, "The time I lost my job we ate beans six weeks in a row. But I got back on the payroll!" In the same list of trials, he states, "The night we got the telegram about our boy, we thought the sun would never shine again. But . . . we're carrying on!" He goes on to suggest that America's strength can be measured both by its past feats of military valor and by the grit and determination of its families. He pledges on behalf of all American families to sacrifice whatever is necessary to bring the war to a victorious end: "Take everything we've got to win this war, and welcome! Because there's one thing no one's ever going to take from you and me, and that's America!" This ad, which features a white breadwinner whose commitment to family is paramount in his life, but who also sees his role as larger than his own home, was mirrored in countless other advertisements during the war.

As the locus of family life, the home also assumed patriotic proportions. An October 1942 ad for the *Chicago Daily News*—described as "America's *Home* Newspaper"—called the home the "most inspired of all man's creations." It declared, "Now, here in America, there is a great mass movement toward the *home-way* of living. Big town-dweller and small-town dweller alike has rediscovered home." The text continues with a patriotic vow: "From this hour on we shall spend more time in the home. Find deeper pleasure in the home. Be more regardful of the home and its daily blessings which sustain us in our strivings and comfort us in our sorrows."[14]

In celebrating "America, home-made style," ads like this one implicitly criticized American housewives who had become too dependent on mass-produced goods to lighten their domestic burden. Marquis Childs, author of *This Is Your War*, castigated "millions of American women," who before the war "apparently spent whole afternoons wandering about the cathedral-like corridors of American department stores" making "needless and foolish purchases." For such women, the wartime imperative to conserve household resources and produce homemade goods provided a much-needed opportunity for self-improvement.[15]

Along with rediscovering their "home-way of life," commentators suggested, Americans were also rediscovering the virtues of neighborliness and close-knit community ties. "Big town dweller and small town dweller alike" were finding common ground in their shared commitment to winning the war. Childs predicted that "we shall get to know the next-door neighbor a good deal better, and we shall see a lot more of that nice couple in the next block."[16] Similarly, urban sociologist Louis Wirth stated, "World War II . . . is giving a rebirth to the social organization of our communities." He added, "Many people who were formerly strangers to one another though living in adjoining apartments are for the first time making one another's acquaintance."[17]

Such statements resonated with widely circulating internationalist texts, such as Henry Luce's *The American Century*. Luce maintained that Americans must be "Good Samaritans" to less privileged members of the international "family of nations."[18] President Roosevelt likewise championed the cause of neighborliness, both in statements on the Good Neighbor Policy with Latin America and in his pleas for U.S. support for the Allied cause. America must take heed of the needs of its "world neighbors," Roosevelt argued repeatedly. He likened the Axis enemies to the "gangsters" and "hoodlums" who menaced America's urban neighborhoods. And in his war messages following the Pearl Harbor attack, he invoked the image of a community or neighborhood whose tranquility had been ruthlessly violated. America must champion the cause of peace and security not only for its own residential communities, Luce and Roosevelt argued, but for the international community of nations as well.[19]

The rhetoric of neighborliness thus developed alongside the rhetoric of homeliness during the war. As Rogers Smith argues, both sets of images occupy a central place within the United States' ascriptivist political tradition. Smith notes that ascriptive Americanism draws on backward-looking, racialized images of family and close-knit community to define civic membership in relational, role-oriented, and difference-based terms.[20]

Such backward-looking images of family and community evoked feelings of comfort and reassurance at a time that Susan B. Hirsch and Lewis Erenberg have characterized as a "liminal period for people's personal lives."[21] They note that the vast social dislocation of the war period, combined with changes in U.S. domestic and foreign policy, "made extraordinary demands on people and their values." Several factors altered Americans' civic consciousness during the war. First, the unequal distribution of political labor between soldiers and civilians privileged military sacrifice, thus compromising the traditional authority of mature male breadwinners. Second, soldiers' departure for military service and civilian men's and women's migrations to war production centers generated a range of gender, racial, and sexual anxieties. And third, changes in men's and women's civic and economic roles disrupted gender and family conventions.

Racial conventions were also disrupted by the war. Soldiers of color generally served in segregated military units, while their civilian counterparts encountered racial discrimination as applicants for war production work.[22] Throughout the war, nonwhite men and women struggled with the paradox of fighting a war against racial intolerance abroad while enduring intense racial prejudice at home. Too often, domestic racial tensions erupted into overt conflict: between white servicemen and Mexican American zoot suiters in Los Angeles; between white and black war workers in Detroit, Harlem, and along the Gulf Coast; and between white civilians and African American servicemen in the environs of Southern U.S. military bases.[23] John Dower also notes that U.S. civilians experienced World War II as a "race war" waged most dramatically in the Pacific Theater; certainly, as Luis Alvarez notes, it was a war in which questions of national loyalty and civic belonging came to be answered in racial and gender terms.[24]

Finally, at a time when World War I (the so-called War to End All Wars) was a vivid memory for many Americans, mobilization for yet another global conflict met with marked ambivalence. Certainly, developments in the Pacific Theater facilitated a racialized rhetoric of national unity and fortified white civilians' support for the war. Yet the daily imperatives of wartime, along with the barrage of news reports from war-torn regions abroad, significantly challenged Americans' national consciousness and propelled them, often reluctantly, onto the stage of world affairs. By using residual, gendered and racialized themes of family and neighborhood to link domestic and international developments, total war ideology offered U.S. civilians a familiar and emotionally reassuring frame of reference. Not only did it ease social and sexual anxieties borne of wartime changes on the home front; it also helped to enlist U.S. citizens in the role-oriented, difference-based project of U.S. global leadership.

Among the domestic sources of civic uncertainty was the valorization of soldiers over all other social groups, as evident in numerous official statements during the war. "A waste of our food resources now will prolong the war and cause the death of thousands upon thousands of American boys," one government bulletin admonished.[25] In an implicit critique of civilian workers, a Naval officer remarked, "Our well-disciplined and heroic soldiers and sailors . . . never question the amount of their wages, nor the hours they must fight, nor do they protest the orders under which they serve." Instead, they "risk their lives," so that American democracy might be secure.[26] Perhaps the most potent symbol of Americans' preoccupation with military sacrifice was the stars that Americans hung in the windows of their homes, indicating that a young member of the household was fighting in the war. The stars indicated the vicariousness of civilian claims to sacrifice in a culture that was absorbed in military developments.

Yet even as civilians praised the nation's soldiers, they worried over the military mobilization of young men. Particularly widespread were concerns about the effacement of individuality that characterized military life. Such effacement had considerable resonance at a time when civilians, too, were being asked to sacrifice individual freedoms for the sake of a common, national cause. Recognizing that concerns about individuality existed, government officials assured Americans that army life was not so different from civilian life. A government pamphlet stressed that individually operated machines, not huge masses of men, enabled modern armies to achieve their goals. Yet the pamphlet also acknowledged the military's "lack of privacy," "strictness of discipline," and rigid assignment of time. As if to confirm civilian fears about the strange effacement of individuality that characterized military life, the pamphlet added, "The serviceman learns to subordinate the self-centeredness and self-indulgence that he probably allowed himself in civilian life. He learns . . . how to put the welfare of the unit above personal welfare."[27]

The military mobilization of masculine youth evoked other concerns as well. Some questioned the capacity of young American men who had come of age in the Great Depression to withstand the rigors of military service. Considerable public alarm followed what one social scientist called "the recent shocking revelation" by the War Department that a "high proportion of youths of draft age . . . are rated as unfit for military service."[28] Others expressed concern about the gender and sexual problems the military created. Sociologist Ernest W. Burgess noted that most military recruits were "single and mainly in their twenties and thirties," adding that "this withdrawal of men from the primary group controls of the home and the neighborhood removes restraining influences against socially disapproved forms of behavior."[29] Stated another sociologist, "The soldier who is withdrawn from civilian life . . . achieves a certain anonymity." He expressed concern that "the wearing of the uniform is rationalized to confer upon the individual a different set of moral precepts."[30] Whereas mature men, situated within the stabilizing institutions of civilian life, might be expected to abide by established "moral precepts," no such expectation applied to militarized youth. Burgess cited an extensive body of research indicating that "Drinking, gambling, prostitution, and illicit sex behavior has been higher among men in military than in civilian life."[31]

As mobilization for war undercut the stability of families and communities on the home front, gender and sexual anxieties spilled over from the military into civilian life. Early in 1942, research criminologist Eleanor T. Glueck warned that Americans "must expect an increase in our . . . rate of juvenile crime."[32] In October 1942, J. Edgar Hoover declared that juvenile delinquency was rising quickly, and a juvenile court judge in New York City noted, "There seems to be a crime wave among young boys here."³³ Others noted a rise in female delinquency, specifically sex delinquency. Burgess noted that the "glamour of the uniform" and "patriotic justification in acceding to the desire of a man about to give his life for his country" accounted for much of the increase in female sex delinquency during the war.³⁴ As Kevin Allen Leonard notes, such concerns about juvenile delinquency were also racialized. Anxieties about the young white citizen-soldier were often displaced onto African American and Mexican American "zoot suiters" and their female counterparts, who loomed large in the representation of juvenile delinquency during the war.³⁵

According to social scientists, a whole host of social and sexual problems derived from the military mobilization of young men. As men left civilian life to enter the military, they also created openings for white women and men and women of color in the civilian workforce. In November 1940, ten and a half million women were in the labor force; by November 1942, the number exceeded fifteen million.³⁶ Although discriminatory hiring plagued African Americans and Mexican Americans throughout the war, labor shortages and pressure from civil rights leaders helped them to overcome some barriers to military and civilian employment. By 1945, African Americans comprised almost 8 percent of workers in defense plants, and roughly 700,000 black families had migrated out of the South to realize wartime economic opportunities. Mexican Americans also took advantage of wartime opportunities for occupational mobility and military service.³⁷

The vast economic and demographic shifts of the war period engendered sexual anxieties. According to sociological experts, the departure of married soldiers left wives prone to the temptations of extramarital sex. "Adultery, and the thought of it, flourish upon opportunity," one sociologist warned.³⁸ Migratory war workers, like soldiers, achieved "a certain anonymity." As Wirth commented, "The relatively large proportion of unattached individuals among the in-migrants who are being uprooted from their home communities creates problems of vice and social disorganization which are difficult to control in a boom atmosphere."³⁹ Concerns about homosexuality also escalated, as wartime migration brought gays and lesbians into urban gay communities.⁴⁰

Mobilization for war thus catalyzed a wide range of social and sexual anxieties, many of which related, directly or indirectly, to the military enlistment of millions of young American men. The centrality of the soldier as a figure of wartime sacrifice and loyalty suggests that America's fighting forces, organized together in the nation's military, helped to model important national values. Their commitment to sacrificing personal well-being on behalf of a transcendent national cause powerfully affected American concepts of citizenship. Yet as wartime concerns about the social and sexual consequences of military mobilization suggest, the national values that America's fighting forces modeled were in some ways at odds with, and induced tremendous gender and generational anxieties within, the same civic culture that generated them. By emphasizing family and the wartime contributions of white civilian breadwinners, total war discourse compensated for the volatile influence of military society.

The metaphors of home and close-knit civic community were useful in garnering popular support for the wartime state. However, as they had been in the 1930s, they were also tremendously consequential, reinforcing divisions in the polity that defined citizenship in gender, racial, and generational terms. All of these metaphors crystallized in the relatively short-lived but sweeping and inclusive OCD. More than any other wartime agency, the OCD stood at the center of popular and official discussions of total war.

↵ Office of Civilian Defense

Established by Executive Order on May 20, 1941, the Office of Civilian Defense coordinated the volunteer defense activities of millions of U.S. civilians. Like so many New Deal programs, its mandate was large and ill-defined, and it took its place within a lineup of similarly ill-defined, sometimes overlapping agencies. Its specific charter was to engage "the united action of every civilian" in a "home front march to victory." It sought to unite U.S. civilians behind the "strong leadership" of the national administration, and it envisioned a harmonious collaboration between the nation's soldiers and civilians that would last "until the guns now pointing at Germany and Japan have ceased to fire."[41]

As a national project, the OCD functioned on several levels. First, it worked to assuage civilian ambivalence about the selective imposition of military obligation on masculine youth. Particularly for mature white civilian men, it provided a simulation of military experience that worked to bridge the gulf between soldiers and civilians. The OCD also worked to organize civilians under the leadership of a *national* defense organization. It brought widely scattered Americans into a defense effort that was national in scope and that linked national concepts of leadership and power to the family-based forms of power and authority with which civilians were familiar. Finally, it involved civilians in a process of national redefinition. Through their OCD participation, civilians were implicated in national politics and global military developments. The agency's rhetoric of total warfare cultivated a siege mentality that tied individual households into a struggle of national and global proportions.[42]

The OCD did not include everybody on equal terms. Like the military it did so much to emulate, the OCD was largely racially segregated and afforded fewer opportunities to African Americans, Mexican Americans, and other nonwhite groups. These exclusionary practices were consistent with the agency's privileging of mature white men who came to occupy the most authoritative roles of air-raid wardens, auxiliary policemen, and auxiliary firemen within the OCD setup.

At the federal level, the OCD consisted of a small Washington-based staff, headed first by New York City Mayor Fiorello H. La Guardia, and then by Harvard Law School Dean James M. Landis after La Guardia resigned in February 1942. In the agency's early months, Eleanor Roosevelt served as assistant director, administering the OCD's Volunteer Participation Committee. Beyond the national level, the OCD operated through nine regional offices, each headed by a regional director. The areas and jurisdictions of the nine regional offices corresponded to the nine Army Corps areas set up during the war. Regional OCD offices worked closely with the forty-eight state defense councils and countless local defense offices that coordinated civilian participation during the war.

At the national level, OCD administrators reviewed plans and progress for civilian defense throughout the nation, developed national policy, and coordinated the agency's efforts with those of other wartime agencies. Initially, as outlined in Roosevelt's executive order, the function of OCD was threefold: (1) to prepare the civilian population to withstand enemy attack, (2) to coordinate volunteer participation in the defense effort, and (3) to preserve national morale. The OCD's "protective" branch oversaw civilian preparation for enemy air raids and other threats to domestic security, whereas the "nonprotective" branch worked to provide opportunities for full civilian participation in the war.[43]

The morale-boosting function of the OCD was more diffuse, finding expression in the agency's rhetoric of total war, which prescribed a central place for civilians alongside soldiers in the war effort. It also found expression in the OCD's rhetoric of "home defense." "Civilian defense is defense of the home," OCD director James M. Landis told audiences. The OCD sponsored National Family Week, and it designated households in full compliance with civilian defense measures "Victory Homes."[44] The OCD also reinforced the sanctity of American family life by establishing gender- and generationally-appropriate tasks for civilian men, women, and children. Most significantly, perhaps, the OCD divided civilian defense into male-dominated "protective" and female-dominated "nonprotective" activities. So explicitly gendered were the protective and nonprotective branches that in many localities, Boy Scouts were automatically incorporated on the protective side, whereas Girl Scouts were channeled into nonprotective work. By providing gender-specific tasks for all family members and by emphasizing defense of the home front as a task equal in importance to that of the military fronts, the OCD sought to boost the morale of the general civilian population while reserving a privileged place for the nation's white civilian breadwinners.

The OCD had a tremendous impact on civilian life during the war. Samuel Rosenman writes that "probably no single civilian Federal agency enlisted the services of so many American people and came so closely into their homes and their daily lives as the OCD."[45] According to *Scientific American*, the OCD was "a volunteer program as broad as the United States itself and as American as Lexington's Minute Men." Its editors remarked, "There's room for everybody in Civilian Defense."[46]

Nearly everybody seemed to join the OCD. In the fall of 1941, even before Pearl Harbor, defense councils had formed in every state, in more than six thousand cities, and in countless neighborhoods and smaller communities. Communities of color tended to organize their own racially specific civilian defense operations. By the summer of 1942, nearly ten million volunteers had enlisted in civilian defense, and by 1943, over twenty million OCD Victory Gardens had been planted.[47] Throughout the war period, air-raid drills, salvage drives, and other OCD events drew millions of participants. Philadelphian Thomas Scott recalled, "Everybody participated, people in all kinds of occupations. . . . There was a job for everybody from ten years old on up . . . So everyone felt they were actively participating in the war effort."[48]

OCD administrators made efforts to encompass even unenthusiastic civilians in its activities. Toward those who did not contribute, the agency made special overtures. An OCD bulletin encouraged neighborhood organizers to use extra persistence and diplomacy with residents who were skeptical of civilian defense, and civilians who engaged in behaviors that undermined the war effort were exhorted to mend their ways. Within the OCD's rhetoric of total warfare, any unproductive behavior was tantamount to sabotage. For civilians who drank and drove, the Oklahoma State Defense Council coined the term "cocktail saboteurs." One OCD bulletin called the black market patron "as much a saboteur as though he dynamited a gun plant," and another warned, "When you hoard, you help Hitler."[49]

Certainly, there were limits to OCD inclusiveness. African Americans and other U.S. people of color were excluded from defense activities in many localities. Official OCD guidelines stipulated that neither race, nor creed, nor color should be a factor in the assignment of OCD jobs, but full racial integration was rare in an agency that did much to emulate the nation's segregated military establishment.

Although African Americans and other people of color answered the call to participate in civilian defense, state and local defense councils did not always welcome their contributions. In many places, African Americans organized separate civilian defense operations that met the defense needs of their own racial groups and were tangential to the main OCD organization in their communities. Moreover, African Americans who sought to enroll in training courses to become air-raid wardens, auxiliary police, and auxiliary firemen were often made to wait indefinitely for the requisite training, whereas whites were trained expeditiously. Particularly during Eleanor Roosevelt's tenure as OCD assistant director from May 1941 to February 1942, African Americans received national and regional appointments to serve as race relations advisers and to encourage African American participation in OCD. But Mrs. Roosevelt had little sway over the more celebrated protective branch, which was more racially restrictive. Her efforts to use the OCD as a platform to advance black civil rights likely contributed to a conservative backlash that resulted in her resignation from the agency.[50]

OCD officials were not above using a racist turn of phrase. The agency's rhetoric freely targeted the Japanese, as when one OCD adviser declared that "the only difference between a Jap and a too-complacent American is that the Jap has slant eyes."[51] But antiblack racism was also pervasive. In New Jersey, white occupants of a bomb shelter refused entry to an African American couple during an air-raid drill. When the president and faculty members of all-black Lincoln College in Missouri attempted to participate in a local civilian defense parade, they were told that they could only march if they moved to the rear of the procession. (They chose not to march.) In many locations, civilian defense courses took place in segregated facilities, prompting some African Americans to resign from their posts as OCD educators. Groups closely affiliated with the OCD, such as the American Red Cross and the American Women's Volunteer Services, routinely engaged in segregationist practices.[52]

Robert Earnest Miller notes African American leaders in Cincinnati, Ohio, sought greater defense roles for members of the black community, on the grounds that they, too, had a stake in national survival.[53] In other communities like New York's Harlem and Chicago's South Side, African Americans formed independent OCD groups, but their active and enthusiastic participation took place within racially segregated bounds.[54]

Leonard notes that although some OCD officials and many participants used total war ideology to define the war effort in discriminatory terms, African American civil rights leaders interpreted that ideology differently. Leonard notes that black newspapers invoked the rhetoric of total warfare when they referred to U.S. racism as "'Hitler's secret weapon' and to racists as 'fifth columnists.'"[55]

Civil rights leaders also specifically targeted OCD racism. With Eleanor Roosevelt's support, they worked to establish a Race Relations Division under the auspices of the "nonprotective" Volunteer Participation Committee. Crystal Bird Fauset, former African American congresswoman and veteran New Dealer, was appointed to head the division. Fauset was assisted by two secretaries—both African American—and charged with appointing race relations advisers in each of the nine civilian defense regions. Although Eleanor Roosevelt supported Fauset's work, many OCD officials did not, and like so many of the First Lady's initiatives, her appointment was controversial. Critics alleged that Fauset's appointment was costly and misguided in light of the agency's central mission, which was not to correct American social ills but to defend the nation against enemy attack. Fauset succeeded in appointing race relations advisers in only five of the nine civilian defense regions. The other four regions, which included the Deep South, lacked race relations advisers throughout the war.[56]

The principle of nondiscrimination was fundamentally at odds with much of the rhetoric and practice of civilian defense. Not only did the OCD fashion itself the civilian arm of the still-segregated military establishment; its practical commitment to localism and to the national kinship metaphor of the (all-white) male-headed home precluded an authentic commitment to racial justice. OCD officials empowered white men to perform the most highly valorized Civilian Protection tasks; when it came to defense against air raids and other wartime emergencies in African American communities, agency officials told residents that they must take care of their own.

Although doing little to challenge racial discrimination, the OCD worked, quite explicitly, to revise the way that civilians conceived of American nationhood. In literature and speeches, OCD leaders sought to dispel the popular notion that the United States was an insular and well-fortified landmass remote from enemy attack. They drew frequent comparisons between the United States and Great Britain, and they modeled the OCD's protective branch on the British Home Defense organization. Officials also implied that the United States, like Britain, was situated in the thick of global events and similarly vulnerable to territorial attack. They reiterated time and again the danger posed to the U.S. home front by air raids, and they used the fearsome specter of modern military technology to encourage civilian vigilance. In January 1942, Director La Guardia sought to mobilize public anxiety when he warned civilian audiences that with modern military techniques, "the war will come right to our cities and residential districts." Similarly, President Roosevelt informed the media that the enemy "can come and shell New York tomorrow night, under certain conditions. They can probably drop bombs on Detroit tomorrow night, under certain conditions."[57] Even late in 1943, when the threat of enemy attack seemed remote, the OCD warned complacent civilians that the United States could still become like the vanquished nations of Europe. A pamphlet on sabotage and espionage admonished readers that "the 19 countries invaded by Germany in this war . . . [were] each . . . lulled into a false sense of security, only to discover a sudden outburst of well organized sabotage that disrupted domestic, industrial, governmental, and military life."[58]

Pamphlets such as that just quoted were among the more important products of the OCD. One historian has described the agency as "an information and publicity mill, producing thousands of pamphlets, newsreels, regulations, and instructions each month."[59] Indeed, what the agency lacked in the capacity to provide material support to state and local defense councils it made up for in publicity. The agency also provided countless guidelines and directives to state and local branches. As a frustrated Community Chest executive from Reading County, Pennsylvania, observed, "Few programs . . . emanated from Washington unaccompanied by a specific title, an organization chart, a suggested list of appointments, and a chain of command leading back to the originator." He objected to the OCD's disregard for local initiative, expressing the hope that the "deluge" of "programs, complicated charts, titles, and superior officers" would stop.[60]

Although the OCD had fairly grand nationalizing claims, its authority to enforce its directives was minimal. *Time* remarked that "about all OCD could do was provide blueprints and fatherly advice."[61] The OCD itself admitted that the agency "[did] not exercise direct control over State or local defense councils" but could only "impose requirements in connection with the loan of Federally owned equipment and the use of officially prescribed insignia."[62] Substantial intervention by the federal office would have compromised the very emphasis on localism and traditional family-based authority that was central to OCD rhetoric and practice.

Even had the OCD been committed to exercising greater central authority, its effectiveness was compromised by the poor credibility of its Washington leadership. Both La Guardia and Eleanor Roosevelt served for less than a year, resigning early in 1942, and both came in for considerable media and congressional criticism. *Time* called Eleanor Roosevelt "OCDiva" to La Guardia's "OCDemon."[63] Conservatives criticized La Guardia primarily for his poor judgment in assuming two full-time jobs, whereas they criticized Roosevelt for her New Deal–style administrative incompetence, for promoting the interests of women and blacks, and for the inappropriateness of her appointment to an official role in her husband's government.[64] Only when James M. Landis, Harvard Law School dean and regional director of New England Home Defense, took over the directorship of the agency in February 1942, did the agency recover its credibility with the public. Yet even under Landis's more palatable leadership, the OCD's powers of enforcement remained small.

For all its limitations, the OCD did a masterful job of organizing civilian defense activities throughout the United States, particularly in 1942 when the danger of enemy attack seemed greatest. And the thrust of OCD organizational efforts was to bridge the gap between soldiers and civilians. Landis explained that soldiers and sailors "have not ceased to be members of families and communities . . . despite their uniforms [and] their weapons." Therefore, he stated, "Their morale is not likely to rise higher than its civilian sources. It is a duty of Civilian Defense to raise this morale high and keep it high, so that the men in the forward ranks may receive from their homes a continuous refreshment of zeal and determination; so that they will feel themselves watched, applauded, and reinforced by a solid nation."[65] A journalist favorable to the OCD similarly remarked that "the line between fighter and civilian has been erased and the war job of each is only a matter of circumstance and degree."[66]

Specific activities of the OCD also worked to bridge the gap between soldier and civilian. The OCD collaborated with the Selective Service System and the Pre-Induction Training Branch of the War Department, organizing pre-induction meetings in which OCD participants helped to prepare recent conscripts for the realities of war. In the process, civilian defenders themselves received measured doses of OCD propaganda about the relationship between military and civilian life. One OCD pamphlet stressed the commonalities between the soldier and the civilian individual, assuring readers that "Army life" does not "mean the end of the individual," but that in the military, "Individual initiative is as important as in civilian life."[67]

The OCD's effort to blur the boundaries between civilians and soldiers sometimes had unintended consequences, as when a group of air-raid wardens in New York City asked that their unit be placed under War Department authority because they objected to local OCD leadership.[68] Following Pearl Harbor, many Americans shared Walter Lippmann's sentiment that the

OCD "should all be put under the jurisdiction of the War Department" because "the facts of the situation and the morale of the people require lucid and authoritative commands."[69] Even the House of Representatives called for greater blurring of the boundaries between civilian and military forces, voting in January 1942 to entrust the OCD's $100 million budget to the War Department rather than allowing the agency's civilian leadership to take charge of it. After Landis's appointment the next month as executive director, the House of Representatives relented and voted to restore budgetary authority to the OCD.[70]

Those who favored greater militarization of the OCD also tended to favor the agency's protective activities over those of its nonprotective branch. For Civilian Protection came closest to approximating military service; its activities bore a clear and distinct relationship to the nation's military effort; and its participants were predominantly mature white male citizens. Civilian Protection also accorded considerable affective power to white civilian men; its rhetoric and practices struck a properly grim and determined tone. The agency's nonprotective branch, on the other hand, had much greater female and African American participation; a number of its national administrators were women and blacks; and it bore the mark, now deemed effeminate, of New Deal social planning. Particularly under Eleanor Roosevelt's leadership, OCD nonprotective work was more cautious and reflective; it lacked the assertive anger that made participation in the protective branch such an effective morale-building activity. Indeed, the affective dissonance between the protective and nonprotective branches of OCD tells us much about the gender, racial, and sexual dimensions of U.S. civic culture in the wartime years.

✥ Civilian Protection

From its very beginning, urgency and drama animated the protective branch of the Office of Civilian Defense. At a time when national attention focused on overseas military developments, the OCD's protective branch gave civilians the opportunity to defend their households and communities from enemy attack by joining auxiliary police and firefighting units and by serving as air-raid wardens. Beginning in the summer of 1941 and increasing dramatically after the bombing of Pearl Harbor, the OCD's protective branch trained millions of Americans to assist the nation's military in case of enemy attack. In particular, it trained hundreds of thousands of Americans to act as air-raid wardens. For a time, especially in the weeks and months immediately following Pearl Harbor, air-raid wardens went door-to-door, educating neighbors on what to do in an aerial attack. Because of its dramatic, highly visible nature, OCD protective work drew far too many applicants for the positions available, and participation in the air-raid warden's unit and other protective fields was a sought-after distinction. Selection criteria for membership in the protective branch were locally determined, but at a time of vast social dislocation, they tended to reinforce existing hierarchies of generation, race, and gender.

Pageantry was central to the OCD's protective branch. Its members enacted a script of national loyalty—one that centered on the ideals of the white-male-headed home and well-ordered community—and that found expression in frequent parades and defensive drills. Focal to the OCD's script of national loyalty were its gender arrangements. Just as total war ideology privileged paternal grimness and determination as the appropriate responses to totalitarian aggression, the OCD's protective branch imagined the nation as a community of grim and determined family breadwinners, awakened to an enlarged sense of civic responsibility by the war. Whereas totalitarian nations forced their civilian populations to participate in national defense without regard for family structure, the United States' defensive effort was predicated on the family as the basic unit of national civic life.[71] The OCD assigned defense roles on the basis of family position, reserving its most important jobs for mature household heads. In this way, the OCD shored up the dignity and importance of the family breadwinner at a time when many factors threatened to undermine that authority.

OCD officials did their utmost to promote the civic importance of civilian protection. Membership in the Civilian Protection Branch organized according to a complex system of rank and insignia, and representatives of the Department of War, Department of the Navy, and the Department of Justice held positions on the Civilian Protection Board. Civilian Protection volunteers also trained, drilled, and worked closely with established law enforcement and fire prevention authorities in their local communities. Respected community leaders assumed positions as air-raid wardens, auxiliary police, and auxiliary firefighters and took part in emergency rescue and decontamination squads.

More than any other facet of civilian defense, the Civilian Protection Branch approximated military experience. According to one OCD official, Civilian Protection was the "combat phase" of civilian defense, and President Roosevelt described its operations as "quasi-military."[72] Landis declared that volunteers "unaccustomed to the rigors of command must learn new lessons in how to act as units and not as individuals."[73] Before one crowd of OCD volunteers, he stated that the key to successful civilian defense was

"Drill, drill, and more drill."[74] Both La Guardia and Landis believed that the purpose of Civilian Protection was to unify national support along military lines. The American public would be a grim and purposeful "army, not a mob," thanks to its experience of self-discipline and preparedness in the OCD.

Colonel R. Ernest Dupay and Lieutenant Hodding Carter also stressed the important place of Civilian Protection within the nation's overall military effort. "Though its army remains physically intact," they stated, "a nation's means and will to win can be destroyed by the reduction of its supply centers, its productive capacity, and the morale of its citizens." Of the civilian defender, they remarked, "In his sector, the civilian defender must stand squarely on his own feet. . . . Diversion of the federal forces to civilian centers for general defense only fritters away our armed strength and thereby assists the enemy."[75]

If the military's role was to defend the nation from external attack, OCD officials contended, the civilian defender's role was to take over the job of protection once the home front had been penetrated. By providing a secondary system of defense, civilian protectors contributed to the war effort. Some OCD officials even suggested that the work of the civilian defender was *more* important than that of its fighting troops because it entailed preservation of a cherished civic ideal: the American home. "This is Civilian Defense, the defense of the home, of ways of living, of the little luxuries that we prized and the great freedoms that are our heritage," Landis declared.[76] OCD rhetoric merged with the broader rhetoric of total war in promoting the American home as a sustaining civic ideal. OCD publications dramatized the perils that confronted the family in a world at war, and they proposed a revitalization of traditional family roles as a means of combating those perils.

The OCD's practice of reserving valorized protective roles for mature household heads, while assigning lesser civic roles to other family members, is evident in *What to Do in an Air Raid*, an OCD pamphlet published in 1942. On the cover of the pamphlet is a strong and determined but clearly middle-aged man. Below the image is the inscription, "Read and Keep This Pamphlet. It May Save Your Life." The pamphlet provides simple illustrations of the safety measures that families might take in an air raid. Large illustrations accompany brief passages of text, each image foregrounding a protective white male figure. One image shows a mother, daughter and son crouched under a table in the background; in contrast, the father stands upright, in the foreground, wielding a flashlight as though it were a weapon. On another page of the pamphlet, readers are advised that a variety of volunteers are needed, including air-raid wardens, auxiliary firemen, rescue squads, road repair units, and demolition and clearance squads. Reflecting the gendered nature of OCD activities, following each volunteer category is a parenthetical statement indicating whether the task requires men or women. Although several of the categories call for men only—and some call specifically for "strong, husky men"—only two categories call specifically for women: nurses' aides programs, and emergency food and housing units, which needed "women who can cook or serve."[77]

The value of Civilian Protection in affirming mature masculine citizenship is also evident in the centrality of the air-raid warden as a figure for civilian defense. "The Warden is the embodiment of all Civilian Defense," one OCD pamphlet stated.[78] Another claimed, "The Air Raid Wardens Unit is one of the most vital parts of the entire civilian defense organization."[79] Because air-raid wardens were so vital to national defense, the pamphlet stated, "The utmost care must be taken in the selection, training, and maintenance of morale of the Wardens themselves."[80] Candidates must be "reliable and responsible, [and] have the needed qualities to lead, direct, and help the people entrusted to [their] care."[81] Male household heads were thus ideal candidates for warden work. Civic leadership experience was also helpful. As one pamphlet informed candidates, "Leadership, as demonstrated by taking an active part in local civic affairs, is an especially desirable quality."[82] At a time when many Americans lamented the increasing self-importance of war workers whose incomes had shot up as a result of the war, OCD role assignments could be used to shore up the traditional authority of the professional class. One OCD publication noted, "Good Warden candidates will be found among the professional people of each community . . . particularly those . . . who, because of age or physical characteristics, are not subject to military call."[83] The OCD thus reinforced a hierarchical vision of civic community that subordinated other groups to the category of mature white middle-class manhood.

"How-To" manuals for other protective services also emphasized the manly accents of Civilian Protection work. Giving participants a sense of active, important responsibility in the war effort, *A Handbook for Auxiliary Police* stated, "The performance of a well-organized, reliable, and capable force of Auxiliary Police . . . is one of the best answers to the dictator nations." It added, "It is a working example of free men disciplining themselves." Accordingly, membership in the Auxiliary Police was "an honor, a distinction—and a responsibility."[84]

Drawing on Republican-era notions of family and civic life, OCD officials likened the ideal civilian defender to the figure of the minuteman, whose independence and civic virtue derived in part from his protective relation to household dependents. The minuteman analogy appeared repeatedly in the rhetoric of civilian defense. OCD protective personnel were "as American as Lexington's minutemen." They posed a compelling "answer to the dictator nations" because their participation in national civic life was not coerced from above, as it was in totalitarian states, but self-generated. Their common enterprise was not a military one but rather one shaped by both martial and democratic ideals.

The OCD also authorized its protective forces to intervene in a range of home-front problems. Indeed, the major wartime accomplishments of the Civilian Protection Branch lay in mundane rescue and firefighting missions unrelated to the war. Such activities, while failing to confirm administrators' predictions about the imminence of enemy attack, nevertheless reinforced the status of mature white civilian men as leaders and protectors in their communities.

Even more significantly, perhaps, the Civilian Protection Branch licensed home-front defenders to investigate any "suspicious-looking characters" whom they suspected of sabotage or espionage in their communities. The day-to-day routine of the air-raid warden certainly meant monitoring blackouts and watching the skies for enemy aircraft, but it also meant assuming authority over five hundred fellow citizens and walking a nightly neighborhood beat in search of unusual activity.[85] And in accordance with the rhetoric of "total war," almost any activity that did not actually *contribute* to the war effort could be broadly construed as unpatriotic. Thus air-raid wardens' mandate to investigate threats to civilian security was very broad.

At a time when most American cities were racially segregated, African Americans, Mexican Americans, and other nonwhite groups were generally responsible for organizing the civilian defense of their own communities. At the same time, many were denied the training and resources to implement a full range of defensive measures. Also, they often lacked representation on local defense councils that made decisions about citywide defense planning, though they were answerable to those councils in cases of emergency. In spite of such discrimination, many people of color answered the call to participate in civilian defense. Encouraged by OCD race relations adviser Fauset, they regarded civilian defense participation as an opportunity to demonstrate their patriotism and enlarge their claim to U.S. civic membership.

Anger and the urge to violence were not the only emotional states aroused by the OCD; at a time when wartime social dislocations prompted considerable anxiety, OCD publicists and other agency supporters evoked feelings of comfort and reassurance in their portrayal of American small-town life.

Images of picket fences and picturesque Main Streets countered fears of gender, sexual, and generational instability by offering the alternative image of a static and familiar social world. As the popularity of Norman Rockwell's wartime illustrations suggests, Americans were particularly attracted to images of traditional New England life. Stories of New England civilian defense recalled the ties between America's martial heritage and its long-standing democratic traditions. Writing for the *New Republic*, Barbara Parmelee described the workings of civilian defense in small New England towns. In "ARP School, Massachusetts," she described a town meeting for civilian defense attended by a purposeful, stereotypically New England crowd: "Half a dozen dignified businessmen . . . several solid attorneys . . . [and] the entire local male staff of the high school" participated, along with "three lean, horse-faced men from one uncontaminated Puritan family" and "a dark and ruddy foreigner with workman's hands." Invoking New England's popular martial tradition, Parmelee declared, "New England was ready in '76, and '61, and '17. It is ready again."[86]

In an article on airplane spotters, Parmelee again invoked idealized images of New England life. Suggesting the valor and fortitude of the civilian defender, she wrote, "There in the bitter, creeping New England cold . . . civilian watchers, two by two, kept a constant twenty-four-hour vigil with the sky." Although the airplane spotters' unit included some women, Parmelee accentuated men's protective role. "The deep night hours at the post belong, by common consent, to men volunteers," she noted. Parmelee envisioned the OCD as an all-male melting pot embodying national ideals: "Louie from the filling station, Mac from the garage, Martin from the parsonage, Tony from the store, kicked and stamped numb feet, hugged frost-stung fingers under their armpits, and reported to the army by telephone."[87]

The military accents associated with men's nighttime work at the post contrasts with its domestic accents during women's daytime watches. In Parmelee's account, women were not "Sentinels in the Army of the United States," even when performing the same defensive duties as men. Instead, they were stereotypical New England housewives who kept the post tidy during daylight hours when nobody expected an enemy attack to occur.

Stories and images of New England life were captivating during the war because they helped to concretize an ethnically diverse, racially homogeneous American way of life grounded in the traditional home and small-town ideals. Yet some accounts focused on civilian protective work in cities such as New York and Los Angeles. Strikingly, accounts of OCD activities in urban areas emphasized the value of civilian defense in helping small groups of city dwellers to recreate civic ideals more typically associated with small-town life. Civilian defense forged atomized blocks of apartment dwellers into neighborhoods, complete with shared civic ideals and methods of policing social behavior characteristic of the New England small town.

At the center of that process of civic revitalization stood the air-raid warden. The *New York Times Magazine* ran a series of articles on air-raid wardening, focusing on a typical warden, "Mr. Smith." Air-raid wardens, journalist Jack Bechdolt stated, wore "no uniforms," but were "just people like your neighbor, Mr. Smith."[88] Although neither "romantic" nor "soldierly"—too preoccupied was he with providing for his family—Mr. Smith was reassuringly familiar, and he held an important place in the life of his community. As air-raid warden, Mr. Smith came to "know the neighborhood as you know the back of your hand . . . [learning] facts about his neighbors that even the Police Department was too polite to ask for." He also gained an appropriate sense of his own civic authority. His affect was transformed. Previously a "shy man" who "evaded making public speeches," Mr. Smith was propelled by civic obligation to speak persuasively to his neighbors, and his affect was transformed. Smith's wisdom and authority contrasted with the less impressive performance of younger members of the air-raid warden group. In his third article on Warden Smith, Bechdolt characterized him as a veteran who had seen many other wardens come and go. "There are many faces seen no more since Warden Smith first attended a post meeting . . . faces of pretty girls in fancy skiing suits; of various young men of various professions." The departure of gender and generational "others" left only "veterans" like Mr. Smith. Possessing maturity and family leadership experience, such "veterans" were equipped to instruct their neighbors in how to reform their wartime ways and protect their families from aerial bombardment.

Writing about wartime Chicago, Perry Duis notes that imperatives to contribute to the civilian war effort had a profound influence on family life. He argues that the principle of family privacy was violated as families underwent civic scrutiny to determine the extent of their contributions and sacrifices on behalf of the war effort. World War II Chicagoans felt considerable public pressure to participate fully in OCD activities ranging from scrap collection, to home canning, to nighttime air-raid drills. The family's day-to-day existence also changed as Americans took on war jobs that left them with diminished leisure and family time. If it had ever been a haven from the larger civic sphere, the home no longer served that function during World War II. From the imperative to create a "refuge room" in its interior, to pressure to post emblems of family vigilance and sacrifice in the front windows, the home was thoroughly penetrated by the public imperatives of war.[89]

CIVILIAN PROTECTORS AND MEDDLESOME WOMEN 159

The air-raid warden and the broader system of Civilian Protection that he symbolized were central to this process. As in the broader rhetoric of total war, OCD protective rhetoric promoted a backward-looking ideal of family and community life, even as it contributed to the interpenetration of the civic and familial spheres. Air-raid wardens like Bechdolt's Warden Smith stood for traditional American values, particularly the values of home and paternal civic leadership. Yet placed within the broader discourse of total war, and particularly viewed in light of the internationalist thrust of U.S. wartime policy, the paternalistic model of civic community that flourished in the protective branch also facilitated major political changes. In supporting the OCD's protective branch, Americans consented to principles of male family headship and civic obligation that also suffused foreign policy statements such as Roosevelt's Good Neighbor Policy and Henry Luce's "American Century."

The protective branch of the OCD struck a chord with the American public. Particularly in the weeks and months following Pearl Harbor, the agency's challenge was not how to enlist Americans in its programs but how to keep program membership within reasonable limits. OCD officials were compelled in mid-1942 to inform the public that not everybody could be an air-raid warden. The *OCD Newsletter* informed readers that there were many valuable ways to contribute to national defense by signing up with the OCD's Volunteer Office. Such suggestions were generally unpopular, because the same Americans who lauded civilian protection work tended to be highly critical of the OCD's "nonprotective" branch.

❧ Nonprotective Branch

In a 1942 ad for General Electric, Mary, a young wife, sits by the shore with her son in front of her "small, storm-tight house." Her soldier-husband has charged her with the task of "keeping their dreams alive" while he fights for their shared family and civic ideals overseas. Published before the 1943–44 campaign to enlist women in war industry, this ad celebrates women's domestic confinement and the gulf that separates men's from women's wartime roles. Mary's status as a small-town New England wife further illustrates the wartime preoccupation with reaching into the gendered and racialized past for models of collective civic identity appropriate to the imperatives of waging total war.[90]

New England women also appeared in supportive roles in accounts of civilian defense. In Barbara Parmelee's articles for the *New Republic*, "rose-petal blondes" and "housewives comfortable with dinner" sat side by side with farmers, lawyers, and gas station attendants in a Massachusetts Air Raid Protection School. Young "housewives in undistinguished clothes," lady schoolteachers, and mothers dragging little boys in tow held daytime shifts in Parmelee's description of a rural New England airplane spotters' unit. Practical, satisfied to play a supportive role, and enterprising enough to bring along a bottle of Windex to clean "the rough room smelling of men," such women gladly ceded the post to male OCD volunteers during the dramatic nighttime hours.

In general, the OCD celebrated civilian defense activities that were consistent with women's traditional domestic roles. OCD publicity emphasized women's important family-based role in salvaging household wastes, preparing homes for blackouts, cultivating Victory Gardens, and engaging in other forms of home production. By endorsing the broader cultural enthusiasm for America's "home-way of life," the agency afforded an important defensive role to women, albeit one circumscribed by domesticity. Not only within their individual homes, but as participants in the OCD's "Block Plan" and other neighborhood defense activities, women received recognition and opportunities for civic participation during the war.

Although good, domestic women, sensibly operating their households for the greatest national benefit, were sometimes celebrated in the rhetoric of civilian defense, women who exceeded their traditional domestic roles were frequently maligned. Just as the broader discourse of total war criticized women who hoarded, gossiped, and behaved opportunistically, stories of civilian defense criticized women who meddled in OCD protective activities or approached OCD work as an opportunity for personal gain. Parmelee described "fluttery club women dressed for tea and scones at the Ritz" who preferred "the cosy chattiness of the Red Cross sewing room" to more meaningful defensive duties. The *OCD Newsletter* criticized housewives who spread rumors and hoarded scarce commodities.[91] Significantly, in representations of OCD nonprotective work, such negative female stereotypes came to be associated with the inefficiency and effeteness of New Deal liberalism. At a time when "Dr. New Deal" had made way for the decisively masculine "Dr. Win-the-War," negative representations of the nonprotective branch were part of a gendered backlash against New Deal social policy.

Notwithstanding the unpopularity of their work, some officials did their best to promote the activities of the nonprotective branch. In a radio program, Federal Security administrator Paul V. McNutt made the agency sound like a glorified extension of the New Deal, stating that "Many of the activities we shall carry on in the name of defense are the same sorts of things we have always done to protect our communities against disease, malnutrition, and other social ills." Seeking to inject the OCD's nonprotective activities with urgency and importance appropriate to wartime, he added, "We must never forget that, important as such activities may have been in ordinary days, they are imperative now. Now we have no time to lose, and now we cannot fail!"[92]

McNutt made his statement while introducing a radio dialogue between OCD director La Guardia and Volunteer Participation head Eleanor Roosevelt in September 1941. In a rare moment of consensus, La Guardia and the First Lady discussed the kinds of defense jobs that were appropriate to different kinds of people. They agreed that "a young businessman, twenty-eight years old" should enroll as "an air-raid warden or firefighter," while "a young woman who supports her family" should do volunteer work "typing, [or] filing," and jobless young girls should train to be nurses' aides. A housewife with several children, La Guardia suggested, might volunteer at "a day nursery," and older women might "knit or sew garments to be used for the Red Cross."[93]

A University of California survey examining civilian defense activities in the nation's urban areas, conducted early in 1942, showed a similar pattern of sex segregation in the OCD. The survey found that opportunities for women in Civilian Protection were extremely limited, and the only protective field dominated by women was that of nurses' aides. Based on the survey results, Miller remarks, "While the federal government encouraged women to assume a non-traditional role in the defense plants, volunteer civilian defense work seemed to reinforce traditional sex roles."[94]

Indeed, while the rhetoric of total war ostensibly held a place for *all* civilians—men, women, and children alike—many women confronted obstacles in obtaining defense roles. One woman who visited her local OCD office to enlist as an air-raid warden was informed by the director that air-raid wardening was physically strenuous and therefore unsuitable for women. He suggested that she clean the office instead. Another woman, frustrated that she and her female acquaintances had completed numerous OCD training courses without being placed on specific tasks, wrote to national headquarters to suggest that an OCD placement service be established. No such service existed at any time during the war, and decisions about volunteer placement were left to local offices. As if to discourage female participation in OCD's protective branch, *Time* poked fun at women who participated in civilian defense. In January 1942, the magazine reported, "By last week hundreds of thousands of [women] were . . . driving automobiles, thundering in airplanes, jumping into fire nets." Particularly amusing to the magazine's editors were a group of "militant women" in Boston, who "practiced firefighting, had firemen worried over their possibility of turning up at a fire, to get tangled up in hoses." Women who wanted to avoid ridicule, *Time*'s editors suggested, might pursue three gender-specific courses: "First Aid, Home Nursing, Nutrition."[95]

Such negative portrayals of women's civilian defense roles must be placed within a broader discursive context. As Maureen Honey notes, images of parasitic and opportunistic women pervaded popular adventure and romance stories during the war years.[96] In addition, public warnings not to spread rumors, waste scarce resources, or engage in other inimical practices more often pictured female culprits than male ones. Such images pervaded wartime popular culture in part because of the unequal distribution of political labor between older and younger men on the one hand, and between men and women on the other. At a time when soldier's political roles were in some ways more highly valued than civilians', the civilian breadwinner gained political stature through his opposition to civilian women. In OCD rhetoric and practice, that opposition often tended toward hostility. The OCD, and particularly its protective branch, worked to reinforce a masculinist narrative of collective civic identity through the pageantry of Civilian Protection. In their capacity as civilian defenders, white male OCD members enacted a script of American loyalty that centered on the vital, well-ordered community and the white-male-headed home. Women's nonprotective activities, particularly those that advanced New Deal corrective themes focusing on urban social ills, were at odds with that civic story.

In September 1941, Eleanor Roosevelt publicly criticized the defense program for not giving women volunteers sufficient opportunity to participate in civilian defense.[97] As the OCD's assistant director and head of its Volunteer Participation Committee, Roosevelt worked to create opportunities for women in the defense program. Evidence of her success can be found in the *OCD Newsletter* for November 1941. In a list of "Regional Appointments" for the OCD, female appointees predominated in the Volunteer Office, although women rarely obtained leadership in other categories. Also included in the issue was a report about "a conference held last week in Washington" at which "representatives of nearly 70 women's national organizations" discussed "women's activities in the Civilian Defense program." Finally, the issue included an article about the V-home campaign, which focused specifically on the housewife's role as salvage, conservation, and consumer agent for her household. "Every American home has been affected by the war," the article claimed, thus making the housewife, as home manager, a crucial contributor to the war effort.[98]

In addition to creating opportunities for women to participate in civilian defense, Eleanor Roosevelt used her post at OCD to ensure the continuation of New Deal health and welfare objectives. She explained, "I . . . could not help feeling that it was the New Deal social objectives that would make it possible for us to fight the war, and I believed it was vastly important to give people the feeling that in fighting the war we were still really fighting for these same objectives."[99] Under her direction, the nonprotective branch became a haven not only for women, but for social workers and other welfare professionals intent on pursuing New Deal social objectives.

Joanna C. Colcord, director of the Russell Sage Foundation's Charity Organization Department, discussed the need for wartime welfare services, noting that "many towns and cities have suffered from the closing of industries. . . . Selective service has taken sons and husbands from the homes of all localities, frequently leaving social problems to be met by the local agencies."[100] One of the functions of Volunteer Participation, Colcord observed, was "to place volunteers in . . . social work enterprises" where they could assist in managing wartime social problems. Volunteers helped to combat the lack of child care available to working mothers, the inadequacy of existing health and welfare services in communities adjacent to booming war industries, and the spread of prostitution and juvenile delinquency. In 1943, OCD administrators reported that a typical nonprotective committee in a war impact center had subcommittees on topics ranging from health and medical services, to social protection, to salvage and war savings. Reflecting the gender composition of the nonprotective branch, other nonprotective fields included issues of specific interest to women, such as consumer problems, nutrition, and family and children's services.[101]

The nonprotective branch's commitment to welfare advocacy and leadership roles for women and African Americans ran counter to the OCD's broader tendency to gloss over wartime social problems and celebrate the benefits of the air-raid defense system for national morale. The OCD's protective and nonprotective branches were premised on competing models of American civic life. The nonprotective branch envisioned a nation that was modern, complex, and beset by a range of social problems that could be solved, New Deal–style, through social scientific expertise. The protective branch envisioned the nation along simpler, more cohesive lines, revitalized by shared anger at Axis aggressors and sundry home front enemies, and premised on the racialized and gendered civic ideals of the small town and the male-headed home.

The OCD's nonprotective branch differed from its protective branch not only in affect but in form. According to one OCD publication, the protective branch was "an authoritative line-operated program" with a highly developed command structure, whereas the nonprotective branch had "an entirely different type of function and operation" characterized by maximum participation and horizontal community organization.[102] Also, whereas Civilian Protection relied on some federal funding to support its activities, an OCD publication pointed out that "sources of funding" for nonprotective services "will be largely local."[103]

In January 1942, Congress stipulated that the OCD's $100 million budget could only be used to purchase "firefighting equipment, protective clothing, helmets, medical supplies, gas masks, and training facilities" and not to support activities related to the nonprotective branch. This congressional decision came at a time of growing hostility toward the nonprotective services, and particularly toward Eleanor Roosevelt, who was seen to typify "the earnestness and confusion with which U.S. women have stampeded into defense work."[104] An African American newspaper editorialized that demands for Roosevelt's ouster also stemmed from her efforts to enlist African Americans in civilian defense.[105] In a typical example of Eleanor-bashing, columnist Raymond Clapper stated early in 1942 that "half the trouble around [OCD] could be got rid of if the President would haul [Mrs. Roosevelt] out of the place."[106] So heated were debates over the nonprotective branch that congressional hearings were convened to address allegations of the subagency's negative impact on national morale.

Hostility toward Eleanor Roosevelt and the nonprotective branch grew intense in the aftermath of Pearl Harbor. As one welfare professional observed, "After Pearl Harbor the focus of defense councils veered sharply in the direction of civilian protection, while welfare problems were relegated to the background."[107] She noted that "in most of the cities . . . air raid precautions had the center of the stage with the local defense councils proper; activities for men in service came next in appeal to the general populace; and few but those persons connected professionally or otherwise with the health, social, and educational agencies, felt a responsibility for community war services."[108]

Responding to such indifference, Eleanor Roosevelt remarked, "It is evident that many people do not yet grasp the fact that civilian defense cannot really be accomplished by adding auxiliary police and firemen to the existing forces, or even by appointing air raid wardens." She predicted, "If we should ever be unfortunate enough . . . to have a bombing, the protection side of civilian defense will very quickly be swamped by the need for community services of every kind."[109] Frustrated by her ineffectiveness in promoting the cause of OCD health and welfare services, Roosevelt resigned her post as assistant director under considerable pressure in February 1942. Although the nonprotective branch continued to exist, Roosevelt's departure as its lead administrator deprived civilian women and other disadvantaged groups of a powerful advocate.[110] After Roosevelt's departure, Fauset remained as race relations adviser to the OCD, though her staff was cut dramatically. In seeking fuller African American participation in OCD, she faced an uphill battle. Some local defense councils seized the opportunity afforded by the conservative shake-up in Washington to further restrict African American participation in the agency.[111]

Throughout the history of the OCD, conflict more often than cooperation characterized relations between the protective and nonprotective branches. Civilian Protection volunteers complained that the credibility of the OCD was undermined by the "piccolo-playing, basket-weaving, folk-dancing, community singing, and broccoli-growing activities" of the nonprotective branch, and the press assailed its Washington staff in gendered terms as "fussbudgets" and "flibbertigibbets."[112] Significantly, the brush most often used to tar OCD's nonprotective activities was that of New Deal–style make-work, inefficiency, and "boondoggling." Even though most of the OCD's minor budgetary expenditures went to finance equipment for civilian protection, nonprotective activities were criticized for providing little tangible benefit for the time and money expended. Reflecting a common viewpoint, one man observed that the OCD's protective branch performed important work, but its efforts were undermined by the fact that "there seems to be a lot of women and politicians running around and making a noise," miring the entire OCD operation in "confusion and red tape."[113]

When civilian defense activities came in for political or media criticism, the focus was generally the activities of the nonprotective branch. The press had a heyday with the mountains of scrap metal, collected under the auspices of the OCD salvage program, that were left to rust in public spaces because plans had not been made for their disposal. Yet rarely did politicians or the press challenge the necessity of repeated air-raid drills, even in remote hamlets and towns of the nation's interior.

Such disparaging descriptions of women's civilian defense activities must be viewed on a continuum with wartime propaganda that positioned women as unwitting traitors and saboteurs. In terms that recall the woman-blaming practices of the Great Depression, a 1944 propaganda poster featured a photograph of a white American woman. In the image, she stares remorselessly at the viewer, her face surrounded by the words, "WANTED! FOR

MURDER—*Her <u>careless talk</u> costs lives.*"[114] Images of treacherously careless and selfish white women proliferated during the war. Such propaganda used women to symbolize values antithetical to the war effort.

As such images suggest, within the role-oriented, difference-based discourse of total war, valorized traits like selflessness and sacrifice could be generalized to all American men (and not restricted to actual fighters), precisely through their opposition to nonvalorized feminine traits such as selfishness and moral weakness.[115] This opposition was particularly important in homefront rhetoric and practice because civilian men's status as protectors was compromised by their distance from the actual battlefronts of the war. Moreover, as in Depression-era woman-blaming narratives, wartime figurations of insubordinate and unpatriotic womanhood served to sustain civilian men's angry and authoritative affect, thus dovetailing with positive figurations of civilian manhood during the war.

By the fall of 1943, the OCD had begun a gradual demobilization of the protective branch. As the Allies' strategic situation improved in 1943, some suggested that the OCD might even be abolished. President Roosevelt argued against such a course of action on the grounds that dismantling the agency before the war's end would damage civilian morale.[116]

Yet even as more of the OCD's emphasis shifted to nonprotective activities, air-raid drills continued in many parts of the nation. As one contemporary observed, the activities of Civilian Protection had always been much "more spectacular than the rest."[117] As Mary Ryan argues, patriotic spectacles have long helped Americans to span harrowing transitions by creating temporary tableaux of order and harmony.[118] Certainly, the ritual and pageantry of OCD protective work enabled participants and spectators alike to grapple with the myriad dislocations of wartime and to span the harrowing transition from an isolationist to an interventionist nation-state. When OCD protective work could no longer be justified on practical grounds, the agency crumbled. Federal, state, and local governments ceased to support OCD activities when the agency's protective work was scaled back. A much-diminished OCD survived the president who conceived it and was terminated by President Truman's executive order of June 30, 1945.

Like other New Deal agencies before it, the OCD deftly drew on widely circulating gender, racial, and generational representations to render new forms of state power more palatable. But although earlier New Deal programs aligned those representations with an expansive welfare state, the OCD used them to enlist popular support for the United States' expansive role in the global "family of nations." Indeed, the vigilant white civilian air-raid warden, exercising traditional masculine authority to protect his family and neighborhood from aerial bombardment, had a potent parallel in the image of the United States as a just and determined world leader, paternalistically guiding other, less civilized members of the "family of nations" toward a safe and democratic future.

Also like other New Deal agencies, the OCD evoked popular sentiments of anxiety and anger, comfort and longing. In particular, OCD protective work evoked feelings of grimness and determination, watchfulness and anger, and it aligned those emotions with the figure of the mature white civilian defender. Within OCD rhetoric and practice, and in dialogue with the broader discourse of total war, such emotional states helped to constitute a gendered and racialized American public that readily embraced the shift from isolationism to interventionism. Anger promotes openness to risk taking, whereas fear promotes caution and retreat.[119] OCD narratives of civic preparedness encouraged an angry and vigilant response to the war by invoking Axis atrocities, but also by invoking negative figurations of wartime womanhood. Like their Depression counterparts, such negative figurations unified civilian men in shared hostility toward women and feminized racial "others."

Certainly, the OCD propelled U.S. civilians into the fray of world events. But for all of their drilling, OCD participants never got the opportunity to implement their defensive tactics against invading enemy forces. While the predicted bombings never happened, civilian defenders did utilize their skills in cases of natural disaster and other domestic crises. Some of the most dramatic events that called for OCD participation were race riots that took place in several U.S. cities in the summer of 1943. In the midst of severe rioting that began on June 20, 1943, in Detroit, Michigan, OCD volunteers donned air-raid helmets and joined police and federal troops in attempting to quell the battle. Black civilian protection forces, many of whom had been hastily transferred from the "nonprotective" branch, were sent into the hardest-hit black neighborhoods in an effort to restore peace. Before the riot ended, twenty-five black residents and nine white residents had been killed and several hundred more had been injured. Explanations for the riot ranged widely, from the National Association for the Advancement of Colored People's (NAACP's) emphasis on discriminatory housing, education, employment, and law enforcement policies, to House Un-American Activities Committee chairman Martin Dies's allegation that Japanese Americans "had infiltrated Detroit's Negro population to spread hatred of the white man and disrupt the war effort."[120]

When rioting broke out in Harlem on August 1, 1943, leading to six deaths and several hundred more civilian injuries, air-raid wardens and other Civilian

Protection personnel were again deployed to assist police and federal troops. Black and white OCD volunteers worked together in a rare instance of interracial cooperation. They were joined by five hundred hastily deputized African American women, whom municipal authorities equipped with clubs and armbands so that they could assist in the peacekeeping effort.[121]

The disconcerting fact of five hundred African American women, patrolling Harlem's riot-torn streets with clubs and OCD armbands, contrasts strikingly with the popular image of mature white civilian defenders that garnered so much attention during the war. The Harlem race riot also contrasts strikingly with the New York at War Parade that had taken place in an adjacent section of the city the previous summer. Like countless other rituals of wartime civic preparedness, the New York at War Parade had promoted the image of a unified civilian war effort defined in role-oriented, difference-based terms. Drawing on long-standing ideals of close-knit civic community and the male-headed home, that image prescribed distinct roles for soldiers and civilians, as well as for civilian men, women, and children. Civilian participation thus defined in gender and generational terms was further differentiated in terms of class, race, and nationality. Yet quite a different story of civic collaboration unfolded during the Harlem riot.

In the wake of the Harlem riot, Mayor La Guardia and other city officials downplayed the role of race discrimination, attributing the melee to the bad acts of young African-American "hoodlums."[122] Like the conflation of the traditional male-headed home with the emergent principle of U.S. leadership in the global "family of nations," the rhetoric of hoodlumism had domestic and international political significance. Not only did it devalue the civic claims of African American protesters, Mexican American zoot suiters, and Japanese American draft resisters during the war; it also justified a high-handed international posture by applying that same "hoodlum" epithet to foreign governments that challenged U.S. global authority.

The next chapter takes up the theme of hoodlumism as it relates to the rhetoric and practice of Japanese American internment. Denied opportunities to participate in popular civilian defense activities, Japanese Americans were compelled to prove their loyalty in other, intensely punitive ways. Although some internees proved "good pupils" by embracing the racially specific criteria for civic membership imposed by the War Department and War Relocation Authority, many others resisted, leaving themselves—like so many other groups in mid-twentieth-century U.S. civic culture—open to allegations of hoodlumism, juvenile delinquency and other behaviors "antithetical to familialism."

CHAPTER 6

The Citizen-Soldier and the Citizen-Internee
Fraternity, Race, and American Nationhood, 1942–46

When an enemy submarine allegedly shelled Goleta, California, in an effort to destroy oil installations there, Japanese Americans were accused of collaborating with the enemy. How else, their accusers reasoned, would the enemy have known that a changeover of the shore battery would leave the installations defenseless that very day? According to one government official, when a sweep of the Japanese community ensued, "Innocent appearing fishermen were found to be reserve officers in the Japanese armed forces." He added, "It is fair inference that for every person caught, many others have evaded apprehension." Moving from this particular incident to a more general discussion of wartime loyalties, the official continued,

> Indeed, in time of war it is only inference upon which the country may safely rely. A fifth column exists by virtue of successfully pretending loyalty and successfully concealing evidence of its activities from the constituted authorities. The existence of a fifth column in every democratic country that has found itself at war with a fascist country is proof that there is no necessary identity of citizenship and loyalty, but that in periods of ideological struggle loyalties to class or race cut across or ignore national boundaries.[1]

Revealed in this passage is much of what was at stake in the government's overwhelmingly popular decision to intern Japanese Americans during World

War II. At stake was the meaning of loyalty, and the capacity to distinguish "true" loyalty from loyalty that is "pretended." At stake as well was the possibility that loyalty to the nation might conflict with "loyalties to class or race"; and finally, at stake was the specter of fifth columnism, and the necessity of curtailing constitutional rights in order to police it, while holding up an image of American democracy at war with foreign fascism.

The threat of fifth columnism was a potent ideological tool by which ordinary civilians could be made to feel a greater stake in the military mobilization of World War II.[2] The notion that enemy agents might be anywhere, posing a threat to national security, gave civilians a heightened sense of their own significance to the war effort, thus helping to bridge the gulf between civilian and military experience in wartime. Statements like "Loose lips sink ships" were commonly reiterated during the war, and agencies like the Office of Civilian Defense stressed that consciousness of fifth-column activity was the responsibility of every civilian.

Eager to play a more authentic part in the war, many Americans drew on existing racial and gender distinctions in their efforts to define the terms of loyalty and disloyalty for the nation. Luis Alvarez argues that when white servicemen assaulted Mexican American and African American youth and stripped them of their zoot suit attire, they asserted a white masculine version of national loyalty while denigrating the patriotism and masculinity of their victims.[3] Moreover, with public attention drawn repeatedly to the dangers of sabotage and espionage, the Japanese American community became a compelling site of public interest and concern. More so than any other location within the nation, the threat of fifth columnism was perceived to be concentrated there.

During World War II, widely circulating terms like loyalty and disloyalty were seemingly straightforward, yet they lacked obvious or apparent meanings. For their meanings to be persuasive, they had to be generated, at least in part, by the public at large. The question of what the government should do with the West Coast Japanese became a context in which concepts of "loyalty" and "disloyalty" could be popularly negotiated. And indeed, popular interest in the so-called Japanese problem was extensive. Public opinion polls administered early in the war indicate that hostility toward the Japanese American community ran high, particularly in the western United States. And in hundreds of letters to the Justice Department early in 1942, white citizens expressed their support for drastic governmental action against Japanese Americans living on the West Coast. Such writers emphasized both the threat of fifth columnism and the racial kinship of Japanese Americans with the enemy Japanese. Some lent their support to the idea of placing Japanese Americans in "concentration camps" for the duration of the war, and a handful, caught up in the unique ethical climate of wartime, suggested secret extermination by a variety of means. Concerned that camps might become "breeding grounds" for Japanese Americans, some proponents of the concentration camp idea recommended sterilization of internees, while others suggested that camps be segregated by sex.[4]

Racism was a central feature in almost all of citizens' calls for drastic action and was invariably linked to claims about the meaning of political loyalty. The vehemence with which so many weighed in on the issue of what should be done with West Coast Japanese Americans reflects how deeply bound up white Americans' own conceptions of loyalty and national belonging were with how the "Japanese problem" might be resolved.

At a time when so much was at stake politically, Japanese Americans were an appealing social and symbolic resource. On the West Coast, they counted for only about 112,000 of the total population and a third of them were classified as "aliens ineligible to citizenship"; many were isolated from the mainstream and maintained a low profile politically; and they shared racial features with the enemy Japanese. These characteristics left them relatively defenseless against all kinds of popular and governmental inference. And as the concept of loyalty came increasingly to be separated from legally defined citizenship, even Japanese Americans who were U.S. citizens by birth became vulnerable to allegations of political disloyalty.

In the months leading up to internment, the American-born second generation (Nisei), and specifically *men* of that generation, captured the popular imagination. Immediately following Pearl Harbor, the Federal Bureau of Investigation (FBI) made a sweep of the Pacific Coast, removing all first-generation (Issei) males who were leaders in their communities or who otherwise were considered threats to national security. The leadership of the largest immigrant organization, the Japan Association, was categorically removed at this time, as were many other influential figures. Some critics of internment would later ask why the roundup could not have stopped there. Setting aside the obvious question of whether *those* arrests were justified, it is clear from the record of pro-internment sentiment that animosity toward the citizen Nisei was extremely strong, and would not have been alleviated by the removal of selected Issei leaders.[5]

The nature of anti-Nisei animosity is reflected in *Little Tokyo, U.S.A.* (Twentieth Century Fox, 1942), in which the American-born Ito Takimura (Harold Huber), archvillain and avid fifth columnist, oversees a Japanese American espionage ring in Los Angeles.[6] Takimura is effective as an espionage agent because he is partially assimilated to American culture and his status as a citizen gives him political freedoms that he can use to promote Japan's war aims. Fluent in Japanese and English, Takimura feels as much at home in Tokyo as he does in California. Takimura is also stereotypically perverse. Sexually indifferent to his vixenlike female counterpart, he kills her when she fails as a spy. According to the film and to other anti-Japanese imagery on the West Coast, Japanese American fifth columnists like the fictive young Takimura knew about Pearl Harbor well before December 7, 1941. And in the film, Takimura and other young Japanese Americans like him plot to supply information to Japan that would make Los Angeles the next Pearl Harbor.

As Hollywood would have it, the film also features a strong-willed white protagonist, Mike Steele (Preston Foster), who in spite of being saddled with a meddlesome, liberal-minded fiancée named Maris Hanover (Brenda Joyce), manages not only to crush the spy ring, but to break Takimura's nose and Maris Hanover's spirit as well. Takimura gets punched in the face, and Hanover gets swept off her feet. In the final scene, she recants her views about the inviolability of civil rights over the radio, arguing that in times of crisis all Americans must make sacrifices. The film implies that Hanover herself will sacrifice her position as a radio journalist to become Steele's wife. In this way, the narrative brings together racial and gender themes in a celebration of grim and determined, heterosexual white manhood.[7]

Although other films blended long-standing anti-Asian stereotypes with wartime racial themes, evidence of anti-Nisei animosity could be found in many other places. In the Tolan Committee hearings, held on the West Coast in February and March 1942, witness after witness echoed California attorney general Earl Warren's statement that "the consensus of opinion is that . . . there is more potential danger in this state from the group that is born here than from the group that is born in Japan."[8] The Nisei posed more of a threat, Warren and others argued, because they were younger and stronger and therefore more menacing than their enemy alien fathers, they were generationally indistinguishable from and therefore likely to feel an affinity with invading Japanese forces, and their partial assimilation to American customs made them likelier candidates for successful fifth-column activity.

Hearings participants seemed to assume, rather uneasily, that while Nisei youth were conversant with American conventions, their deeper loyalties were identical to those of their fathers, and were therefore fundamentally Japanese. Stated the district attorney of San Diego County, "It is a well-known Japanese family tradition that the father of the family is the dominant and guiding factor for the formulating of ideas in his children." Thus, he continued, the Nisei "is, to a great extent, imbued in the same ideas as his parents."[9]

For the situation to be otherwise—for the Nisei to be loyal to the United States as against the country of their fathers—would have posed an uncomfortable affront to commonly held assumptions about the terms of *white* American loyalty and racial group identity; it would have challenged a conception of paternal control and filial respect that hearings participants were eager to associate with *white* family conventions. Hugh Gallagher of the Federal Security Agency made explicit the comparison between Japanese and white American family patterns in explaining his suspicions of the citizen Nisei. He asked the committee, "If you were sent to Japan to work and you had children born there, would you expect them to be loyal to Japan? No; absolutely no. Neither can we expect a Jap to be loyal to the white race that he has eternally, for generations, been taught to despise. Nope, just because a Jap is born here does not make him white, loyal, trustworthy, or even a citizen."[10]

In this way, Gallagher defined citizenship in terms of race, but also in terms of the male-headed home. Concerns about paternal control and filial respect were very much at issue in an era of military mobilization that relied on its masculine youth both to "defend democracy abroad" and to enforce, through example, a system of stringent wartime political obligations at home. Within this context, the Nisei might have been temporarily reassuring in his alleged deference to paternal authority, but he was simultaneously depicted as a threat to national community. The Nisei was more threatening than his Issei father because he dramatized the possibility that "there is no necessary identity between citizenship and loyalty" but that "in periods of ideological struggle loyalties to race or class cut across or ignore national boundaries."[11]

At the time the Tolan hearings were taking place, Selective Service boards across the country were changing the military classification of the Nisei. Immediately following Pearl Harbor, Kibei soldiers (second-generation Japanese Americans who were educated in Japan) were categorically expelled from the military, and Nisei inductions came to a halt. Over a period of months, a policy was devised whereby Nisei Selective Service registrants were classified either as IV-F, ineligible for service for reasons of mental or physical condition, or more commonly as IV-C, ineligible for service for reasons of ancestry.[12]

Some Japanese Americans vocally objected to the abridgment of their military obligations. Mike Masaoka, secretary of the Japanese American Citizens League, assured the Tolan Committee that the "American-born Japanese . . . know that the Axis aggressors must be crushed and we are anxious to participate fully in that struggle."[13] Responding to proposals that would exclude Nisei and Kibei from military service and lead to the wholesale evacuation of Japanese Americans, *Current Life* editor James M. Omura asked the Tolan

Committee, "Are we to be condemned merely on the basis of our racial origin? Is citizenship such a light and transient thing that that which is our inalienable right in normal times can be torn from us in times of war?" Asserting the loyalty of Japanese American citizens, he added, "We in America are intensely proud of our individual rights and are willing, I am sure, to defend those rights with our very lives. I venture to say that the great majority of Nisei Americans, too, will do the same against any aggressor nation—though that nation be Japan."[14] Omura's testimony that Nisei would fight any aggressor nation that sought to deprive them of their civil rights is poignant, given his arrest two years later for supporting Nisei draft resisters at Wyoming's Heart Mountain camp.[15]

Even as Nisei witnesses proclaimed their willingness to take up arms against Japan, witnesses hostile to Japanese Americans alleged that second-generation Japanese American men possessed dual citizenship and were thus under military obligation to the emperor of Japan.[16] Many Nisei did not possess dual citizenship, were unaware of it, or had renounced their Japanese citizenship prior to the war, yet their status did not deter West Coast politicians and nativist groups from highlighting the indeterminate loyalties of young Nisei men.

Certainly, the anti-Nisei allegations of some Tolan Committee witnesses were motivated by a nativist desire to exclude second-generation Japanese Americans from citizenship. The Issei were already excluded from citizenship under U.S. law. To some nativists, the war afforded the opportunity to extend that exclusion to the American-born Nisei, and a series of legislative proposals was initiated to achieve that end. The Nisei posed more of a threat than the Issei, nativists openly declared, partly because their status as citizens undermined the racial homogeneity needed to maintain a strong American nation.[17]

Racism and nativism were at the heart of anti-Nisei sentiment during the war. But anti-Nisei rhetoric also had important gender and generational accents. Like the "wandering youth" of the Depression, Nisei youth raised the specter of improperly socialized masculine youth. Also like the wandering youth, Nisei males became a social and symbolic resource that government administrators used in their efforts to revise concepts of citizenship and national belonging during the war. Specifically, the rhetoric and policies that administrators applied to Nisei youth worked to contain anxieties about military socialization and about the unequal distribution of political obligation in wartime. Images of Japanese American youth also became a resource for defining the complex terms of membership in a new, more internationally focused model of national collectivity that was emerging during the war.

⌁ War Relocation Authority

A brief period of voluntary resettlement followed President Roosevelt's Executive Order 9066, issued February 19, 1942, which called for the removal of Japanese aliens and "non-aliens" from California, Oregon, and Washington.[18] But voluntary resettlement was unsuccessful; many Japanese Americans clung desperately to their coastal homes, and some who migrated faced open hostility at their inland destinations. In Salt Lake City, Utah, and Denver, Colorado, civic leaders objected to a relocation policy that "dumped" Japanese Americans onto their communities.[19] If Japanese Americans posed a threat to communities on the Coast, they argued, what was to prevent them from posing just as great a threat to the nation's inland communities? In localities whose citizens had taken the wartime rhetoric of "total war" to heart, sharing space with Japanese Americans was a daunting prospect. The political unpopularity of voluntary resettlement soon resulted in the policy's abandonment. It was replaced by a policy of forced relocation to government-run internment camps located in remote areas of the inland West.[20]

The U.S. Army's Western Defense Command, directed by Lieutenant General John L. DeWitt, oversaw Japanese Americans' removal from their homes. During the spring and early summer of 1942, Japanese Americans were gathered at coastal evacuation centers under less than humane conditions. In Portland, Oregon, the evacuation center was a converted fairground, and evacuees were housed in livestock buildings where whole families shared cramped stalls intended for cattle. The Army held Japanese Americans in such facilities until plans for their subsequent relocation could be finalized.[21]

While Japanese Americans waited in evacuation centers under military guard, policymakers in Washington worked to formulate a constitutionally acceptable plan for their internment. After much deliberation, they proposed the WRA, which would operate under civilian rather than military leadership. Despite widely expressed support for military internment, policymakers realized that the military could not reasonably detain over 100,000 U.S. citizens and legal residents without positive proof of their disloyalty. The WRA's status as a civilian agency was intended to fortify the dubious constitutionality of internment.

The WRA's first director was Milton S. Eisenhower, formerly a bureaucrat with the Department of Agriculture. As historian Richard Drinnon notes, Eisenhower soon developed misgivings about the ethics of internment and resigned his post. He was replaced by a former associate, Dillon S. Myer of the Soil Conservation Service. As WRA director for most of the agency's tenure, Myer oversaw the administration of ten relocation camps. He worked closely with representatives of the War Department and the Office of the Solicitor, and he met regularly with Western politicians who contested relocation policy throughout the war. Much of Myer's Washington staff was composed of former associates from the Department of Agriculture and related agencies.[22]

At the camp level, WRA administration had several components. At each of the ten camps, a staff of WRA administrators oversaw camp operations and was headed by a camp director. Many camp directors had prior administrative experience in the New Deal. Although WRA staff had jurisdiction *inside* the camps, their authority ended at the barbed-wire fencing that surrounded them. At the periphery, guard towers were stationed at regular intervals, and military police monitored border activity. Often, the men who worked as military guards were "limited service men" whose minor disabilities disqualified them for overseas service.[23]

Other components of WRA camp administration were the Community Welfare and Community Analysis sections. Staffed by social workers, the Community Welfare section addressed family and social problems that emerged in the camps. The Community Analysis section was made up of social scientists who saw the internment as an opportunity to analyze human behavior. Whereas many women worked in the Community Welfare section, Community Analysis was a male-dominated field. Community analysts worked independently of the WRA staff to further social scientific knowledge, but they also advised WRA staff on how to administer the camps.[24]

At the national level, the WRA also developed a formidable publicity machine. WRA publicists disseminated favorable reports about the agency to sympathetic journalists, and they wrote pamphlets and prepared newsreels designed to combat the negative publicity that the WRA received. That the WRA developed such an elaborate publicity policy reflects national administrators' awareness that the agency had a symbolic as well as a social function. National administrators responsible for devising WRA information policy, including Myer, were clearly aware that considerable national attention focused on the agency. Some WRA policies, like the decision to recruit an all-Nisei combat team, were devised specifically with their publicity value in mind.

In several ways, then, the WRA conformed to the contours of New Deal administration. Like earlier New Deal agencies, the WRA stood at the center of national attention, and Roosevelt administrators used publicity about the agency to make gendered and racialized claims about citizenship and national belonging that had relevance for groups beyond the Japanese American community. Many WRA administrators, both in Washington and in the camps, had prior experience in New Deal bureaucracies. Some facets of WRA administration drew explicitly on New Deal models. The services afforded by social workers in the Community Welfare section were reminiscent of early New Deal relief practices, and as soon as internment camps were established, WRA administrators set up a Work Corps to provide jobs to dislocated Japanese Americans.[25]

The WRA resembled the New Deal rhetorically as well. During his brief tenure, Eisenhower had espoused a vision of positive community building and long-term social planning within the WRA. The purpose of the agency, he asserted, was to provide social uplift for dislocated Japanese Americans. To his successor, Myer, the WRA would become "a story of human conservation," an agency intended not to *punish* but to *protect* its target population. Despite the abridgment of Japanese American civil rights entailed in the internment, administrators often celebrated the positive Americanizing features of the program.

Of all the New Deal agencies, the WRA most resembled the Civilian Conservation Corps. Like the CCC, WRA administration involved a complex and sometimes contentious collaboration between civilian and military officials. Also like the CCC, the WRA originated in proposals to house a nationally menacing group in military-run "concentration camps." Finally, both CCC and WRA administrators asserted their agencies' value in conserving the nation's human resources and in socializing young male citizens for constructive citizenship.

And yet the WRA did not match the CCC in popularity—far from it. Indeed, the WRA was more like the Federal Transient Program in the amount of negative publicity it generated. Nisei and Kibei youth, like inveterate hoboes in transient perversion narratives, were scapegoats whose objectionable gender, racial, and sexual characteristics, detailed in stories of camp unrest, helped a white American public to cohere. As the agency charged with managing the unpopular internee group, the WRA was also unpopular. Sensational narratives depicted WRA officials as feminized, "mollycoddling" bureaucrats who lacked the masculine grimness and determination to properly control unruly Japanese American youth.[26] The latter were characterized as social and sexual outsiders, but also as "loafers" and "chiselers" who reaped the benefits of federal largesse while other civilians endured wartime austerity measures.

➳ Nisei Manhood

Although the WRA had charge of *all* elements of the dislocated Japanese-American community—citizens and aliens, men, women, and children, representatives of every occupation and all political persuasions—administrators' primary preoccupation was the socialization of masculine youth. For like so many other Americans, WRA administrators believed that questions of Japanese American loyalty or disloyalty hinged on the outlook and behavior of young men. This preoccupation can be seen in administrators' initial plans for internal camp governance. Whereas Issei men were the conventional leaders of the Japanese American community before internment, the system of political representation that WRA administrators devised favored the younger Nisei. Issei men could be elected to councils within their residential blocks, but representation on the community-wide governing body that met directly with WRA authorities was restricted to the citizen group.

In formulating national WRA policy, administrators also relied substantially on input from the Japanese American Citizens League, a body restricted to Nisei citizens and dominated by young Nisei men. The JACL was a relatively small, patriotic organization whose members repudiated Japanese culture in favor of full assimilation to American customs and values.[27] College students and recent college graduates predominated among the JACL's leadership. Given their high level of educational attainment, their commitment to patriotic Americanism, and their avowed willingness to cooperate with the government, it is not surprising that JACL leaders became unofficial consultants to the WRA. No other Japanese American group was as vocally enthusiastic about sacrificing its members' civil rights and assisting the agency that interned them. Administrators praised JACL members as model Japanese American citizens, and many of the educational programs they implemented in the camps were designed to instill JACL-style Americanism in the entire second-generation group.[28]

In their assessment of social problems developing in the camps, WRA administrators routinely addressed youthful problems first and foremost. They dwelled repeatedly on the adverse consequences of the large generation gap that separated Issei and Nisei males. "Among the Japanese there are few persons who can bring together the polar views of raw, impetuous, but plastic youth and older age that is experienced, but rigid and inclined to act and think in terms of other days and other ways," a staff social scientist at the Poston camp stated.[29] During his brief tenure as national director, Eisenhower told a group of administrators that "the age breakdown of these people presents a special social problem. By no means do the Japanese families break down into the same nice age levels as the average American family."[30] Later, in attempting to explain the extent of internee disloyalty and the need for a segregation center to house disloyal internees, another administrator cited the "abnormal age characteristics" of the internee group, particularly the "wide and distinct difference in age between the citizen and alien groups."[31]

At a time when concerns about juvenile delinquency were increasing throughout the nation, camp administrators reported increases in juvenile delinquency and gang formation in the camps, as well as weakened family cohesion and parental authority due to the military-style residential and dining arrangements. A report by the Community Analysis section noted that "eating in mess halls, bathing in community bath houses, and utilizing common laundry and toilet facilities have already strained the normal ties of family life and threaten to weaken if not destroy the authority of parents over their children." In particular, the report stated, "The weakening of parental authority . . . has made it more difficult for law-abiding parents to restrain the activities of young men who may form gangs which can easily drift from antiproject administration to anti-American in attitude."[32] Allegations of Japanese American youthful misbehavior, which also appeared in popular press reports, contributed to and capitalized on the broader racialization of juvenile delinquency during the war. Indeed, unruly Nisei internees, like "zoot suiters" and other African American and Mexican American youth, came to symbolize a broader crisis of generational authority during the war.

Residential concentration of so many Japanese Americans together, administrators noted with concern, also led to greater exposure of Nisei youth to allegedly immoral elements. These included the so-called old bachelors or fruit tramps, first-generation migratory workers who had a reputation for "hard-living" and troublemaking, who dominated a separate set of barracks in each camp known as the "bachelor's quarters" where some Nisei youth also gathered.[33] Recalling Depression-era concerns about relations between inveterate transients and wandering youth, WRA administrators feared that the "old bachelors" would corrupt Nisei youth, undermining their commitment to American values of family, work, and civic responsibility. Other elements that drew official concern were Japanese-style fraternal organizations, such as athletic clubs and the much-discussed Butoku-kai, or Japanese Military Virtue Society of North America. Judo instructors were placed in the same category with the "old bachelors" as negative role models for impressionable Nisei males.[34]

In 1943, when the Dies Committee investigated the internment camps, its members placed particular emphasis on the subversive homosocial activities of young Nisei men. Groups that were alleged to breed subversives were judo clubs, youth gangs, and other "pro-Axis" fraternal organizations within the camps.[35] Although WRA administrators were not in sympathy with the Dies Committee, they too sought to redirect Nisei participation into American-style fraternities like the Boy Scouts and even the Japanese American Citizens League. They also encouraged Nisei participation in the WRA Work Corps as a means to combat idleness and instill positive citizenship values and skills. Yet in spite of these approved activities, WRA administrators were concerned that internment cut off important avenues of assimilation to the Nisei and encouraged participation in subversive fraternal activities. As one administrator observed, "There is a grave danger that the desirable trend toward Americanization might be halted or even reversed" by the internment.[36]

The WRA had good reason to be concerned about maintaining the outward appearance of administrative success, for in addition to the internal problems of social disintegration, the agency also had to contend with a constant stream of criticism from political forces outside the camps. Both anti-Japanese forces and groups traditionally hostile to the New Deal criticized Japanese American internees and WRA administrators for exemplifying the pitfalls of New Deal–style government administration. Such critics sought to promote harder, more efficient and militarized modes of administration, which would also entail a different, more virile and militarized construction of manhood. They depicted WRA administrators as "two-bit men pitchforked into four-dollar jobs," whose previous experience as New Deal bureaucrats, far from making them competent administrators, made them less able to deal with untrustworthy Japanese Americans. According to the WRA's critics, the agency's approach to internees was too solicitous and not sufficiently pragmatic. The internees, they argued, were recalcitrant government dependents who spurned productive labor and allowed WRA administrators to cater to their every whim. In the ideological climate of wartime, in which inefficiency and waste were tantamount to treason, allegations of internee overconsumption and refusal to work engendered considerable public outrage.

Outrage is what the *Denver Post* was aiming for in 1943 when it charged that internees (all implicitly male in the *Post*'s account) received meat, eggs, and milk while white women and small children could obtain none. Male youth were particularly vilified. The *Post* accused Nisei males of willfully destroying government property, vandalizing their surroundings, and "joyriding" in official vehicles outside of camp bounds, at a time when a rubber shortage restricted civilian automobile use. The *Post*'s allegations that internees violated austerity measures sparked a public outcry. Far from deserving privileged treatment, critics argued, the internees should receive only what was required for subsistence.[37]

Although an internal government investigation debunked the *Post*'s allegations, many continued to regard the WRA as an agency that knew no mode of operation other than solicitousness, resulting in an internee population characterized by the worst traits of New Deal dependency. Except that internees were worse still because in addition to being dependent, they were also disloyal. The *Post*'s allegations exemplify how, during a period of heightened anxiety about the meanings of loyalty and sacrifice, the terms of disloyalty, dependency, wastefulness, and improper masculinity often came to be lumped together, and defined in relation to the internee group.[38]

The unpopular WRA was oddly positioned in relation to the broad range of political forces that favored Japanese American evacuation and internment. Its status as a civilian agency was crucial to the federal government's claim that it was not violating the constitutional rights of internees. Although internment camps were designated as military areas and were surrounded by military guards, the civilian character of internal camp administration allowed the government to claim that it was preserving the rights of Japanese American internees who, as civilians, could not be subject to direct military rule. Less attuned to legal details, many who had supported placing Japanese Americans in "concentration camps" were frustrated by administrators' reluctance to impose a more explicitly military regime on internees.[39] Much of that frustration was directed at the WRA itself, but it also found expression in assaults on Japanese American manhood, as reflected in the widely publicized *Denver Post* allegations and in the Dies Committee findings on Japanese American subversion.

Throughout the history of internment, surprisingly little administrative attention was focused on the Nisei's elders, the Issei. And yet the consequences of internment were at least as devastating for the Issei as they were for the younger Nisei. Traditional authority figures within the West Coast Japanese American community, Issei men had been separated from their homes and livelihoods; their families had been forcibly dislocated; and when not imprisoned in Department of Justice internment camps, they were placed along with other members of the Japanese American community in vast, inland relocation camps. Once inside the camps, they were deprived of opportunities to act as breadwinners for their families. The WRA provided food and shelter, and most jobs available to Issei men paid low wages and entailed menial tasks to which many were unaccustomed. In addition to disrupting their conventional family roles, internment stripped Issei men of political authority within the evacuated community.

Some social scientific observers within the camps noted the shortsightedness of WRA policy that focused intensively on the second generation while ignoring the older Issei.[40] WRA administrators' apparent indifference to the altered status of Issei males illustrates that concerns for the preservation of adult masculine authority, so clearly reflected in other New Deal agencies, were racially specific and did not extend to Japanese "aliens ineligible to citizenship" during the war.

Only the Nisei, who were U.S. citizens though racially distinct from the white majority, occupied the attention of WRA administrators. And the terms of that attention reflect the very particular ways in which Roosevelt administrators constructed youthful, masculine citizenship. Far more like the CCC than either the OCD or WPA, the WRA promoted fraternal concepts of citizenship and national community within the internment camps. In so doing, it used traditional gender imagery to convey new political meanings appropriate to the circumstances of global war.

Leave Clearance

Administrative fears about juvenile delinquency, family breakdown, and general social disintegration leading to subversion and other social problems culminated in the fall of 1942. At that time, disturbances at a number of camps, most notably Poston and Manzanar, focused national attention on internment and caused WRA authorities to reevaluate the general thrust of relocation policy. Out of this process of evaluation and redirection, a set of opposed, mutually defining images emerged: the images of the loyal Nisei soldier and the disloyal Kibei troublemaker. These images, and the contrast between them, also helped to define the terms of political loyalty and national collectivity in the wartime United States.

The division of young Japanese American manhood into "loyal" Nisei and "disloyal" Kibei was not an immediate effect of internment, but began to take place after the fall disturbances of 1942. Brian Masaru Hayashi notes that anti-Kibei sentiment had been evident among JACL-affiliated Nisei as early as the 1920s.[41] Before the war, the JACL's anti-Kibei stance led to its break with the Japan Association, which objected to the JACL's intolerance. The War Department had also treated Kibei differently prior to internment, expelling them from the Armed Services sooner than it excluded other Nisei. Some individuals who testified at the Tolan Committee hearings had also referred to the Kibei as a particularly troubling group because of their early exposure to Japanese militarism. Such examples suggest that apprehensions about the Kibei had a complicated history, just as those Japanese Americans who had visited Japan as children were a diverse and multifaceted group.

Yet in the wake of the fall 1942 disturbances, the socially marginal Kibei became symbolically central. These disturbances, in which many young Japanese American men were perceived to make their debut in antiadministration politics, fanned already caustic public hostility toward the camps and exacerbated the public's already pronounced tendency to confuse Japanese American internees with the enemy Japanese. Administrators began to grow concerned about the extremes to which anti-Japanese sentiment had risen, especially since more and more of that hostility was being turned on the WRA itself—at the same time as internees were beginning to show signs of organized resistance to unsatisfactory camp conditions. In the wake of these events, administrators decided that a plan was needed to counter anti-Japanese sentiment and to smooth the way for internee resettlement outside of the camps in so-called normal communities across the middle and eastern sections of the nation. It was at this point that the division between "loyal" Nisei and "disloyal" Kibei became critical.

WRA administrators' plan had several components. First, it entailed a streamlined process of leave clearance that would facilitate internee resettlement outside of the camps. By the fall of 1942, WRA administrators had abandoned the idea that camps were vital communities that would last for the duration of the war. In September 1942, administrators began granting some internees "indefinite leave," but the resulting outmigration was negligible and largely restricted to the citizen group. Moreover, it elicited protest from anti-WRA critics who questioned whether leave recipients had been adequately screened. To expedite the leave process and dispel white racist concerns about leave recipients' possible disloyalty, WRA administrators introduced a mass loyalty oath in January 1943, whereby all internees who declared themselves "loyal" and who were not otherwise disqualified could receive leave clearance more easily.[42]

But this new policy of escalated internee resettlement outside the camps was secondary to another feature of the WRA's plan in the winter of 1943. Reflecting the extent to which the terms of U.S. political obligation during World War II revolved around the gender-exclusive realm of the military, *the* central feature of the plan WRA and War Department officials devised to combat the mounting problems of internment was the formation of an all-Nisei combat team. The mass loyalty oath which WRA administrators applied to all internees as part of its leave clearance procedure was actually a military registration form devised by the War Department. It contained two questions (initially asked of *all* internees, regardless of sex, age, or citizenship status) that were specifically directed at Nisei males:

27) Are you willing to serve the armed forces of the United States on combat duty, wherever ordered?
28) Will you swear unqualified allegiance to the United States of America and faithfully defend the United States from any or all attack by foreign or domestic forces, and foreswear any form of allegiance to the Japanese emperor, to any foreign government, power or organization?[43]

As a mass loyalty questionnaire, the military registration form devised by War Department officials posed obvious problems. Questions about willingness to serve in combat were absurd when posed to women or to elderly Issei men who were categorically excluded from such service. Asking Issei men and women who were Japanese citizens to "foreswear any form of allegiance to the Japanese emperor or any foreign government" was equally absurd. And, as many Nisei who refused to complete the loyalty questionnaire argued, it was absurd to ask any interned individual to defend American democracy from behind barbed wire. The absurdity of the questions 27 and 28 as applied to Japanese aliens gradually dawned on WRA officials who administered the tests, and other questions were substituted when interviewing Issei. That such questions had been universally applied reflects insensitivity to groups besides Nisei males that ran throughout the history of the WRA.

Certainly, WRA administrators could see no greater tool for demonstrating Japanese American loyalty than allowing Nisei males to volunteer for combat. They placed tremendous faith in the combat team as a means of rectifying the agency's troubles, calling it "a fork in the road for the evacuated people." Administrators reported that "the War Department's decision to accept Army volunteers from the populations at the centers . . . [is] an excellent opportunity to provide the American public with dramatic proof of their essential patriotism and loyalty."[44]

Yet neither War Department nor WRA officials intended to redeem the political status of *all* Japanese Americans. Rather, their efforts were focused on a very particular subset of the internee population, whom WRA director Dillon Myer referred to as "the cream of the draft-age group," meaning the most highly assimilated Nisei men. The combat team was also conceived less as a meaningful social movement than as a potentially powerful propaganda tool. "This is a bit of propaganda in part. It will be a sort of 'corps d'elite,'" Myer explained. As he told a group of WRA administrators, "We are working on plans for radio programs, movie shorts, newspaper articles. . . . Until we got this army thing established we would have been running into snags right and left. Now we are ready to go." He called January 28, 1943— the date the combat team was announced—"a most significant date for persons of Japanese ancestry in the United States."[45]

The combat team could only fulfill its intended propaganda function, WRA and War Department officials contended, as long as it remained a racially segregated group. To Nisei internees who expressed a desire to enter the military on equal terms with whites, officials argued, "If your strength were diffused throughout the Army, you would be important only as manpower. . . . But united, and working together, you would become a symbol of something greater than your individual selves, and the effect would be felt both in the United States and abroad."[46]

Indeed, the WRA, the War Department, and the pro-WRA press did everything they could to ensure that the Nisei soldiers "would become a symbol of something greater than their individual selves," and to efface the extent to which, *as individuals*, the Nisei failed to conform to this idealized image of their collective masculinity. Myer was true to his word that "plans for radio programs, movie shorts, [and] newspaper articles" were under way even before the combat team was formed, and accounts of Nisei valor circulated widely long before the 442nd Regimental Combat Team ever left training camp in Shelby, Mississippi. In these accounts, WRA publicists depicted the Nisei soldier almost invariably as a figure of superlative loyalty, sacrifice, and valor. But his role was also servile; his abilities were generally attested to not by Nisei battle-mates, but by white soldiers and officers.

Perhaps the most celebrated, joint campaign of the 442nd Combat Team and the all Japanese-Hawaiian 100th Battalion was the rescue of the "Lost Battalion," a unit composed of white Texan soldiers in Italy. In this campaign, the 442nd combat team and the 100th Battalion suffered extraordinarily high casualties. Their extreme dedication to the rescue mission resonated with representations of Japanese national soldiers, in ways that suggest that the figure of the Nisei soldier was linked to the extreme nationalistic fervor attributed in media accounts to Japanese militarized manhood. What made that fervor acceptable in the case of the 442nd Combat Team and the 100th Battalion was that it was harnessed to the interests of the predominantly white, segregated armed forces.

WRA and War Department accounts of Nisei heroism also tended to lack individuality and depth; they functioned not so much as personal profiles as profiles of an entire racial and generational group. In 1944, when 442nd Staff Sergeant Kazuo Masuda died after walking through two hundred yards of enemy fire and single-handedly setting up an improvised mortar position that aided his fellow soldiers, his story became a media event. Masuda's sister had been in the news previously as one of the first Nisei to relocate back to California, where she had been accosted by a group of nativist "vigilantes." In an effort to discourage such vigilantism against returning Japanese American civilians, General Joseph Stilwell personally delivered a posthumous citation to the Masuda family, trailed by cameramen and reporters.

Yet Stilwell made no attempt to describe Masuda as a heroic individual. Instead he remarked, with generality characteristic of accounts of Nisei valor, "I've seen a good deal of the Nisei in service and never yet have I found one who did not do his duty right up to the handle." The case of Sergeant Masuda illustrates how, from the very outset of the recruitment program, WRA and War Department officials imagined the valiant Nisei soldier less as an individual, and more as a representative figure. He represented the potential valor of his fellow Nisei soldiers, grouped together with him in a segregated unit, as well as the political worthiness of all Japanese Americans who claimed to be "loyal and law-abiding." That publicists sought to link Mary Masuda's civil rights to her brother's military sacrifice reflects how, in the WRA's complexly calculated media campaign, the political claims of other members of his community were contingent on the Nisei soldier's willingness to serve the military fraternity in racially specific ways.[47]

That media accounts of Nisei valor were only partially dependent on actual Nisei military accomplishments is reflected in the effectiveness with which WRA publicists effaced Nisei resistance to recruitment. In fact, approximately 26 percent of male citizens "failed to provide unqualified affirmative answers" on the loyalty questionnaire that would have qualified them for recruitment. Of the initial complement of 5,000 recruits for the 442nd, only slightly over a thousand came from the internment camps, whereas the rest came from Hawaii and from the ranks of Nisei on the mainland whose families had managed to avoid internment.[48] Media accounts of the 442nd disregarded the minority status of evacuees in the combat team by highlighting the experiences of soldiers who had undergone internment.

Although Hawaiians and other Nisei were also represented, many published accounts told the story of Nisei soldiers on leave who returned to WRA camps to visit their parents, wives, and sweethearts. WRA publicity photos showed Nisei soldiers at United Service Organization (USO) centers inside the camps, socializing with young Nisei women, or spending time with parents and other kin.[49] Such accounts reassured readers that although some Nisei might be in uniform, they were not frequenting white USO centers or fraternizing with white women. Yet at the same time, they *were* engaging in appropriate filial and heterosexual pursuits—all the more appropriate, perhaps, by virtue of their enactment within the restricted bounds of the internment camp. Profiles of Nisei wounded likewise recognized former internees disproportionately. In addition to describing the soldier's malady, such accounts also stated his parents' names and camp affiliation.

In spite of the impression that WRA publicists presented to the media, many internees refused to cooperate with registration and recruitment. Organized resistance to the loyalty questionnaire and later to the draft when it was reinstated was marked at a number of centers, including Heart Mountain and Tule Lake segregation camp in California. At the Heart Mountain camp in Wyoming, members of a group calling itself the Fair Play Committee headed by Kiyoshi Okamoto answered the loyalty questionnaire affirmatively but did not volunteer for the combat team.[50] Later, when the draft was reinstated for Japanese Americans in January 1944, members of the Heart Mountain group resisted, and sixty-three were ultimately imprisoned for their stand. With Okamoto as their spokesperson, they articulated a different conception of American citizenship from that which emphasized self-sacrificing loyalty above all else. Claiming that they could not be bound by the obligations of citizenship when they were barred from exercising its rights, they refused to comply with the draft. Indeed, they declared such compliance to be un-American. Two years of WRA-administered loyalty "tests" had perhaps convinced the draft resisters at Heart Mountain that there was conceivably no end to the cycle of discrimination and mistrust that shaped both official and popular conceptions of Japanese American citizenship during the war. They took the stand that citizenship must be defined in terms of civil rights, equally, for all citizens, regardless of race or ancestry. And they recognized that the alternative emphasis on loyalty and contingent citizenship rights lent itself to the exclusionary and racist politics that were at the heart of WRA internment.[51]

While the Heart Mountain draft resisters were imprisoned in local jails and then in federal penitentiaries, other Japanese American youth who protested against camp conditions were housed at an abandoned CCC camp in Moab, Utah.[52] The connections between CCC and WRA are many, and they are especially evident in the WRA's efforts to enlist Nisei internees in the military. Just as the CCC had promoted a martial ideal of embodied masculine citizenship for white working-class youth, the Nisei combat team advanced a racially specific version of embodied martial idealism during the war. Just as CCC youth would "knuckle down to hard work and like it," Nisei soldiers would train their bodies to the imperatives of combat, putting life and limb on the line as a demonstration of national loyalty. If the CCC youth had become "heavier and hard-muscled" as a result of his national labors, press accounts made much of the Nisei soldier's diminutive status, noting the mismatch between his allegedly child-sized body and the usual G.I. uniform. And just as the CCC's "loosely clad forestry worker" garnered national acclaim, the returning Nisei veteran, bandaged and possibly dismembered, likewise met with public approbation. Finally, in both the CCC and the WRA, the heterosexual family ideal loomed over the activities of young recruits. Just as CCC officials encouraged a sense of family obligation by requiring enrollees to send cash allotments to family members, WRA officials stressed that Nisei soldiers' military sacrifices were a boon to mothers, fathers, siblings, and wives in internment camps back home.

Although some groups of Nisei within the camps, most notably those affiliated with the JACL, eagerly accepted the opportunity to "prove" their loyalty through combat, they by no means a spoke for an undifferentiated majority. The true range of Nisei responses to their government's racially specific call-to-arms was not evident and was in fact covered up by the glowing media coverage of the 442nd Combat Team, and in this way the response of one group of internees was made to assume majoritarian proportions. The other extreme was equally overdrawn and misrepresented in the WRA's media campaign: that which came to be associated with the figure of the disloyal Kibei troublemaker. At the same time that the WRA formulated its plan for a Nisei combat team, it devised a policy to segregate those who answered the loyalty questionnaire in the negative. As WRA officials would later explain, "The admixture of a disloyal minority in the population at relocation centers was undoubtedly confusing the public mind about the loyalties of the entire group. Once the patently disloyal had been weeded out, the problem of gaining public acceptance for relocation of the remainder would be greatly simplified."[53]

The so-called disloyals who gave negative loyalty statements in the winter of 1943 and thereby committed themselves to remaining in a separate segregation camp for the duration of the war, by WRA's own admission, did so for a range of reasons, and they were characterized by tremendous age, gender, political, and cultural diversity. Yet in the politics and imagery of WRA segregation, the Kibei troublemaker stood at the forefront of the disloyal group, as a menacing figure of political duplicity and cultural hybridity.

More so than Nisei youth, whom authorities had generally characterized as "plastic and impressionable," Kibei youth was represented as a problem. "[The Kibei] group of 10,000 is . . . regarded as containing some of the most dangerous elements in the Japanese community," the Tolan Committee report had stated. It added, "Youths thus educated are essentially and culturally Japanese. It is reasonable to assume that most of these students were inculcated with Japanese nationalistic philosophy and were exposed to religious training which identifies the Emperor as a deity."[54] In line with these nationalistic accents, the Kibei were represented as dissolute and aggressive and as lacking the social skills that would have ensured good relations with the Issei and with other Nisei. Their unconventional upbringing, apart from nuclear family ties, also allegedly fostered social maladjustment. According to one WRA source, "Whatever the parents' reasons, the returning Kibei often exhibited the psychology of a rejected child who finds it difficult to adjust himself to the parents and siblings who had rejected him earlier. Some Nisei claimed that the Kibei were like bats in the old folktale of the war between the mammals and the birds: whichever side was winning would be joined by the bats."[55]

Certainly, as this reference to folk wisdom suggests, there was some basis in Japanese American culture for the stigmatization of the Kibei. Differences of experience did hamper smooth relations between the Kibei and other second-generation Japanese Americans.[56] Yet what is perhaps most interesting about the characterization of the Kibei as "bats" in this passage is the way in which this imagery was appropriated from Japanese American culture and embellished by WRA officials. Like some Nisei, the WRA viewed Kibei as akin to bats in the folktale about the battle between the mammals and the birds. Social scientists employed in the camps described Kibei as "marginal men," possessed of indeterminate loyalties and irregular social bonds.[57]

The one group with whom WRA officials sometimes identified the Kibei was their fellow troublemakers, former migratory workers known as "the old bachelors," for like them, they were typically single and lacked the stabilizing influence of family ties.[58] This bachelorhood made them more vulnerable to WRA attack because their isolation would not elicit protest from family members and also marked them as in some ways perverse or unnatural.

Accounts of relations between "Kibei troublemakers" and the "old bachelors" appear frequently in the record of internment. An examination of such accounts reveals the role that allegations of improper homosociality played in establishing Kibei disloyalty. WRA administrators routinely tarred Kibei with the brush of deviant homosociality, further undermining their claims to civic entitlement. WRA director Myer characterized Kibei as "the most maladjusted group of Japanese in this country," adding that "the girls didn't like to dance with them—they were social outcasts."[59] Barred from wholesome heterosocial pursuits, WRA officials implied, the Kibei found companionship among the "old bachelors," who shared their subversive outlook.[60]

Popular and official accounts of life in the Tule Lake segregation camp particularly emphasized the unwholesome collaboration between Kibei and "old bachelors." Some accounts portrayed Kibei as the instigators of conflict who used pressure tactics to enlist the bachelor Issei in their cause. Other accounts reversed the generational influence, depicting the older "fruit tramps" as spreading antisocial viewpoints to the receptive Kibei. Accounts of Kibei–old bachelor collusion obscured a broader culture of homosocial leisure pursuits that flourished in the camps. In fact, that culture was more concerned with sponsoring *goh* tournaments and fielding baseball teams than with plotting against the U.S. government.

The narrative of Kibei–old bachelor collusion is significant on two levels. First, it recalls narratives of inveterate transients and wandering youth in the Depression. Like inveterate transients in the thirties, bachelor Issei had spent most of their lives apart from heterosexual family norms. Speaking broadly about Asian American immigrants, David Eng observes, "Antimiscegenation and exclusion laws worked to produce . . . exclusive 'bachelor communities,' which exerted great influence on questions of sexuality."[61]

"Questions of sexuality" were at the heart of a 1940 article in the *Portland Oregonian*, which explained, "Most of the immigrant Japanese were youths of 16 to 20 when they came to the Western world. To them it was a land of strange new faces, unfamiliar customs, foreign philosophies and religions and puzzling tongue . . . and for many years, no Japanese women."[62] Consigned by antimiscegenation and exclusion laws to lifelong bachelorhood, Issei migrant laborers had been "historically disavowed . . . as full members of the U.S. nation-state" and thus rendered "queer."[63]

The Kibei's maladjustment was similarly sexualized in WRA rhetoric, not the least through insinuations of their close relations with the bachelor Issei. In this way, WRA administrators further stigmatized the Kibei, increasing their effectiveness as scapegoats and preempting public concern about the mistreatment in the camps.

How officials viewed the Kibei can also be seen in the kinds of changes that took place at the Tule Lake camp following its designation as the WRA's segregation center. The military guard at the camp was more than doubled, security facilities were expanded, and residents of the segregation camp were denied even the limited role in camp governance that had existed at other centers. Moreover, segregation was alleged to bring heightened social problems, such as juvenile delinquency and disrespect for soldiers in uniform.[64] Media accounts represented Tule Lake as a place totally out of control and overrun by rebellious young men.[65] There was some real basis for these claims; Tule Lake was the site for pro-Japan cultural and political demonstrations, and one political faction within the camp sponsored a young men's Japanese militaristic organization, in addition to promoting other Japanese cultural activities. Other political factions also existed in the camp, and political loyalties tended to correspond to residential blocks. Such political and social differences were by no means unique to Tule Lake, nor was Tule Lake the only camp characterized by conflict between camp residents and WRA administrators. Although such conflicts were common to all camps, in the case of Tule Lake, political conflicts were frequently sensationalized on the grounds that they were instigated by members of the "young hoodlum group."[66]

One such conflict, which would lead to the serious incidents of early November 1943, was a labor dispute between internee farmworkers and the camp administration over workplace safety, following a truck accident that occurred en route to a work site, killing one worker and injuring several others. Workers refused to return to work until their safety concerns were addressed. WRA administrators, instead of addressing the workers' concerns, minimized the accident and brought in replacement workers from other internment camps to harvest the crops. When Tule Lake residents learned this, they protested, and their protests coincided with a visit to the camp by national director Myer. The "November incidents," as these protests came to be known, became the focus of intense political scrutiny nationwide and led to a two-month Army takeover of the camp that some politicians argued should have been permanent. The November incidents were vastly distorted in the press, attributable in part to the Army's policy of strict censorship, which contributed to reporters' reliance on rumor and hearsay.[67]

Press reports generally vilified Kibei youth as instigators of the protests. A photo-essay featured in *Life* magazine described the Kibei menacingly as "pressure boys."[68] The essay's opening photograph, shot from below, presented a lineup of prisoners—a mixture of young and old men—staring down ominously at the camera. In another photograph, a single "pressure boy" idly strums his guitar, eyes averted, while on the wall behind him, pinup images of white women are clearly visible. Although attracted to women, this Kibei's object choice is portrayed as racially inappropriate. The text accompanying the image portrays Kibei youth as idle, aimless, and filled with pent-up bitterness toward the government that interned them.

If newspaper and magazine accounts sensationalized the November incidents, governmental accounts were a bit more accurate, stating that three main incidents occurred: one was the beating of the white chief medical officer at the internee hospital by a handful of young men; second was a meeting between an internee-appointed grievance committee and top administrators including Myer, which was held at the administration building while

FIGURE 9. Portrait of a line of men at Tule Lake Segregation Center, an internment camp for Americans of Japanese descent, Tule Lake, CA, March 1, 1944. Published in *Life*, March 20, 1945. Photo by Carl Mydans / The Life Picture Collection / Getty Images.

thousands of peaceful demonstrators waited outside and white personnel were prevented from leaving the premises; and third was a confrontation between male internees and WRA staff members that arose when white workers attempted to remove food supplies from the camp storage depot for use by strikebreakers housed outside the camp. After this final incident, during which irate internees gathered first at the supply depot and then moved to the project director's house, the Army was called in.[69]

Internees' demands in attempted negotiations with the administration were multiple and complex, involving problems with particular administrators and grievances about food quality, dust control, medical care, and workplace safety. Yet the media reduced camp events to a standoff between incompetent, overtolerant WRA administrators, characterized as "theorists and crackpots," and unruly Kibei youth, who took advantage of a weak administration by "wielding bats and pickhandles" and wreaking havoc generally. Press accounts glo-

THE CITIZEN-SOLDIER AND THE CITIZEN-INTERNEE 193

FIGURE 10. Young Kibei playing guitar in the stockade at Tule Lake Segregation Center. Note pinups of white women visible on wall behind him. Published in *Life*, March 20, 1945. Photo by Carl Mydans / The Life Picture Collection / Getty Images.

rified the Army takeover; a *Los Angeles Times* report described how the Army was called onto the scene just in the nick of time, as irate young hoodlums, not content to wreak havoc at the camp supply depot, converged on the private residence of Project Director Ray Best, where Best's defenseless wife and children were housed.[70] In this way, what was really a dispute over workplace safety and the WRA's decision to employ strikebreakers became an assault by unruly Kibei youth against the white-veteran-headed American family. (In addition to being a less-than-scrupulous WRA administrator, Best had been a marine in World War I.) The incidents also showcased WRA incompetence and the relative virtues of military rule.[71]

That several thousand internees participated in the November demonstrations did not deter journalists from representing the events as a contest between a handful of Kibei troublemakers and weak, New Deal style administrators. Rather, the fact that so many internees turned out for demonstrations was depicted as evidence of the Kibei's formidable pressure tactics.

In his retrospective evaluation of the internment program, Myer acknowledged that the November incidents represented the nadir of WRA public relations.[72] No other single event did more to damage the WRA's credibility than the moment at which top administrators were incarcerated in their own administration building and forced to negotiate with a committee of internees. Hostile politicians and the media were outraged. In the wake of the November incidents, Myer was called before a congressional committee to answer charges that the WRA was an agency incapable of dealing with the allegedly "vicious" sorts of internees who were housed at Tule Lake. Legislation was proposed that would permanently transfer administration of the internment program to the War Department. Seeking to prevent this, Myer emphasized the role of an isolated group of Kibei troublemakers and suggested that order might be restored simply if "an area [were] fenced off, with a man-proof fence around [it], whereby this group of people [could] be placed away" from the rest of the camp.[73]

In explaining these plans for an all-male stockade before the congressional committee, Myer elaborated on the figure of disloyal Kibei manhood, whom he and others also referred to collectively as "the young hoodlum group." Characterizing them as being "malcontents at the center from the time we received them," volatile young men between eighteen to twenty-five years of age, and as being "real Japanese from the standpoint of culture," Myer also cast suspicion on their motives for returning to the United States after living in Japan. He stated, "They came back to this country, why, we will never know. I will give you my opinion. I think most of them came back to keep out of serving in the Japanese Army. They capitalized on their American citizenship to that extent."[74]

In this way, Myer painted an image of the Kibei troublemaker not only as a malcontented "young hoodlum," but as a two-time evader of military service, giving new meaning to his status as a "no-no boy." Not only had the troublemaking Kibei answered "no-no" to the two crucial loyalty questions posed by the WRA and the War Department about allegiance and willingness to serve, but they answered "no" first to Japan's call to arms, then "no" again to that of the United States. By representing Kibei manhood in this way, Myer attempted to divert the committee's hostile concern away from WRA administrative weaknesses onto the always-handy figure of the Kibei troublemaker.

Indeed, Myer had every reason to vilify the Kibei "young hoodlum." In his view, this improperly socialized figure of Japanese militarism and disregard for political obligation had always been the thorn in the side of the WRA. And yet, paradoxically, the WRA had helped to construct the image of the Kibei troublemaker. In the official rhetoric of gender, race, and political obligation during World War II, the Kibei troublemaker was a necessary and fruitful image of young Japanese American manhood.

❦ Soldiers and Headhunters

If the Nisei soldier was a reassuring figure in the context of the WRA, then the Kibei troublemaker was a dystopian figure. The Nisei soldier represented the appropriate degree of socialization; he accepted his racially specific place in the context of military fraternity; and he served with valor. Sometimes, he even served with too much valor: the superlatives with which Nisei military exploits were usually discussed had a ring of unreality about them; they hearkened to the images of Japanese military zealotry; it was as though a racial trait imputed to the Japanese had been harnessed to the American war effort. Moreover, one wonders if the images of Nisei wounded and the widely disseminated statistics about Nisei casualties and deaths were not partly intended to be read by a hostile American public as retribution for Japanese atrocities against the Allied Forces—were not intended, partly, to be read as Japanese wounded, as Japanese dead.[75]

George H. Roeder Jr. has emphasized the care with which visual imagery of combat and military life was monitored during the war.[76] Although government censors withheld images of African American wounded in order to discourage civil rights claims by black leaders, the same was not true of images of injured Japanese Americans, which were frequently shown, thanks largely to publicists at the WRA.[77] A particularly poignant example is the story of Private Yoshinao Omiya, whose eyes were blown out by a land mine when he and his unit were crossing a field. In addition to the short narrative, an article about Omiya presents a large photograph of him sitting barefoot and cross-legged, in civilian clothes, on a hospital bed. The image shows Omiya with his arms wrapped around himself, his eyes covered with large, white bandages. The overall effect is one of impotence and vulnerability. The audience can examine Private Omiya but he cannot look back. His defensive posture seems to acknowledge this. The picture is larger than the brief written text that accompanies it. It is titled "Pfc. Omiya Proves His Americanism."[78]

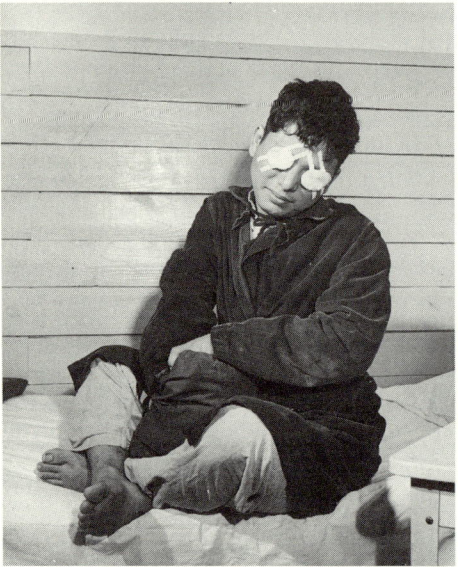

FIGURE 11. Portrait of blind American soldier Yoshinao Omiya as he recovers from his injuries at Stark General Hospital, Charleston, SC, 1944. A member of an all Japanese-American division of the U.S. Army, he was blinded by a booby trap while crossing the Volturno River. Photo by Jack Wilkes / The Life Picture Collection / Getty Images. Reprinted with accompanying text in *Nisei in Uniform* (U.S. Government Printing Office, 1944).

That Private Omiya was compelled to "prove" his Americanism through injuries sustained in combat whereas African Americans were denied opportunities to represent their loyalty visually to the American public suggests the very different terms in which the wartime politics of race affected Japanese American and African American men. What is evident in WRA imagery of Nisei wounded is the hostility and punitive intent with which such Japanese American demonstrations of loyalty were regarded. Just as white Americans used the derogatory term "Jap" to refer to both Japanese Americans and the enemy Japanese, they also tended to regard Nisei sacrifices as *compensation* for Japanese atrocities in warfare. This kind of ambivalence in representations of Nisei sacrifice in battle is perhaps obvious, but it bears mentioning. For it speaks to the extent of confusion about the terms of nationalism and racial identity, and about the racial limits of military membership, that were inseparable from the politics of WRA internment and Nisei military service in the war.

But within the rhetoric of the WRA, if the Nisei soldier was in some sense a figure for the Japanese national soldier, he was also a figure of exemplary American citizenship. His sacrifices, borne on the battlefield, outweighed and overshadowed the sacrifices of men and women on the home front, though that front was also mobilized for war. Certainly, the Nisei soldier was a figure of patriotic excess; in part, that excess was self-generated, a reflection of some Nisei's frustrated sense of entitlement and their determination to do something about it.[79] Their valor was a challenge to those who had questioned their loyalty, their capabilities as soldiers, and their very status as citizens and as men. But relative to the Kibei segregant, the Nisei soldier was also a figure of moderation. Like his white American counterpart, the terms of his participation in the fraternity of military life were finite and carefully contained. According to the WRA's media campaign, whether accurately or not, he too fought on behalf of wives, mothers, and sweethearts back home; he too had a home to return to; he too looked forward to a life after military service of patriarchal family prerogatives and economic prosperity consistent with the American Dream.

Yet in evaluating the privileged status of the Nisei soldier, it is worth returning for a moment to media treatments of his place within the military brotherhood. Late in the war with Japan, a white officer commenting on a visit to the 100th Battalion was reported by WRA publicists as saying, in a typical account of Nisei valor, "These [Nisei] soldiers are as far away from the stereotyped picture of the evil-doing sons of Japan as the all-American boy is from a head-hunter."[80] Although this statement marks a clear division between the Nisei soldier and his Japanese national counterpart—one that puts the latter in some odd relationship to the primitive figure of the head-hunter—it nevertheless retains a distinction between the Nisei soldier and the image of all-American boyhood. Within the rhetoric of the WRA, Nisei soldiers were not represented fully as brothers to their white military counterparts. Indeed, the only way that the two could be placed in the same category is through their opposition to similarly but not identically racialized "others."

Within this complex system for reckoning the gender and racial terms of U.S. national collectivity, the Kibei troublemaker also had his place. If the Nisei soldier occupied a kind of intermediary status, revealing the profound racial limits of military fraternity by which national collectivity was sometimes imagined during the war, then the Kibei troublemaker was the true "other," the enemy whose figuration gave participation in the military brotherhood meaning, even as it unsettled it.

In some ways, the Kibei troublemaker is more menacing than the "evil-doing son of Japan"—indeed, he was perhaps more like the headhunter—in his defiance of the political claims of *two* nations. Although every effort was made to distinguish Japanese nationalism from U.S. nationalism by depicting the former as an odd amalgam of emperor-worship, Buddhism, and military zealotry, nevertheless U.S. soldiers and Japanese national soldiers presumably shared the common characteristic of commitment to a national cause. Whereas the Kibei's loyalties, although extreme, were less definable in precisely *national* terms. Indeed, the Kibei troublemaker represented the possibility that loyalty *need not* be defined in national terms at all—that it might rather be defined in terms of race, of class, or even possibly of defiant homosociality. For the Kibei, in addition to defying the terms of national belonging, also was an affront to the proper terms of masculine socialization into adulthood that would have led to other, nonmilitarized masculine attainments.

In this sense, the Kibei was a compelling figure for the dystopian potentiality immanent in all political cultures that rely on "plastic but impressionable youth" as figures of national collectivity. That the Kibei, as such a figure, should be marked as racially and nationally "other," as an aberrant "cultural hybrid"—and that he should be imprisoned in a segregation camp—helped a white American culture with its own ambivalences about the gendered consequences of militarized political obligation to steady itself. And perhaps the segregated Nisei soldier, too, the terms of whose political obligations and entitlements were so excessively sacrificial, helped to relativize the sacrifices that other Americans were required to make.

What happened to the Kibei troublemaker after the war? Some members of the diverse group that came to be lumped together in this troublingly imprecise category renounced their U.S. citizenship and were deported to Japan; others who resisted the draft once it was reinstated for Japanese Americans in 1944 were imprisoned.[81] Eventually, many avowedly "loyal" and avowedly "disloyal" Japanese Americans returned to West Coast communities and picked up the pieces of their lives. This course of action was more possible after the war because—whatever the consequences for Nisei and Kibei manhood of WRA internment, Army recruitment, and segregation had been—their role as a symbolic resource for the articulation of broader cultural concerns about gender, generation, and national belonging shifted at war's end. Although individual Kibei had diverse and complicated personal histories, it would be a mistake to confuse personal experience with the kinds of cultural figurations described in this work. Kibei manhood will always be something of a fixed image—an image fixed between two nations and two cultures—an image fixed in homosociality. The trajectory of figurative Kibei manhood is difficult to fathom because its whole point is about fixity, about masculine socialization unnaturally forestalled. In contrast, the Nisei soldier connotes progress, forward motion toward maturity, and the promise of successful transition to still racialized masculine adulthood. Finally, in the rhetoric and practices of the WRA, both figures helped to represent a masculinized and militarized concept of national collectivity—the inherently unstable meanings of "true loyalty" and "heartfelt" citizenship—that neither could fully attain.

Bad Boys and Good Pupils

WRA images of Japanese American manhood were also useful to the United States in helping to define its role as a global power of unparalleled strength in the postwar political economy. Reflection on the significance of those images reveals that it was not only Kibei youth who were likened to gangsters and juvenile delinquents during the war. The same rhetoric was applied, as historian John Dower suggests, to the nation of Japan. Japan was characterized as "a land of diminutive distances," it was a "small urchin in the family of nations," and its soldiers and officers were likened to a "gang of badly behaved boys."[82]

After the war, Dower argues, as racism took on a more benign face, the United States' propensity for attributing the characteristics of white male adolescents to the Japanese national character took a different turn, and the "bad boy" became a "good pupil." As a more mature and powerful member of the "family of nations," the United States could help to redeem Japan, its delinquent "younger brother," whom social scientific experts had come to know in the context of the WRA camps.[83]

Indeed, what happened on the postwar global stage of U.S.-Japanese relations bore significant relation to the politics of WRA internment, particularly from the standpoint of social scientific experts in the policymaking process. One of the functions of the internment camps was international: internees were seen as hostages whose treatment would materially affect the fate of American prisoners of war in Japan, and social scientists in the camps believed that by studying the internee population, noting its personality traits and habits of living, they could learn something about the Japanese national character.[84]

After the initial round of disturbances took place late in 1942, administrators created a subagency of the WRA called the Community Analysis section. The purpose of Community Analysis was to undertake social scientific research into social problems at the camps. Staffed by anthropologists and sociologists, most of whom had both government experience and some field experience with nonwhite or non-Western populations, the Community Analysis section was designed to anticipate and prevent the kinds of conditions that provoked strikes and other disturbances at the camps. It provided information to WRA administrators to assist them in communicating their objectives to internees, and it identified social forms and managerial strategies that were conducive to internee cooperation. It also analyzed different social groups within the camps, such as the Nisei and the Kibei, and it extrapolated from those studies to make claims about the Japanese national character. Underlying the Community Analysis section was a profound faith in the salutary effects of social science, and participating experts viewed their role as akin to that of social science experts in industrial management or in colonial regimes, whose job it was to understand the outlook of "administered populations" and to mediate between "administrators" and the "administered" from a position of scientific objectivity.[85]

Although the real value of Community Analysis was arguably negligible (the only major policy decision that followed its inception was the plan for segregation at Tule Lake), it espoused a model of administration and an approach to racial and cultural difference that its proponents regarded as superior to those of the military or welfare arms of WRA administration. Significantly, almost all of the participants in Community Analysis were men whose high level of training in anthropology or sociology, combined with experience in government service, distinguished them from the less auspicious, more typically female social workers of the Community Welfare section. And their enlightened approach to policymaking, supposedly based on a *consensual* rather than a *coercive* model of administration, differed from the divisive, militaristic approach to solving problems that emerged during the November incidents at Tule Lake.

As part of a redirection of social science that coincided with the war years, the Community Analysis section indicates much about the United States' approach to colonial administration in the immediate postwar era. Directly following the war, WRA administrators and foreign policymakers distanced themselves from the coercive military model that had been so influential in the politics and imagery of internment. Yet it is important to recognize the continuities between the coercive, militaristic and more consensual, nonmilitaristic approaches to race, culture, and national difference in the war and immediate postwar years. Both approaches utilized young male internees as a resource for understanding Japanese cultural and racial characteristics, and both sought to justify unequal relations between the Japanese people and the people of the United States.

Late in the war, it was considered altogether appropriate that social scientific "experts" whose primary experience had been with Japanese American internees should be transferred from the WRA to the State Department to assist in planning the United States' postwar occupation of Japan. Indeed, experts who worked in the camps were perceived to have a wealth of knowledge about Japanese national characteristics. A handful of community analysts published studies of the Japanese national character, based on their brief sojourns in the internment camps.[86] Such studies reflected especially the stereotyped perceptions of the Kibei, characterizing the Japanese as a people emotionally stunted in childhood, immature, aggressive, and fanatical. The model of administration deemed appropriate to such a population was a benignly superior one—one that would help the Japanese to become more like their Western "elder brothers." As such administrative developments reveal, a rhetoric of youthful manhood and fraternal kinship articulated in the WRA—and otherwise evident throughout the record of the Roosevelt administration—once again helped to found a major shift in U.S. policy at the end of the Roosevelt years.

At the end of World War II, community analysts had come a long way from the fall of 1942, when they were called into the internment camps to help the WRA deal with its "administered population." So too had the national consciousness of the majority of Americans transformed by leaps and bounds. From reluctant participants in the war effort before Pearl Harbor, Americans had become avid observers of world events, and they supported the government's interventionist foreign policy following the war.

In that sense, if not in others, the WRA had been successful. As with other Roosevelt administration agencies, it used the population under its authority to articulate national political meanings appropriate to the changing contours of the U.S. nation-state. Specifically, it used the resource of masculine youth to define new terms of civic obligation and entitlement, of national loyalty, and of state action during a period of rapid political change.

In that sense, the WRA had much in common with the Depression-era CCC. In both instances, a Roosevelt agency combined civilian and military models in approaching a youthful, masculine group that was widely perceived as nationally threatening. Through policies that involved considerable military participation, both agencies worked to imbue their target populations with civic values appropriate to their racial, gender, and generational location within the nation. The populations targeted by both agencies became resources for unofficial figurations of citizenship and national collectivity as well. Certainly, as the wide range of representations of Nisei and Kibei youth suggest, government officials did not have exclusive purchase on the image-making process. Nationally significant images of CCC youth were more uniformly positive than the questionable fraternal imagery that circulated around the WRA, but in both instances, representations of properly and improperly socialized youth were used to articulate concepts of citizenship and national community during moments of rapid political change.

Contrasting the gender imagery and kinship models generated within agencies such as the CCC and WRA to those created by the WPA and OCD suggests the very different ways in which youthful and mature men figured in official constructions of citizenship and national community during the Roosevelt years. If youthful, masculine groupings more frequently came to represent the *obligations* of political membership, mature male groupings more frequently came to represent citizenship *entitlements*—the prerogatives of earning an honorable living and providing for dependent family members that characterized the breadwinner ideal.

Like Nisei and Kibei men during the war, American women of all races were largely excluded from wartime civic ideals. Placing wartime depictions of Nisei and Kibei manhood alongside unsympathetic constructions of wartime womanhood invites us to think complexly about what Anne McClintock has termed "the uneven gendering of the national citizen."[87] Among other things, it compels us to consider the complex interplay of race and gender in sustaining the nationally productive kinship metaphors of military fraternity and the male-headed home. Moreover, it prompts us to consider how the affective bonds of civic community map onto differently gendered and racialized bodies in order to produce a coherent and compelling body of the nation.

Stories of Homecoming
Deserving GIs and Faithless Service Wives

As Allied victories in 1943 and 1944 prompted Americans to contemplate the postwar world, narratives and images of the soldier's homecoming came to the forefront. Some were optimistic, like Norman Rockwell's illustration on the October 1946 *Saturday Evening Post* cover that featured Willie Gillis as a mature and purposeful veteran-scholar. In this final Gillis illustration (a total of nine others had appeared since 1941), Gillis returns home safely and reaps the educational benefits afforded by the GI Bill. Whereas Rockwell presents a veteran success story, other reconversion texts expressed considerable foreboding. Many Americans feared that demobilization would bring back prewar unemployment levels; the vast social dislocations of wartime had permanently undermined American values; and soldiers, who had borne a disproportionate share of the war's violence, would not adjust to the economic, social, and sexual imperatives of postwar civilian life.

Indeed, the veterans' return to the home front at the end of World War II evoked many of the same fears that attended the plight of Bonus veterans and other forgotten men in 1932. In a Fireside Chat on June 28, 1943, Roosevelt advised his radio audience that in order to meet the needs of its veterans, the nation must continue to remember the forgotten man. "They [the veterans] must not be demobilized into an environment of inflation and unemployment, to a place in a bread line, or on a corner selling apples,"

FIGURE 12. Cover. *Saturday Evening Post*, October 4, 1946. Printed by permission of the Norman Rockwell Family Agency. ©1946 the Norman Rockwell Family Entities.

Roosevelt declared. He continued, "I have assured our men in the armed forces that the American people would not let them down when the war is won."[1]

Roosevelt's words set the stage for what many regard as the last piece of New Deal legislation, the 1944 Serviceman's Readjustment Act, or GI Bill. Like federal relief programs of the 1930s, the GI Bill both expanded the scope of national government in providing for its veterans and promoted a masculine model of civic community.[2] Emergent state policies were joined to residual race and gender concepts, just as they had been in early New Deal programs that purported to restore dignity to the forgotten man.

Despite Roosevelt's allusions to forgotten manhood in the waning years of his administration, the contours of U.S. civic community looked very different as the war drew to a close. Whereas strong isolationist sentiments had animated U.S. civic culture in the 1930s, wartime experiences had convinced a majority of Americans of the need for military production at home and interventionism in foreign affairs.

Among the experiences that had altered Americans' civic consciousness during the war was their participation in civilian defense. Through its sponsorship of air-raid drills, scrap drives, Victory Gardens, and parades, the Office of Civilian Defense helped countless U.S. civilians to organize their contributions to the war effort. But the OCD also did more than that. Through its engagement with widely circulating narratives of soldiers and civilian defenders, meddlesome women and dutiful wives, it helped to compose a compelling vision of civic community defined in role-oriented, difference-based terms.

OCD officials' insistence that the nation was constantly under threat of aerial attack gave civilians a valuable emotional investment in the war, providing a focus for their anger and anxiety and fortifying their sense of kinship with young military troops. Scapegoating meddlesome civilian women and African American and Mexican American "hoodlums" also authorized white male civilian defenders' angry and authoritative affect. Likewise, the War Relocation Authority's incarceration of Japanese Americans, so often sensationalized in the press, was widely available for popular controversy and comment. Dramatic stories of Japanese American disloyalty, set inside and outside of the camps, helped to constitute a racialized American public that derived considerable pleasure from the stories' negative depictions of young Japanese Americans manhood. WRA representations of disloyal Kibei troublemakers were particularly evocative, enhancing civilians' feelings that they were living with a clear and present danger to the nation's gender, racial, and sexual ideals.

If Americans' outlook on world affairs had changed dramatically by 1945, so too had their outlook on federal welfare policy. Early in the war, relief agencies such as the Works Progress Administration and the Civilian Conservation Corps had been abolished, partly in response to wartime reemployment, but also because of increasingly effective conservative attacks on the New Deal. Gender and racial scapegoating played a central role in wartime attacks on the New Deal. As a figurehead for New Deal liberalism, Eleanor Roosevelt was roundly abused for her progressive gender and racial politics, as reactions to her tenure as director of the OCD's "nonprotective" branch reveal. Even New Deal officials who did not share Mrs. Roosevelt's progressive politics, such as Dillon S. Myer of the WRA, were cast as effeminate "mollycoddlers" and "crackpots" who lacked the masculine resolve to control "Kibei troublemakers." Although some welfare advocates had hoped that the CCC and even the WPA might be reinstated after the war, those agencies were superseded by the GI Bill of Rights.

Touted as the nation's "greatest single piece of legislation," the GI Bill was designed to aid all servicemen who had been on active duty at least ninety days without dishonorable discharge. It did this through four provisions: job placement assistance; a year's worth of unemployment compensation; loans to purchase homes, farms, or businesses; and educational or vocational training. Proponents framed these provisions as the "GI Bill of Rights," thus separating veterans' benefits from any taint of "welfare" and locating it rhetorically in the long American democratic tradition.

But the GI Bill followed the trajectory of earlier New Deal programs in promoting a less-than-democratic conception of U.S. social citizenship. As in the case of federal emergency relief, racial discrimination in the GI Bill was partly the result of administrative power sharing between the federal government, on the one hand, and state and local governments, on the other. According to David H. Onkst, African American veterans in Mississippi, Georgia, and Alabama struggled to access the law's provisions because of white control over local Veterans Administration (VA) and U.S. Employment Service offices and over state lending and educational institutions.[3] Steven Rosales notes that Mexican American veterans encountered similar discrimination in California and Texas.[4]

The discrimination embedded in GI benefits had much to do with state and local officials who sought to differentiate among veterans on the basis of race.[5] Yet to attribute the discriminatory features of veterans' legislation wholly to state and local influences is overly simplistic. Edward Humes points out that returning African American servicemen encountered discrimination all over the country, though nowhere as intensely as in the Deep South. He notes that General Omar Bradley, who directed the VA in its first two years, was a segregationist who later resisted President Harry Truman's order to desegregate the military.[6] Ascriptivist interpretations of veterans' benefits thus operated at the federal level, as well as state and local levels of governance.

Margot Canaday observes that the GI Bill was the first federal social policy explicitly to define social citizenship in heterosexual terms. Banned from military service in World War II, homosexuals were denied access to veterans' benefits. Those who did serve risked exposure, which often resulted in general or even dishonorable discharge. Although veterans who had received general discharges were technically eligible for GI benefits, VA officials claimed the right to determine the eligibility of soldiers granted general discharges on a case-by-case basis. This policy led many who had been discharged as homosexuals, along with African Americans who had been discharged as "troublemakers," to be denied the "democratizing" benefits of the GI Bill.[7]

Other excluded groups included the Merchant Marines, Women's Air Force Service Pilots, and, of course, the vast majority of American women who had not been soldiers during the war.[8] In terms that recall the gender provisions of the WPA, most women could access GI benefits only secondarily as the wives and daughters of eligible men. Japanese Americans, whose relationship to military service and other forms of civic sacrifice was extremely fraught during the war, were likewise underrepresented among the beneficiaries of the GI Bill.

In spite of these limitations, the GI Bill was heralded as a democratizing piece of legislation—one that transcended traditional ethnic, religious, and regional differences and facilitated ascendance to respectable middle-class status for countless veterans and their families.[9] Together with the reinstitution of universal (male) military service in 1948, the GI Bill promised to make the nation stronger, more vital, and ideally prepared the nation's future challenges.

Although many praised the GI Bill, some welfare reformers were disappointed to see that its provisions were not extended to other groups of Americans. According to their vision of civic community, all Americans should have the right to health, education, and economic security that the GI Bill provided. They regarded the law as a mere shadow of the promise that New Deal relief and recovery programs had portended.

But if liberal reformers regarded the GI Bill as a betrayal of earlier Roosevelt policies, it was also their logical outcome. The privileging of heterosexual white male soldiers and veterans that characterized the GI Bill had been implicit, at least rhetorically, in earlier programs such as the WPA and the CCC. Even during the war when relief programs were sidelined, agencies like the OCD and WRA continued to cast some white men as soldiers and others as mature breadwinning men. Not only age and gender, but race, sexuality, and class, determined where one stood in popular and official configurations of wartime civic life.

Scapegoating also had its place in gendered narratives of the reconversion period, if not explicitly in the GI Bill. Like the woman-blaming narratives of the Depression, many reconversion stories blamed service wives for their soldier-husbands' postwar difficulties. The most famous variation on this theme is perhaps William Wyler's *The Best Years of Our Lives* (MGM, 1946), in which Air Force Captain Fred Derry (Dana Andrews) returns home to find that his war bride Marie (Virginia Mayo) has begun a new, promiscuous life as a nightclub performer. Fred attempts to redomesticate Marie, even handling her roughly when she proposes using her ill-gotten war earnings to take him out on the town. Also figured as blameworthy in the film is Clarence "Sticky" Merkle (Norman Phillips Jr.), the effete drugstore clerk promoted to floor manager while Fred fought overseas. Along with Marie, Sticky embodies the feminization of the home front and thus shares responsibility for veterans' alienation from civilian life.

Predictably, neither Fred's job at the drugstore nor his marriage lasts. In one dramatic scene, Fred punches Sticky in the face and walks out of the store. Forced to spend long days looking for work, he returns one afternoon to find Marie entertaining another man. When Fred accuses her of having been unfaithful while he was at war, she makes no denial but retorts, "What were *you* up to in London and Paris and all those places, huh?" She continues, "I've given you every chance to make something of yourself.... And what have you done? You've flopped.... So I'm going back to work for myself and that means I'm going to live for myself too. And ... I'm going to get a divorce. What have you got to say to that?"

The Best Years of Our Lives, which won several Academy Awards including Best Picture in 1946, was anything but an isolated expression of postwar fears and longings. Other narratives likewise featured "faithless wives." Newspapers were filled with accounts of injured veterans who returned only to find that their wives had become adulterers and "nightclub habitués." Some courts resurrected the long-ignored letter of adultery law, imposing jail sentences and fines on adulterous service wives when they might simply have granted divorces to their husbands. "I can conceive of no greater blow to the morale of a soldier than to learn that the home he has been fighting for has been broken up thru adulterous conduct," declared William Tuohy, Illinois state's attorney.[10] Justice Matthew F. McGuire of Washington, DC, similarly promised criminal prosecution of wives who were unfaithful during their husbands' military service, stating, "There is entirely too much of this sort of thing going on." He asked, "What has happened to our old standard of morals?"[11] If the old standard had been a double one, punishing women more severely than men, the new outcry against adultery was also significantly one-sided. In *Best Years*, Marie's effort to deflect Fred's accusation of adultery by implying that he too is sexually guilty is ineffective, even though Fred's overseas sexual adventuring is evidenced earlier in the film.[12] Whereas service wives' sexual misconduct was roundly condemned and sometimes even criminalized, marriage experts counseled women to exercise forbearance with unfaithful soldier-husbands. Some courts even denied divorce petitions to service wives who presented proof of their husbands' adultery.[13]

After the breakup of his marriage to Marie, Fred finds a new job that affirms his virile masculinity and promises occupational advancement. Appropriately, Fred's new job is to salvage decommissioned bombers so that the material can be used to build postwar family housing. When Fred approaches the project foreman about a job, the man asks him, "What do you know about building?" "Not much," Fred replies, "but I can learn. Same as I learned that job up there." Fred's assertion of the veteran's desire for education and job training serves as a tacit endorsement of the GI Bill. In the logic of the film, in order to assume their proper civic roles as citizens and breadwinners, white heterosexual men like Fred both needed and deserved special opportunities for occupational and material advancement.

On the strength of his new job, Fred proposes marriage to Peggy Stephenson (Teresa Wright), the true woman of his postwar dreams. A figure for postwar domestic idealism, Peggy is only too happy to sacrifice her independence and stand by Fred "for richer, for poorer, for better, for worse." The film ends as Fred warns his tearful, smiling bride-to-be that there will be plenty of "worse" times ahead. Yet just as Americans had weathered the "worse times" of the Depression and war through a combination of federal intervention, martial fortitude, and family togetherness, those same resources would enable Americans to weather the civic challenges of an uncertain postwar world.

Further research is necessary to document the interplay between veterans' entitlements and gendered reconversion narratives, but the stark contrast between deserving veterans and undeserving women that plays out in *Best Years* and other stories of "faithless wives" clearly supported a system of social benefits that favored male veterans over civilian women. Although such gendered stories are not the *only* things that matter in understanding the course of twentieth-century U.S. civic development, neither are they merely epiphenomenal. In understanding the dynamics of national political power in the Depression and World War II, we would do well to consider not only the causality of politicians and administrators, institutions and policies, but also how those factors interacted with stories about faithless wives and Kibei troublemakers, transient wolves and wandering boys, fallen women and forgotten men.

NOTES

"More Terrible than the Sword"

1. On the history of the Bonus March, see Lucy Barber, *Marching on Washington: The Forging of an American Political Tradition* (Berkeley: University of California Press, 2002), 75–107; Roger Daniels, *The Bonus March: An Episode of the Great Depression* (Westport, CT: Greenwood, 1971); Todd DePastino, *Citizen Hobo: How a Century of Homelessness Shaped America* (Chicago: University of Chicago Press, 2003), 195–220; Paul Dickson and Thomas B. Allen, *The Bonus Army: An American Epic* (New York: Walker, 2004).

2. *BEF News*, no. 1, cited in Gardner Jackson, "Unknown Soldiers," *The Survey* 68, no. 9 (August 1, 1932): 343.

3. Floyd Gibbons, "Food for Europe, but Sabres for Vets, Gibbons Finds," *New York American*, August 1, 1932, repr. in George Kleinholz, *The Battle of Washington: A National Disgrace* (New York: B.E.F. Press, 1932), 30.

4. *New Republic* editorial, August 10, 1932, 328.

5. Ibid.

6. J. Prentice Murphy, "America on the March," *Survey Graphic* (March 1933): 150.

7. My discussion of "civic stories" builds on Rogers Smith's conception of "civic myths" and "compelling stories" of civic identity in *Civic Ideals: Conflicting Visions of Citizenship in U.S. History* (New Haven, CT: Yale University Press, 1997), 34, 497.

8. Lauren Berlant, *The Female Complaint: The Unfinished Business of Sentimentality in American Culture* (Durham, NC: Duke University Press, 2008), 3–4. Various scholars explore the role of emotions and affective experience in constituting individual and collective identities and shaping the dynamics of political power. See, e.g., Sara Ahmed, "Affective Economies," *Social Text* 22, no. 2 (2004): 117–39; Brian Massumi, "The Autonomy of Affect," *Cultural Critique* 31 (September 1995): 83–110; Eve Sedgwick, *Touching Feeling: Affect, Pedagogy, Performativity* (Durham, NC: Duke University Press, 2003); Patricia Ticineto Clough and Jean Halley, eds., *The Affective Turn: Theorizing the Social* (Durham, NC: Duke University Press, 2007).

9. William Ranulf Brock's work on the Federal Emergency Relief Administration, Neil Maher's study of the Civilian Conservation Corps, Martha Swain's analysis of the Women's Division of WPA, and Brian Masaru Hayashi's study of the War Relocation Authority are among the many institutional histories that provide indispensable models and historical insights for this work. William Ranulf Brock, *Welfare, Democracy, and the New Deal* (Cambridge: Cambridge University Press, 1988); Neil Maher, *Nature's New Deal: The Civilian Conservation Corps and the Roots of the American Environmental Movement* (New York: Oxford University Press, 2008);

Martha H. Swain, *Ellen S. Woodward: New Deal Advocate for Women* (Jackson: University Press of Mississippi, 1995); Brian Masaru Hayashi, *Democratizing the Enemy: The Japanese American Internment* (Princeton, NJ: Princeton University Press, 2004).

Nayan Shah, "Policing Privacy, Migrants and the Limits of Freedom" *Social Text* 23, nos. 3–4 (Fall–Winter 2005), 275–84; Nayan Shah, *Stranger Intimacy: Contesting Race, Sexuality and the Law in the North American West*, American Crossroads Series (Berkeley: University of California Press, 2011); George Chauncey, *Gay New York: Gender, Urban Culture, and the Making of the Gay Male World, 1890–1940* (New York: Basic Books, 1995).

10. Eve Sedgwick, *Between Men: English Literature and Male Homosocial Desire* (New York: Columbia University Press, 1985), 7.

11. On working-class bachelor subculture, see George Chauncey, *Gay New York*. On transients and homosexuality, see Peter Boag, *Same-Sex Affairs: Constructing and Controlling Homosexuality in the Pacific Northwest* (Berkeley: University of California Press, 2003); Nayan Shah, "Policing Privacy, Migrants, and the Limits of Freedom," *Social Text* 23, nos. 3–4 (Fall–Winter 2005): 279–81. See also Jennifer Terry, *An American Obsession: Science, Medicine, and Homosexuality in Modern Society* (Chicago: University of Chicago Press, 1999).

12. For the concept of "sex panic," I am indebted to Janice Irvine, "Transient Feelings: Sex Panics and the Politics of Emotions," *GLQ: A Journal of Lesbian and Gay Studies* 14, no. 1 (2008): 1–40.

13. Two exceptions are Maher, *Nature's New Deal*, and Margot Canaday, *The Straight State: Sexuality and Citizenship in Twentieth-Century America* (Princeton, NJ: Princeton University Press, 2009).

14. Canaday, *Straight State*, 91–173.

15. Anthony Badger, "How Did the New Deal Change the South?," *New Deal/New South: An Anthony J. Badger Reader* (Fayetteville: University of Arkansas Press, 2007), 31–44; Patricia Sullivan, *Days of Hope: Race and Democracy in the New Deal Era* (Chapel Hill: University of North Carolina Press, 1996); Lauren Rebecca Sklaroff, *Black Culture and the New Deal: The Quest for Civil Rights in the Roosevelt Era* (Chapel Hill: University of North Carolina Press, 2009).

16. Cybelle Fox, *Three Worlds of Relief: Race, Immigration, and the American Welfare State from the Progressive Era to the New Deal* (Princeton, NJ: Princeton University Press, 2012).

17. Luis Alvarez, *The Power of the Zoot: Youth Culture and Resistance during World War II* (Berkeley: University of California Press, 2009); Kevin Allen Leonard, *The Battle for Los Angeles: Racial Ideology and World War II* (Albuquerque: University of New Mexico Press, 2006); Hayashi, *Democratizing the Enemy*; Eric L. Muller, *American Inquisition: The Hunt for Japanese-American Disloyalty in World War II* (Chapel Hill: University of North Carolina Press, 2007); Alice Yang Murray, *Historical Memories of the Japanese American Internment and the Struggle for Redress* (Stanford, CA: Stanford University Press, 2008).

18. T. H. Marshall, *Citizenship and Social Class and Other Essays* (Cambridge: Cambridge University Press, 1950); Nancy Fraser and Linda Gordon, "Contract versus Charity: Why Is There No Social Citizenship in the United States?," *Socialist Review* 22 (1992): 45–65.

19. Linda K. Kerber, *No Constitutional Right to Be Ladies: Women and the Obligations of Citizenship* (New York: Hill & Wang, 1999); Robert Westbrook, *Why We*

Fought: Forging American Obligations in World War II (Washington, DC: Smithsonian Books, 2010).

20. Benjamin Barber, "The Compromised Republic," in *American Social and Political Thought: A Reader*, ed. Andreas Hess (New York: New York University Press, 2003), 141–48; Sheldon S. Wolin, "Democracy without the Citizen," in Hess, *American Social and Political Thought*, 149–54; Adrian Oldfield, "Citizenship and Community: Civic Republicanism and the Modern World," in *The Citizenship Debates: A Reader*, ed. Gershon Shafir (Minneapolis: University of Minnesota Press, 1998), 75–89.

21. See Smith, *Civic Ideals*; Suzanne Mettler, *Dividing Citizens: Gender and Federalism in New Deal Public Policy* (Ithaca, NY: Cornell University Press, 1998); Canaday, *Straight State*.

22. Smith, *Civic Ideals*, 508.

23. Mettler, *Dividing Citizens*, 1–27.

24. Lauren Berlant and Michael Warner note that "the family form has functioned as a mediator and metaphor of national existence in the United States since the eighteenth century." See Lauren Berlant and Michael Warner, "Sex in Public," *Critical Inquiry* 24, no. 2 (Winter 1998): 549–50.

25. Etienne Balibar, "The Nation–Form: History and Ideology," in *Race, Nation, Class: Ambiguous Identities*, ed. Etienne Balibar and Immanuel Wallerstein (New York: Verso Press, 1988), 100, 102.

26. War Relocation Authority Meeting, verbatim transcript of proceedings, July 23, 1942, Records of the WRA, Washington Office Records, Documentary Headquarters Files, Meetings and Conferences, 1942–43, R.G. 210, U.S. National Archives and Records Administration, Washington, DC (hereafter National Archives).

27. Sara Ahmed, "Affective Economies," *Social Text* 22, no. 2 (2004): 118.

28. Michael Foucault, *The History of Sexuality* (New York: Pantheon Books, 1978), 48, 45.

1. The War to Save the Forgotten Man

1. Franklin Delano Roosevelt, radio address, April 7, 1932, Albany, NY, repr. in *The Public Papers and Addresses of Franklin D. Roosevelt*, ed. Samuel Rosenman, vol. 1, 1928–32 (New York: Random House, 1938), 624.

2. Mike Davis suggests that New Deal relief policy, along with its more general support for workers' rights, "reinforced and extended the hegemony of the political system," in *Prisoners of the American Dream: Politics and Economy in the History of the U.S. Working Class* (New York: Verso, 1986), 5.

3. Lauren Berlant argues that genres play an important role in constituting "affective" publics in *The Female Complaint: The Unfinished Business of Sentimentality in American Culture* (Durham, NC: Duke University Press, 2008), 3–4. Also pertinent is Rogers Smith's formulation of "civic myths" and "stories of civic identity" in *Civic Ideals: Conflicting Visions of Citizenship in U.S. History* (New Haven, CT: Yale University Press, 1997), 13–39.

4. In addition to the print narratives studied in this work, forgotten-man symbolism pervaded other cultural texts during the Great Depression, including fiction by John Steinbeck, Albert Malts, and Edward Anderson; films by Busby Berkeley, Alfred E. Green, and Frank Capra; and music by "Yip" Harburg and Woody Guthrie, among others.

5. Examples include Copley Clarke, *The New Deal for the Forgotten Man* (New York: Barnes, 1933); Jewell Bothwell Tull, *The Forgotten Man: A Drama in One Act* (Chicago: Dramatic, 1934); Ernest G. Shinner, *The Forgotten Man* (Chicago: Patterson, 1933); James H. Guilfoyle, *On the Trail of the Forgotten Man; A Journal of the Roosevelt Presidential Campaign* (Boston: Peabody Master, 1933); Claudius J. Gregory, *Forgotten Men* (Hamilton, ON, CAN: Davis-Lisson, 1933).

6. "The Forgotten Man," *Saturday Evening Post*, February 24, 1934, 22.

7. Julian Aronson, "The 'Forgotten Man' of Yesterday," *Scholastic* 24 (February 3, 1934): 15–16.

8. Pauline Young, "The New Poor," *Sociology and Social Research* 17 (1933): 242.

9. Other sociological works that examine the effects of unemployment on men's broader social roles include the following: Mirra Kamarovsky, *The Unemployed Man and His Family: The Effect of Unemployment upon the Status of the Man in Fifty-Nine Families* (New York: Dryden Press/Institute of Social Research, 1940); James M. Reinhardt and George R. Boardman, "Insecurity and Personality Disintegration," *Social Forces* 14, no. 2 (1935): 240–49; E. Wight Bakke, *The Unemployed Worker: A Study of the Task of Making a Living without a Job* (New Haven, CT: Yale University Press, 1940); E. Wight Bakke, *Citizens without Work: A Study of the Effects of Unemployment upon the Workers' Social Relations and Practices* (New Haven, CT: Yale University Press, 1940).

10. Tom Jones Parry, "We Americans I—Fred Salo, the Forgotten Man," *Forum* (December 1932): 330.

11. Ibid., 331.

12. Nels Francis Nordstrom, "Cinder Snappers," *Survey Graphic* 22 no. 7 (July 1933), 363.

13. Anonymous, "From the Forgotten Man," letter to the editor, *New York Times*, July 31, 1935; Whiting Williams, "But You Can't Let People Starve," *The Survey* 47, no. 9 (February 1, 1932): 460.

14. Franklin D. Roosevelt, "Three Essentials for Unemployment Relief" (March 21, 1933), in *The Public Papers and Addresses of Franklin D. Roosevelt*, ed. Samuel D. Rosenman, vol. 2 (New York: Random House, 1938), 80–81.

15. William R. Brock, *Welfare, Democracy, and the New Deal* (New York: Cambridge University Press, 1988).

16. Walter White, secretary of the National Association for the Advancement of Colored People, to Harry Hopkins, director, FERA (telegram), November 23, 1934; Lawrence A. Oxley, chief, Division of Negro Labor, U.S. Department of Labor, to Jacob Baker, assistant administrator, FERA, September 6, 1934; Records of the WPA, FERA, Old Subject File, Interracial Miscellaneous Correspondence, R.G. 69, National Archives.

17. Forrester Washington to Harry Hopkins, July 30, 1934, Records of the WPA, FERA, Old Subject File, Interracial Miscellaneous Correspondence, R.G. 69, National Archives. See also "No 'Yes Man' Is Forrester B. Washington—Resigns from FERA Rather than Be Puppet in Administration," *Call*, August 10, 1934.

18. Walter White to Eleanor Roosevelt, November 8, 1934, Records of the WPA, FERA, Old Subject File, Interracial Miscellaneous Correspondence, R.G. 69, National Archives.

19. Aubrey Williams, "The Problem of Unemployment" (speech), January 16, 1935, Harry Hopkins Papers, box 13, Franklin Delano Roosevelt Library, Hyde Park, NY (hereafter FDRL).

20. Harold Ickes, "The Social Implications of the Roosevelt Administration," *Survey Graphic* 23, no. 3 (March 1934): 111.

21. Bakke, *Citizens without Work*, 397. See also Bakke, *The Unemployed Man: A Social Study* (New York: Dutton, 1934).

22. Gertrude Springer discusses the pantry-snooper in "What Price the Power of the Food Order?" *The Survey* 69, no. 5 (May 1933): 182–83. On the gender composition of the social work community and its place within the relief apparatus of the New Deal, see Linda Gordon, "Social Insurance and Public Assistance: The Influence of Gender in Welfare Thought in the United States, 1890–1935," *American Historical Review* 97, no. 1 (1992): 19–54.

23. Daniel J. Walkowitz, *Working with Class: Social Workers and the Politics of Middle-Class Identity* (Chapel Hill: University of North Carolina Press, 1999); Linda Gordon, *Pitied but Not Entitled: Single Mothers and the History of Welfare, 1890–1935* (New York: Free Press, 1994), 67–110.

24. Marie Dresden Lane and Francis Steegmuller, *America on Relief* (New York: Harcourt, Brace, 1938), 20.

25. Harry Hopkins in Brock, *Welfare, Democracy, and the New Deal*, 263.

26. *Hearings on First Deficiency Appropriations Bill,* House Appropriations Comm., 74th Cong., 1st Sess. (1936) (statement of Harry Hopkins, FERA administrator).

27. Franklin Roosevelt, "Unemployment Must Be Faced on More than One Front," White House Statement on a Plan for Relief, February 28, 1934, *The Public Papers and Addresses of Franklin D. Roosevelt*, ed. Samuel D. Rosenman, vol. 3 (New York: Random House, 1938), 108–12.

28. Harry Hopkins, radio address on the National Radio Forum, October 11, 1933, Harry Hopkins Papers, box 9, FDRL, paraphrased in George McJimsey, *Harry Hopkins: Ally of the Poor and Defender of Democracy* (Cambridge, MA: Harvard University Press, 1987), 58.

29. Bonnie Fox Schwartz, *The Civil Works Administration: The Business of Emergency Employment in the New Deal* (Princeton, NJ: Princeton University Press, 1984).

30. Harry Hopkins, speech to general meeting of the CWA, November 15, 1933, box 9, Harry Hopkins Papers, FDRL.

31. Franklin Roosevelt, "Remarks on Signing Executive Order Creating Civil Works Administration," November 8, 1933. Online by Gerhard Peters and John T. Woolley, *The American Presidency Project*. http://www.presidency.ucsb.edu/ws/?pid=14547.

32. Harry Hopkins, *Spending to Save: The Complete Story of Relief* (New York: Norton, 1936), 120.

33. Harold Ickes, "The Social Implications of the Roosevelt Administration," *Survey Graphic* 23, no. 3 (March 1934): 111.

34. Ibid.

35. Harry Hopkins, remarks to FERA Emergency Conference on Needs of Women, November 20, 1933, *Proceedings of Conference on Emergency Needs of Women*, FERA Old Subject File, R.G. 69, National Archives.

36. On unemployed women's relationship to the Civil Works Administration, see Martha Swain, *Ellen S. Woodward: New Deal Advocate for Women* (Jackson: University Press of Mississippi, 1995), 45–49.

37. William Zimmerman Jr., liaison officer, Interior Department, to Harry Hopkins, director, CWA, December 8, 1933, and related correspondence, Records of the WPA: WPA, CWA, Administrative Correspondence, Interracial Miscellaneous Correspondence, 1933–34, R.G. 69, National Archives. On Mexican Americans and CWA, see Cybelle Fox, *Three Worlds of Relief: Race, Immigration, and the Welfare State from the Progressive Era to the New Deal* (Princeton, NJ: University of Princeton Press, 2012), 210–12.

38. Russell H. Kurtz, "An End to Civil Works," *The Survey* 70, no. 2 (February 1934): 35.

39. See, e.g., "Demobilizing the CWA," *Washington Post*, February 18, 1934, B6; "CWA Rally Overflows: Committee Named to Protest against Cutting of Funds," *New York Times*, March 13, 1934, 3; "Thomas Warns on CWA: Foresees Serious Trouble and a Fascist Trend if It Is Ended," *New York Times*, March 2, 1934, 3.

40. On the reasons for the end of CWA, see Kurtz, "An End to Civil Works."

41. Elizabeth Frazer, "Bill Meade: Brass-Tag Man: A Story of Emergency Relief," *Saturday Evening Post*, March 10, 1934, 31.

42. Ibid.

43. Ibid., 74.

44. Ibid., 78.

45. Ibid., 81.

46. Ibid., 81.

47. See, e.g., Martha Gellhorn, *The Trouble I've Seen* (New York: Morrow, 1936), 177–78; "They'd Rather Work," *Nation* 144, no. 3657 (August 7, 1935): 144; Gertrude Springer, "Men Must Work," *The Survey* 70, no. 11 (November 1934): 344; Reinhardt and Boardman, "Insecurity and Personality Disintegration," 240–49; Ernest Groves, "Adaptations of Family Life," *American Journal of Sociology* 40 (May 1935): 772; Anonymous, "This Strange New World," *Saturday Evening Post*, July 21, 1934, 72.

48. See Springer, "What Price the Power of the Food Order?," 182–83; Gordon, "Social Insurance and Public Assistance," 19–54.

49. Kurtz, "An End to Civil Works," 35.

50. Winthrop Thornton, "The Danger Point in Giving," *Saturday Evening Post*, May 19, 1934, 26.

51. Ibid.

52. Jeff Singleton, *The American Dole: Unemployment and the Welfare State in the Great Depression* (Westport, CT: Greenwood Publishing Group, 2000), 144.

53. Jessie O. Thomas, "Negro Relief Racket," *Atlanta Daily World*, August 3, 1934, 1.

54. Lorena Hickok in Fox, *Three Worlds of Relief*, 195. See also "Low Wage Scale of U.S. Industry Scored by F.D.R.," *Atlanta Constitution*, August 12, 1936, 1.

55. Bullard's remarks are excerpted in "They'd Rather Live on Relief," *Nation* 141, no. 3657 (August 7, 1935): 144.

56. Margaret Culkin Banning, "Two Billions More," *Saturday Evening Post*, August 11, 1934, 83.

57. Ibid.

58. Brock, *Welfare, Democracy, and the New Deal*, 260.

59. Ibid.

60. Many welfare professionals resisted the WPA because it returned a large segment of the relief population to traditional relief. See Russell H. Kurtz, "No More Federal Relief?," *The Survey* 71, no. 2 (February 1935): 35–37; Gertrude Springer, "Nothing Short of the Nation," *The Survey* 69, no. 3 (March 1933): 67–68; "The AASW Platform," *The Survey* 69, no. 3 (March 1933): 69.

61. Harry Hopkins, "Basic Philosophy Underlying WPA Policies," June 12, 1936, Records of the WPA, General Files, R.G. 69, National Archives.

62. Paul W. Ward comments on administrators' preoccupation with regulating WPA publicity in "Face-Saving in WPA," *Nation* 142, no. 3680 (May 6, 1936): 61.

63. Franklin Roosevelt, Annual Message to Congress, 1935, Rosenman, *Public Papers*, 4: 22; Franklin Roosevelt, "Unemployment Must Be Faced on More than One Front," White House statement on a Plan for Relief, February 28, 1934, Rosenman, Public Papers, 3: 108.

64. Ellen Sullivan Woodward, speech before the Conference of Southeastern Democratic Women, March 19, 1936. R.G. 69, National Archives, Series 737, box 8.

65. Harry Hopkins, "What Is the 'American Way'?" (Washington, DC: Works Projects Administration, 1938). The text is a speech that Hopkins delivered at the Chautauqua Institution, Chautauqua, NY, July 16, 1938.

66. Harry Hopkins, "Federal Emergency Relief," *Vital Speeches of the Day* 1 (December 31, 1934), 210–12. December 31, 1934, in *Vital Speeches of the Day*, 210–12.

67. Harry Hopkins, *Spending to Save*, 168–69.

68. Ibid., 173, 169.

69. Ibid., 178.

70. See also the summary of testimony by WPA administrator Harry L. Hopkins before the subcommittee of the House Committee on Appropriations in charge of deficiency appropriations, April 8, 1936, 74th Cong., 2nd Sess., S. Doc. 226, serial set vol. no. 10016, sess. vol. no. 18.

71. U.S. Works Progress Administration, *Our Job with the W.P.A.* (Washington, DC: U.S. Government Printing Office, 1936).

72. Ibid., 20.

73. Ibid., 26.

74. Ibid., 21.

75. William E. Leuchtenberg, *The FDR Years: On Roosevelt and His Legacy* (New York: Columbia University Press, 1995), 209–35.

76. Roosevelt, "Unemployment Must Be Faced on More than One Front."

77. McJimsey, *Harry Hopkins*, 270.

78. Harry Hopkins in Brock, *Welfare, Democracy, and the New Deal*, 280.

79. Charles F. Ernst, "We Demand . . . ," *The Survey* 73, no. 2 (February 1937): 35.

80. Alfred Edgar Smith, *Interesting Facts about the Negro and the W.P.A.*, 1936, 9, Records of the WPA, Primary File 983 (Negroes Benefited by WPA, 1936–42), R.G. 69, National Archives.

81. Lois Scharf, *To Work and to Wed: Female Employment, Feminism, and the Great Depression* (Westport, CT: Greenwood, 1980), 38.

82. Ibid., 66–109; Martha H. Swain, *Ellen S. Woodward: New Deal Advocate for Women* (Jackson: University Press of Mississippi, 1995), 38–103.

83. Donald S. Howard, *The WPA and Federal Relief Policy* (New York: Russell Sage Foundation, 1943), 279.

84. Ibid.

85. Mary Simkhovitch in Lorena A. Hickok, *One Third of a Nation: Lorena Hickok Reports on the Great Depression* (Urbana: University of Illinois Press, 1983), 49.

86. Pearl Lindner of 35 Glenwood Ave., Buffalo, NY, to Eleanor Roosevelt, n.d., Records of the WPA, Women's Division Files, R.G. 69, National Archives.

87. George Wycherley Kirkman to Eleanor Roosevelt, June 17, 1933, Records of the WPA, Women's Division Files, R.G. 69, National Archives.

88. Leslie Fishel Jr., "The Negro in the New Deal Era," in *America's Black Past*, ed. Eric Foner (New York: Harper & Row, 1970); see also Harvard Sitkoff, *A New Deal for Blacks* (New York: Oxford University Press, 1978); T. H. Watkins, *The Great Depression* (Boston: Little, Brown, 1993).

89. Clark Forman, "What Hope for the Rural Negro?," *Opportunity, Journal of Negro Life* (April 1934): 105. Also see Forman's correspondence as adviser to Harry Hopkins on the Economic Status of Negroes, R.G. 69, P.C. 37, entry 2, box 31, National Archives; Alfred E. Smith, 1935 Report-Summary, "Negro Clients of Federal Unemployment Relief," Records of the WPA, December 31, 1935, R.G. 69, P.C. 37, entry 9, box 31, National Archives.

90. Anonymous, "This Strange New World," *Saturday Evening Post*, July 21, 1934, 72.

91. An unnamed segregationist, quoted in Jesse O. Thomas, "Will the New Deal Be a Square Deal for the Negro?," *Opportunity, Journal of Negro Life* (October 1933): 308.

92. Ibid., 308.

93. "Refusal to Work Jails Bibb Negro," *Atlanta Constitution*, June 10, 1937, 1.

94. An unnamed African American, quoted in "Bare Exploitation Dixie under CWA, PWA: Treatment in South Is Bared," *Atlanta Daily World*, February 14, 1934, 1, 3.

95. U.S. Works Progress Administration, Division of Social Research, *The Negro on Relief* (Washington, DC: U.S. Government Printing Office, 1938), 2.

96. "Roosevelt Says He'll Stick by 'Forgotten Man'; FDR Assures Negroes of Interest; Asserts There Should Be No Such Thing As 'Forgotten Man,'" *Atlanta Daily World*, October 27, 1936, 1.

97. "Roosevelt's The Man," *Atlanta Daily World*, October 29, 1936, 6.

98. *Negro Press Digest*, October 17, 1936, 9.

99. *Negro Press Digest*, August 1936, 5.

100. Anthony Badger, "How Did the New Deal Change the South?," in *New Deal/New South: An Anthony Badger Reader* (Fayetteville: University of Arkansas Press, 2007), 38.

101. Smith, *Interesting Facts about the Negro*, 15.

102. James A. Ross, "What WPA Means to the Negro Worker in New York State," in Alfred E. Smith, *WPA and the Negro* (Washington, DC: U.S. Government Printing Office, n.d.), 1.

103. G. Victor Cools, "Negro Job Relief and the WPA," in Smith, *WPA and the Negro*, 5.

104. *The Rural Negro on the Works Program*, n.d., 2, Records of the WPA, Division of Information, Primary File 983 (Negroes Benefited by W.P.A., 1936–1942), R.G. 69, National Archives.

105. *The Negro and the WPA*, n.d., 14–15, Records of the WPA, Division of Information, Primary File 983 (Negroes Benefited by W.P.A., 1936–1942), R.G. 69, National Archives.

106. "Will the Senate Act?," *Chicago Defender* (national edition), March 16, 1935, 14.

107. "Report of resolutions committee, 27th annual conference NAACP," *The Chicago Defender*, July 11, 1936, 10. See also "New Deal Love Has Limits," *The Chicago Defender*, July 11, 1936, 16.

108. *Amsterdam News*, October 17, 1936, cited in Negro Press Digest, 1936, 9. R.G. 69: W.P.A. Division of Information, Negro Press Digest, 1936–1942.

109. John Robert Moore, "Senator Josiah W. Bailey and the 'Conservative Manifesto' of 1937," *Journal of Southern History* 31, no. 1 (February 1965): 21–39.

110. Michael K. Brown, *Race, Money, and the American Welfare State* (Ithaca, NY: Cornell University Press, 1999), 42–43.

111. David Garland, "Penal Excess and Surplus Meaning: Public Torture Lynchings in 20th Century America," in *Law & Society Review* 39 (December 2005): 793–834. See also Stewart Emory Tolnay and E. M. Beck, *A Festival of Violence: An Analysis of Southern Lynchings, 1882–1930* (Champaign: University of Illinois Press, 1995).

112. Trudier Harris, *Exorcising Blackness: Historical and Literary Lynching and Burning Rituals* (Bloomington: Indiana University Press, 1984).

113. "NAACP Sends Protest on Fla. Wage Slavery: Relief Work for Race Is Urged," *Pittsburgh Courier*, December 30, 1933, A2.

114. Thomas H. Reed and Doris D. Reed, "The Republican Opposition," *Survey Graphic* 29, no. 5 (May 1940).

115. Wendell Willkie, quoted in the *New York Times*, October 17, 1940, cited in Howard, *WPA and Federal Relief Policy*, 711. Former President Herbert Hoover claimed credit for the advent of federal relief, stating that in 1930, he "announced the formation of a national organization for unemployment relief"; *Congressional Record*, June 27, 1939, cited in Howard, 712.

116. Robert Staughton Lynd and Helen Merrell Lynd, *Middletown in Transition: A Study in Cultural Conflicts* (New York: Harcourt, 1937). See also "Middletown—Ten Years After," *Business Week*, June 9, 1935, 12.

117. Smith, *Civic Ideals*; Suzanne Mettler, *Dividing Citizens: Gender and Federalism in New Deal Social Policy* (Ithaca, NY: Cornell University Press, 1998).

2. "Uncle Sam's Wayside Inns"

1. Joseph C. Leyendecker, "Southbound Hitchhiker," *Saturday Evening Post*, October 19, 1935. Frank Tobias Higbie notes that "observers of many political orientations considered laborers 'birds of passage,' migrating from place to place." Higbie, *Indispensable Outcasts: Hobo Workers and Community in the American Midwest, 1880–1930* (Urbana: University of Illinois Press, 2003), 208.

2. See J. C. Leyendecker, "Football Hero," *Saturday Evening Post*, November 3, 1933.

3. Nels Anderson wrote, "The prevalence of homosexual relations was so "generally assumed to be true among hoboes that whenever a man travels around with a lad he is apt to be labeled a 'jocker' or a 'wolf' and the road kid is called his 'punk,' 'preshun,' or 'lamb.'" Dean Stiff [pseudonym of Nels Anderson], *The Milk and Honey Route: A Handbook for Hobos* (New York: Vanguard Press, 1931), 161, cited in George Chauncey, *Gay New York* (New York: Basic Books, 1994), 90.

4. A. Wayne McMillen, "An Army of Boys on the Loose," *The Survey* 38 (September 1932): 389–92; "Boys on the Loose," *Survey Graphic* 69 (February 1933): 71.

5. Rufus Steele, "Homeless Boys Roam the Road," *Christian Science Monitor*, August 18, 1932, 1.

6. "American's Juvenile Hoboes," *New York Times*, September 22, 1932, 14.

7. Towne Nylander, "Wandering Youth," *Sociology and Social Research* 18 (1934): 563.

8. Gertrude Springer, "Step-Children of Relief," *Survey Graphic* 69 (June 1933): 212–13; Benjamin F. Culver, "Transient Unemployed Men," *Sociology and Social Research* 17 (August 1933): 532.

9. Barbara Meil Hobson, *Uneasy Virtue: The Politics of Prostitution and the American Reform Tradition* (New York: Basic Books, 1987); on the longer history of the American hobo, see Higbie, *Indispensable Outcasts*; Todd dePastino, *Citizen Hobo: How a Century of Homelessness Shaped America* (Chicago: University of Chicago Press, 2003); Tim Cresswell, *The Tramp in America* (London: Reaktion, 2001); Kenneth Kusmer, *Down and Out and On the Road: The Homeless in American History* (New York: Oxford University Press, 2002). On the sexual dimensions of hobo life, see also Chauncey, *Gay New York*; Peter Boag, *Same-Sex Affairs: Constructing and Controlling Homosexuality in the Pacific Northwest* (Berkeley: University of California Press, 2003).

10. Stuart Hall, Charles Critcher, Tony Jefferson, John Clarke, and Brian Roberts, *Policing the Crisis: Mugging, the State, and Law and Order* (New York: Hall and Meier, 1978); Stanley Cohen, *Folk Devils and Moral Panics: The Creation of the Mods and Rockers* (New York: St. Martin's Press, 1980); Philip Jenkins, *Moral Panic: Changing Concepts of the Child Molester in Modern America* (New Haven, CT: Yale University Press, 1998); Janice Irvine, "Transient Feelings: Sex Panics and the Politics of Emotions," *GLQ: A Journal of Lesbian and Gay Studies* 14, no. 1 (2008): 1–40.

11. Irvine, "Transient Feelings," 10, 11, 6.

12. Chauncey, *Gay New York*, 79; Kusmer, *Down and Out*, 217; Cresswell, *Tramp in America*, 94–95.

13. Nels Anderson, *The Hobo* (Chicago: University of Chicago Press, 1925), 17, cited in Cresswell, *Tramp in America*, 43. See also Theodore Caplow, "Transiency as a Cultural Pattern," *American Sociological Review* 5, no. 5 (October 1940) 737. On the interracial features of transient life, see Nayan Shah, "Policing Privacy, Migrants, and the Limits of Freedom," *Social Text* 23, nos. 3–4 (Fall–Winter 2005): 279–81. See also Nayan Shah, *Stranger Intimacy: Contesting Race, Sexuality and the Law in the North American West* (Berkeley: University of California Press, 2011).

14. Higbie, *Indispensable Outcasts*, 176.

15. Margot Canaday, *The Straight State: Sexuality and Citizenship in Twentieth-Century America* (Princeton, NJ: University of Princeton Press, 2011), 15.

16. Ibid., 93–94.

17. Ellen C. Potter, NJ State Department of Institutions and Agencies, "Mustering Out the Migrants," *The Survey* (December 1933): 411.

18. A. Wayne McMillen, "An Army of Boys on the Loose," *Survey Graphic* 68, no. 11 (September 1932): 389.

19. Ibid., 392.

20. Thomas Minehan, *Boy and Girl Tramps of America* (New York: Farrar & Rinehart, 1934), 240.

21. McMillen, "Army of Boys on the Loose," 392; Anderson, *The Hobo*.

22. Minehan, *Boy and Girl Tramps*, 142.

23. Ibid., 141–42.

24. Ibid., 143.

25. Nels Anderson wrote, "To write of the transient problem as though it relates entirely to juveniles is to break faith with the scientific spirit to which Professor Minehan presumably owes allegiance." Anderson, "On the Road," *The Survey* (January 1935): 26–27.

26. Towne Nylander, "Wandering Youth," *Sociology and Social Research* 17 (1932): 563.

27. Ibid.

28. Report of the Committee on Migrant Boys, Department of Delinquency and Its Prevention, St. Louis Community Council, September 20, 1933, Records of the WPA, FERA, Transient Division, 1933–36, Memoranda, Miscellaneous Reports, R.G. 69, P.C. 37, entry 16, box 29, National Archives.

29. John N. Webb, *The Transient Unemployed* (Washington, DC: U.S. Government Printing Office, 1935), 12.

30. Ibid., 32.

31. The Civilian Conservation Corps is the subject of chapter 3.

32. Joan Crouse, *The Homeless Transient in the Great Depression: New York State, 1929–1941* (Albany: State University Press of New York, 1986).

33. Ellery F. Reed, *Federal Transient Program: An Evaluative Survey, May to June, 1934* (New York, Committee on Care of Transient and Homeless, 1934), 32–33. See also Clarence M. Bookman, "The Federal Transient Program," *The Survey*, April 1935, 104–5.

34. FERA Press Release, June 6, 1935, Federal Relief Agency Papers, Harry Hopkins Papers, Franklin Delano Roosevelt Library.

35. Fort Eustis, a large transient camp in Virginia, divided the men into age-differentiated "companies." See Jack Burgess, "New Souls for Old at Eustis Transient Camp," *Richmond Times-Dispatch*, January 13, 1935.

36. Nels Anderson was critical of the FTP's preoccupation with transient youth, who were less than 10 percent of the transient population and likelier to find work when conditions improved. He wrote, "The real problem is not the boys, but the aging men. . . . [T]he boys will get work. . . . The older men won't." Anderson, "Forgotten—and Scrapped," *New Republic*, June 21, 1933, 141–42.

37. George E. Outland, "The Federal Transient Program for Boys in Southern California," *Social Forces* 14, no. 3 (March 1936): 428. Outland quotes Anderson's statement that "the boy does not need to remain long in hobo society to learn homosexual practices." Anderson, *The Hobo*, 144–45.

38. Ellen Potter, "Mustering Out the Migrants," *The Survey* (December 1933): 411–12. See also Harry Hopkins, "The Federal Relief Job," *The Survey* (July 1933): 247.

39. John N. Webb, *Depression Pioneers* (Washington, DC: U.S. Government Printing Office, 1939), 4. See also Bookman, "Federal Transient Program," 104–5.

40. Potter, "Mustering Out the Migrants," 412.

41. Ellen C. Potter, "The Problem of the Transient," *Annals of the American Academy of Political and Social Science* 176 (November 1934): 66–73.

42. Katie Louchheim and Frank Freidel, eds. *The Making of the New Deal: The Insiders Speak* (Cambridge, MA: Harvard University Press, 1983), 176–94.

43. Ibid., 238.

44. William J. Plunkert, "Public Responsibility for Transients: The Transient Program," *Social Service Review* 8 (1934), 484.

45. An FTP circular, December 20, 1934, cited in Doris Carothers, *Chronology of the Federal Emergency Relief Administration, May 12, 1933 to December 31, 1935* (Washington, DC: U.S. Government Printing Office, 1937), 69.

46. Potter, "Problem of the Transient," 72.

47. Gertrude Springer, "Men Off the Road," *Survey Graphic* 23 (September 1934): 421.

48. Webb, *Depression Pioneers*, 60.

49. Introduction to the Federal Transient Program Report, December 1934, Records of the WPA, FERA, Transient Division, Narrative reports and correspondence, R.G. 69, P.C. 37, entry 16, box 31, National Archives.

50. Plunkert, "Federal Responsibility for Transients: The Transient Program," 484.

51. Kusmer, *Down and Out*, 215–16.

52. Ben Reitman in Cresswell, *Tramp in America*, 97.

53. Helen S. Hawkins, *A New Deal for the Newcomer: The Federal Transient Service* (New York: Garland, 1991), 178–79.

54. Ibid., 204–5.

55. Webb, *Depression Pioneers*, 31; Hawkins, *New Deal for the Newcomer*, 209.

56. Elizabeth Wickenden, "Transiency: Mobility in Trouble," *Survey Graphic* 73 (October 1937): 362.

57. Herbert C. Jenkins, "The Negro Transient," *Opportunity: Journal of Negro Life* (January 1935). Transient relief was considerably less remunerative and more punitive than other, more privileged forms of federal emergency relief. See J. O. Reade, "Back to Panhandling," *New Republic*, October 9, 1935, 237–38.

58. Evelyn Harvey, "The Unbudgeted Cost of Relief," *Saturday Evening Post*, February 16, 1935, 60.

59. Ernest Groves, "Adaptations of Family Life," *American Journal of Sociology* 40, no. 6 (May 1935): 779.

60. Reade, "Back to Panhandling," 238.

61. Harvey, "Unbudgeted Cost of Relief," 38. Reade noted that "unquestionably the transient service has been taken by some as an invitation to tour the country." Reade, "Back to Panhandling," 238.

62. Wayne W. Parrish, "Federal Camps Tackle Problem of Transients," *Literary Digest*, July 7, 1934, 34.

63. Harvey, "Unbudgeted Cost of Relief," 60.

64. Boyden Sparkes, "A New Deal for Transients," *Saturday Evening Post*, October 19, 1935, 92, 90.

65. Ibid., 92.

66. "Ruin in the Veterans' Camps," newspaper clipping, Records of the WPA, FERA, Transient Division, 1933–36, Memoranda, Miscellaneous Reports, R.G. 69, P.C. 37, entry 16, box 29, National Archives.

67. Sparkes, "New Deal for Transients," 94.

68. Joseph Cartier, client no. 7834, South Schenectady, NY, Records of the WPA, FERA State Series, New York, Complaints, box 421, National Archives.

69. Ibid. Cartier's letter was sufficiently alarming to state Transient Division authorities that they investigated his allegations further. They concluded that he was citing rumors, not facts.

70. Howard Thomas, Syracuse Transient Center, to Charles Alspach, 1935, Records of the WPA, FERA, Transient Division, 1933–36, Memoranda, Miscellaneous Reports, R.G. 69, P.C. 37, entry 16, box 29, National Archives.

71. Harry Hopkins, Letter to all State Relief Administrators, February 7, 1935, Records of the WPA, Records of the FERA, Records of the Transient Division, 1933–36, Memoranda, Miscellaneous Reports, R.G. 69, P.C. 37, entry 16, box 29, National Archives. See also FERA Memorandum on Relief to Transients and Homeless, July 26, 1933, cited in Carothers, *Chronology of the Federal Emergency Relief Administration*, 14: "Shelter care of good quality for unattached males implies that . . . that there shall be proper segregation of the men according to age, etc." See also "Transient Camps Improved," *The Survey* (April 1935), 120.

72. Harry H. Hopkins, *Spending to Save* (New York: Norton, 1936), 134.

73. Franklin Roosevelt to Wilbur Cross, response to telegram, March 19, 1936, Records of the FERA, Records of the Transient Division, 1933–36, Memoranda, Miscellaneous Reports, R.G. 69, P.C. 37, entry 16, box 29, National Archives.

74. Hopkins, *Spending to Save*, 138. One transient complained about the difficulty of obtaining employment after the closure of the transient camps. He stated, "Why, they won't even give us a job if they know we are from the transient bureau— they think we are a bunch of social misfits and morons." Quoted in Case No. 29813, "Five Weeks in a Transient Camp," *Commonweal*, October 18, 1935, 600.

75. On the migrant as a cultural figure, see Linda Gordon, *Dorothea Lange: A Life Beyond Limits* (New York: Norton, 2009), 191–302.

76. David Cushman Coyle, *Depression Pioneers*, Works Progress Administration, Social Problems Series, No. 1 (Washington, DC: U.S. Government Printing Office, 1939), 18, 19.

77. Ibid., 10.

78. Lauren Berlant and Michael Warner, "Sex in Public," *Critical Inquiry* 24, no. 2 (Winter 1998): 549–50.

3. "Builder of Men"

1. William A. Wellman, dir., *Wild Boys of the Road*, Warner Bros., 1933.

2. Other films dramatized the plight of unemployed youth, and transient boys appeared in numerous newsreels. See Gillian Klein, "Wellman's *Wild Boys of the Road:*

The Rhetoric of a Depression Movie," *Velvet Light Trap* 15 (1975); Giuliana Muscio, *Hollywood's New Deal* (Philadelphia: Temple University Press, 1996), 99–100.

3. Norman Taurog, dir., *Boys Town*, Metro-Goldwyn-Mayer, 1938.

4. Nelson Algren, *Somebody in Boots* (New York: Berkley, 1935), 77.

5. "'Wandering Youth' Menace is Described by Atlantan," *Atlanta Constitution*, January 26, 1933, 5. The article quotes Major Arthur Fynn in testimony before a Senate committee.

6. Judge Samuel Blake, quoted in Gardner Bradford, "Ten Thousand Homeless Waifs," *Los Angeles Times*, April 9, 1933, 4.

7. George Chauncey, *Gay New York: Gender, Urban Culture, and the Making of the Gay Male World, 1890–1940* (New York: Basic Books, 1995), 8–9, 13–14. See also Jennifer Terry, *An American Obsession: Science, Medicine, and Homosexuality in Modern Society* (Chicago: University of Chicago Press, 1999), 75, 189. On the interracial aspects of migrant male communities, see Nayan Shah, "Policing Privacy, Migrants, and the Limits of Freedom," *Social Text* 23, nos. 3–4 (Fall–Winter 2005), 279–81.

8. Scholars have noted the erotic appeal of CCC youth. Neil Maher connects the CCC's commitment to American conservationism with its careful husbandry of youthful male bodies. Margot Canaday argues that the CCC was able to avoid condemnation for harboring homosexuals because CCC camps were age-segregated; enrollees received work training of finite duration; and they were drawn from families on relief and not from the transient population. Maher, *Nature's New Deal: The Civilian Conservation Corps and the Roots of the American Environmental Movement* (New York: Oxford University Press, 2008); Canaday, *The Straight State: Sexuality and Citizenship in Twentieth-Century America* (Princeton, NJ: Princeton University Press, 2009).

9. S. 5363, 72nd Cong., 2nd Sess. (1933). A similar piece of legislation, S. 5121, was proposed by Senator Cutting.

10. John A. Salmond, *The Civilian Conservation Corps, 1933–1942: A New Deal Case Study* (Durham, NC: Duke University Press, 1967), 9.

11. Franklin D. Roosevelt, "Three Essentials of Unemployment Relief," March 21, 1933, reprinted in *The Public Papers and Addresses of Franklin D. Roosevelt*, vol. 2, 1933, ed. Samuel Rosenman (New York City: Random House, 1938), 80.

12. *Congressional Hearing on Unemployment Relief*, Joint Sess. of the Senate Comm. on Education and Labor and the Comm. on Labor of the House of Representatives, Washington, DC, 73rd Cong., 1st Sess., (March 23 and 24, 1933), 22–23, 44–61. Connery and Green later came to support the agency. Connery even sponsored legislation in 1939 to incorporate military drill into the CCC training program.

13. *Congressional Hearings on S. 598*, Joint Sess. before the Comm. on Education and Labor, U.S. Senate, and the Comm. on Labor, House of Representatives, 73rd Cong., 1st Sess. (March 23 and 24, 1933).

14. See, e.g., protest resolution submitted to President Roosevelt by members of Lodge 459, International Association of Machinists in St. Paul, MN, Official File 268, Civilian Conservation Corps, FDRL.

15. James J. McEntee, Federal Security Agency, *Final Report of the Director of the Civilian Conservation Corps, April 1933 through June 30, 1942*. Records of the Civilian Conservation Corps, Entry 3: Annual Special, and Final Reports, R.G. 35, National Archives, 5.

16. Press release, Office of the Director, Emergency Conservation Work, Washington, DC, July 1, 1933, Roosevelt Papers Official File 268, Civilian Conservation Corps, FDRL.

17. Robert Fechner, *First Report of the Director of ECW, April 5, 1933 to September 30, 1933*, Records of the Civilian Conservation Corps, Entry 3: Annual, Final, and Special Reports, R.G. 35, National Archives. The Army's jurisdiction did not extend to Native American CCC camps operated under the purview of the Bureau of Indian Affairs.

18. U.S. Department of Labor, "National Emergency Conservation Work: What It Is—How It Operates," *ECW Bulletin*, no. 2, April 20, 1933, Roosevelt Papers, Official File 268, FDRL.

19. Frances Perkins to Franklin Roosevelt, June 1, 1933; follow-up letter from Frances Perkins to Frank Persons, June 1933; Will W. Alexander, Comm. on Interracial Cooperation, to Frank Persons, May 19, 1933. On allegations of venereal disease, see telegram from De La Perriere to Frank Persons, June 1, 1933. On the availability of farm work, see Ed Bethune to Major G. C. Graham, March 2, 1940, Civilian Conservation Corps, Division of Planning and Public Relations, General Correspondence, 1933–42, Negroes, R.G. 35, National Archives.

20. Garth Akridge, Julius Rosenwald Fund, to Frank Persons, March 30, 1935; Garth Akridge to Eleanor Roosevelt, April 19, 1935. Records of the Civilian Conservation Corps, Division of Planning and Public Relations, General Correspondence, 1933–42, Negroes, R.G. 35, National Archives.

21. The CCC actually had about 300,000 men at work by July 1933, but some camps were reserved for veterans and Native Americans, whose work proceeded under an entirely separate administrative substructure. See Merrill, *Roosevelt's Forest Army: A History of the Civilian Conservation Corps, 1933–1942* (Montpelier, VT: Perry H. Merrill, 1981), vii–viii.

22. Battell Loomis, "With the Green Guard," *Liberty*, April 29, 1934, 52–53.

23. Robert H. Fechner, draft of article released to New York *Herald* in late March 1934, Roosevelt Papers, Official File 268, FDRL.

24. A Florida penal farm superintendent, quoted in Charles Lathrop Pack, president, American Tree Association, "Auditing the CCC Ledger," January 1934, Roosevelt Papers, Official File 268, FDRL.

25. Robert H. Fechner, Report to President Roosevelt, July 1, 1933, Roosevelt Papers, Official File 268, FDRL.

26. Ibid.

27. Frances Perkins quoted in "The C.C.C.," *The Pittsburgh Press*, April 17, 1934.

28. A Wisconsin forestry foreman, quoted in Alfred C. Oliver Jr. and Harold M. Dudley, *This New America: The Spirit of the CCC* (London: Longmans, Green, 1937), 80–81.

29. Ibid, 81.

30. "Check CCC Policy of Jim Crow," *Atlanta Daily World*, March 26, 1934, 1; "Charge Jim Crow Plot in Indiana CCC," *Chicago Defender*, December 11, 1937, 7. See also CCC press release, July 24, 1936, Records of the CCC, Division of Planning and Public Relations, General Correspondence, 1932–42, R.G. 35, National Archives.

31. Edgar G. Brown, "Race Gets 14 More CCC Advisors: Total Now Is 70," *Chicago Defender*, September 14, 1935, 12; Peter U. Simmons, "CCC Camps Boon

to Youths: 67,000 Colored Boys Reap Direct Good from Program," *Atlanta Daily World*, April 27, 1935, 1.

32. Edgar G. Brown, *What the Civilian Conservation Corps Is Doing for Colored Youth* (Washington, DC: U.S. Government Printing Office, 1936).

33. McEntee, *Final Report*, 50.

34. Raymond Gram Swing, "Take the Army Out of the CCC," *Nation* (October 23, 1935), 459–60.

35. McEntee, *Final Report*, 8–9.

36. John Dennett Guthrie, *Saga of the CCC* (Washington, DC: American Forestry Association, 1942), 39.

37. McEntee, *Final Report*, 14.

38. Clarence F. Desmond, Company 1942, CA, quoted in Oliver and Dudley, *This New America*, 72.

39. John A. Fox, educational adviser, Company 115, Cummington, MA, quoted in Oliver and Dudley, *This New America*, 159–60.

40. McEntee, *Final Report*, 63.

41. *Advertiser* (Montgomery, AL), September 22, 1940.

42. This policy originated with Robert Fechner, director of Emergency Conservation Work, in the spring and summer of 1935, in response to controversy surrounding racial mixing in some units of the Texas CCC. See Robert Fechner to Frank Persons, special representative to the CCC for the Department of Labor, May 10, 1935. Also see James J. McEntee to Frank Persons, August 17, 1935, Records of the CCC, Selection Division: Policy: Negro Question (Ala.–Wyo.), R.G. 35, National Archives. Olen Cole Jr. discusses the segregation policy in *The African American Experience in the Civilian Conservation Corps* (Gainesville: University Press of Florida, 1999).

43. James J. McEntee, *Now They Are Men: The Story of the CCC* (Washington, DC: National Home Library Foundation, 1940), 28.

44. McEntee, *Final Report*, 18.

45. Roy C. Hoyt, *"We Can Take It": A Short Story of the C.C.C.* (New York: American Book, 1935), 107.

46. Stories that denigrated maternal influence drew on the woman-blaming impulses of the Depression. On mother blaming in the 1930s, see Ruth Feldstein, *Motherhood in Black and White: Race and Sex in American Liberalism, 1930–1965* (Ithaca, NY: Cornell University Press, 2000). See also chapter 4 of this volume.

47. T. Rollins, Relief Comm. chairman, Pulaski County, IL to Mr. Baughman, June 21, 1934, Roosevelt Papers, Official File 268, FDRL; Tom Edwards of the Model Mill Company, Salisbury, MO, to George Baughman, Missouri Relief and Reconstruction Comm., Jefferson City, MO, n.d., Roosevelt Papers, Official File 268, FDRL.

48. Annette Adams, Relief administrator, Emergency Relief Commission, Effingham, IL, to James D. Ellis, Emergency Relief Commission, Chicago, n.d., Official File 268, FDRL.

49. "Benefits of the CCC," statement submitted by Charles M. Wilson, assistant educational adviser, during campaign to gather publicity materials from enrollees in late fall, 1933. See Division of Planning and Public Relations, Benefit Letters, 1934–42, entry 9, box 1, R.G. 35, National Archives.

50. McEntee, *Final Report*, 19.

51. Guthrie, *Saga of the CCC*, 17.

52. Alfred E. Cornebise, *The CCC Chronicles: Camp Newspapers of the Civilian Conservation Corps, 1933–1942* (Jefferson, NC: McFarland, 2004).

53. Harry Woodring, assistant secretary of war, *Liberty*, January 6, 1934.

54. Johnson Hagood, major general, U.S. Army, "Soldiers of the Shield," *American Forests* (March 1934): 103–5.

55. See complaint letters in response to Hagood's and Woodring's articles, Roosevelt Papers, Official File 25, Miscellaneous, FDRL.

56. Guy D. McKinney, personal assistant to the director of Emergency Conservation Work, to Stephen Early, secretary to the president, memorandum of March 7, 1934, Roosevelt Papers, Official File 268, FDRL.

57. *Hearings on H.R. 2990, To Make the Civilian Conservation Corps a Permanent Agency*, Comm. on Labor, House of Representatives, 76th Cong., 1st Sess. (February 9, 23, and 24, 1937) 8–9, 38–39 (statement of Robert Fechner, director of the CCC).

58. McEntee, *Final Report*, 37.

59. Gerald Street, "What the CCC Has Done for Me," *American Forests* 40 (January 1934), 24. Street's essay won Second Prize in a nationwide essay contest on the benefits of the CCC.

60. Guthrie, *Saga of the CCC*, 32.

61. Hoyt, "We Can Take It," 104.

62. Clarence F. Desmond, Company 1942, California, in Oliver and Dudley, *This New America*, 71.

63. *Stars and Stripes* was the newspaper of the American Expeditionary Forces during World War I.

64. Allen Cook, Company 487, CCC, "Dawn of a New Day," *American Forests* 39 (December 1933), 534.

65. Robert L. Miller, "Success Stories," 1937, Records of the CCC, Division of Selection, R.G. 35, National Archives.

66. Keith Hufford, former CCC enrollee, "Success Stories," 1937, Records of the CCC, Division of Selection, R.G. 35, National Archives.

67. Hoyt, *"We Can Take It,"* 83, 84–85.

68. Cook, "Dawn of a New Day"; Nelson C. Brown, "When East Goes West," *American Forests* 39 (November 1933), 501.

69. J. B. Griffing, Camp Educational Adviser, Ninth Corps Area, San Francisco, "The Educational Process in the CCC," *Sociology and Social Research* 19 (1934–35), 377.

70. Battell Loomis, "With the Green Guard," *Liberty* (Spring 1934).

71. "Weak Joes, Grown Strong in CCC Camps, Return to Jobs With Man-Sized Energy," *The Christian Science Monitor*, March 27, 1934, 4. See also "Training the CCC," *The Atlanta Constitution*, June 17, 1940, 4.

72. Loomis, "With the Green Guard," 53.

73. Nelson C. Brown, "The Civilian Conservation Program in the United States," Paper given at the annual meeting of the Woodlands Section, Canadian Pulp and Paper Association, January 25, 1933 (Washington, DC: U.S. Government Printing Office, 1934).

74. Enrollee James O. Billup measured his CCC success with the statement, "When I first enlisted [in] 1933 I weighed 117 pounds[;] at present I weigh 155 pounds[,] so

I think that speaks for itself." Another enrollee stated optimistically, "I have been in but a short time but am gaining weight rapidly." Letters of Commendation from CCC Boys, Records of the CCC, Division of Planning and Public Relations, Benefit Letters, 1934–42, R.G. 35, National Archives.

75. Loomis, "With the Green Guard," 53.

76. Wesley C. Cox, Major Medical Corps, in Oliver and Dudley, *This New America*, 44.

77. Hoyt, *"We Can Take It,"* 57–58.

78. Guthrie, *Saga of the CCC*, 19.

79. McEntee, *Final Report*, 57.

80. McEntee, *Final Report*, 55–56.

81. Ibid., 80.

82. *Emergency Conservation Work Bulletin*, no. 2, April 20, 1933, Roosevelt Papers, Official File 268, FDRL.

83. A CCC official, cited in Maren Stange, "Publicity, Husbandry, and Technocracy: Fact and Symbol in Civilian Conservation Corps Photography," in *Official Images: New Deal Photography*, ed. Pete Daniel, Merry A. Foresta, Maren Stange, and Sally Stein (Washington, DC: Smithsonian Institution, 1987), 68.

84. *Emergency Conservation Work Bulletin*, no. 2.

85. McEntee wrote, "It is not consistent with good policy . . . to force colored companies on localities that have openly declared their opposition to them and where a situation might be created that would prove very serious for both white and colored inhabitants of those localities." McEntee to Persons, August 17, 1935. Records of the Civilian Conservation Corps, Division of Planning and Public Relation Genera Correspondence, 1933–42, Box "N," Negroes, R.G. 35, National Archives.

86. Fechner to Dayton Jones, Director of C.C.C. Department, California Emergency Relief Administration, July 16, 1935, C.C.C. Negro Selection, 500 Series, Box 700, R.G. 94, National Archives, cited in Calvin W. Gower, "The Struggle of Blacks for Leadership Positions in the Civilian Conservation Corps," *The Journal of Negro History* 61, no. 2 (April 1976): 126.

87. George Philip Rawick, "The New Deal and Youth: The Civilian Conservation Corps, the National Youth Administration, and the American Youth Congress" (PhD diss., University of Wisconsin, 1957), 139.

88. Fechner to Dayton Jones, July 16, 1935.

89. See *The Civilian Conservation Corps, "Builder of Men"* (Washington, DC: Happy Days, 1940).

90. Chauncey, *Gay New York*, 65–98.

91. McEntee, *Final Report*, 14.

92. *Official Handbook for Agencies Selecting Men for Emergency Conservation Work* (Washington, DC: U.S. Department of Labor, 1933), 5.

4. "To Wallop the Ladies"

1. Charles Collins, "Shakespeare as Done at Fair Is Roaring Fun: 'Taming of Shrew' Played with Elizabethan Gusto," *Chicago Daily Tribune*, May 28, 1934, 17.

2. Nelson Bell, "The Century of Progress Fair Usurps Show Prerogative of National Capital: Inaugurates a Novel Theater of Folger Type," *Washington Post*, May 26, 1934, 11.

3. Frances Dolan, ed., *The Taming of the Shrew: Texts and Contexts* (Boston: Bedford, 1996), 244, cited in Kevin M. Carr, "Contradicting Shakespeare," http://www.shakespeareismyhomeboy.com/Shakespeare-Paper-Contradicting.htm.

4. *The Taming of the Shrew*, United Artists, 1929. The film was released on November 30, 1929, at the very start of the Depression.

5. Charles Collins, "Enter Lunt and Fontanne as Shakespearean Rowdies: Theater Guild Co-Stars Bring Classic Farce 'Taming of Shrew,'" *Chicago Daily Tribune*, February 2, 1936, D2.

6. Caroline Chatfield, "Friendly Counsel," *Atlanta Constitution*, February 1, 1937, 12.

7. Doris Blake, "Tyrant Type of Wife May Need Stern Handling: Wielding Club of Authority May Cure the Shrew," *Chicago Daily Tribune*, October 14, 1936, 31.

8. "To Slap Wife or Not—That's The Question," *Chicago Daily Tribune*, February 1, 1939, 1.

9. "Dakota Wives Who Get Spanked Form a Hairbrush Club," *Chicago Daily Tribune*, June 26, 1937, 1. A correspondence course originating in Tucson, Arizona, promised prospective subscribers that it would "teach a husband how to properly spank his wife." See "On the Side with E. V. Durling," *Los Angeles Times*, June 19, 1936, A1.

10. Lona Gilbert, "Wife Wields Power by Fine Cooking," *Los Angeles Times*, January 27, 1938, A7.

11. Gail Laughlin, cited in Ruby Hayes, "Independent Women," *Forum and Century* (January 1931).

12. Norman Cousins, "Will Women Lose Their Jobs?," *Current History and Forum* 41 (September 1939): 14.

13. Fannie Hurst, *Imitation of Life* (New York: Collier, 1933); John M. Stahl, dir., *Imitation of Life* (film), Universal Pictures, 1934; Margaret Mitchell, *Gone with the Wind* (New York: MacMillan, 1936); Victor Fleming, George Cukor, and Sam Wood, dirs., *Gone with the Wind* (film), Selznick International Pictures, 1939.

14. Holly A. Crocker, "Affective Resistance: Performing Passivity and Playing A Part in *The Taming of the Shrew*," *Shakespeare Quarterly* 54, no. 2 (Summer 2003): 143.

15. Carole Pateman, *The Disorder of Women: Democracy, Feminism, and Political Theory* (Stanford, CA: Stanford University Press, 1990); Genevieve Lloyd, *The Man of Reason: 'Male' and 'Female' in Western Philosophy* (London: Methuan, 1984).

16. Jesse A. Bloodworth and Elizabeth J. Greenwood, WPA Division of Research, *The Personal Side* (Washington, DC: U.S. Government Printing Office, 1939), 77–78.

17. On Section 213 of the 1932 Federal Economy Act, see Lois Scharf, *To Work or to Wed: Female Employment, Feminism, and the Great Depression* (Westport, CT: Greenwood Press, 1980).

18. Robyn Muncy, *Creating a Female Dominion in America, 1890–1935* (New York: Oxford University Press, 1991), 155. See also Anne Petersen, "New Protest Seen by Wives with Jobs," *New York Times*, November 27, 1938.

19. An unnamed journalist, quoted in John N. Webb and Joseph C. Bevis, *Facts about Unemployment*, WPA Social Problems Series, No. 4 (Washington, DC: U.S. Government Printing Office, 1940).

20. Ibid., 23.

21. "Sees Women Going 'Back to the Home': Mt. Holyoke Dean Tells 'Career' Group of Men's Gentle Plea," *New York Times*, November 8, 1938.

22. "Big Rise Revealed in Women Wage Earners," *New York Times*, October 9, 1938; Webb and Bevis, *Facts about Unemployment*.

23. "Survey Shows 78 Percent Opposed to Wives in Pin-Money Jobs," *New York Times*, November 27, 1938.

24. Crocker, "Affective Resistance," 143.

25. "Embezzlers—Who They Are and Why: Conclusions Reached in a Study of 1001 Cases," *Chicago Daily Tribune*, January 17, 1937, E10.

26. Doris Blake, "Nagging Wife Makes Nervous Wreck of a Man," *Chicago Daily Tribune*, January 25, 1934, 15.

27. "Pleads to Join the Army: Reason? His Nagging Wife," *Chicago Daily Tribune*, February 10, 1940, 1.

28. "'Nagging Wife' Loses Suit," *New York Times*, October 3, 1935, 25; Ralph T. Jones, "Nagging Wives Cause Accidents," *Atlanta Constitution*, October 8, 1936, 6.

29. Peter Levins, "Did Justice Triumph? Death of a Nagging Wife," *Atlanta Constitution*, October 8, 1939, SM5.

30. "Slaying Blamed on Nagging Wife," *Atlanta Constitution*, October 1, 1939, A2.

31. "The Home Port," NBC radio program, September 24, 1938. Described on "Radio Programs," *Atlanta Constitution*, September 24, 1938, 19; James Ronald, *This Way Out* (Philadelphia: Lippincott), reviewed by Isaac Anderson, "A Tale of Murder," *New York Times*, March 30, 1940, BR24; Edmund Goulding, dir., *We Are Not Alone* (film), Warner Brothers, 1939.

32. Katherine Dupre Lumpkin, *The Family: A Study of Member Roles* (Chapel Hill: University of North Carolina Press, 1933), 92; Bloodworth and Greenwood, *The Personal Side*, 240.

33. Lumpkin, *The Family*, 113.

34. Nelson Ackerman, quoted in Irving Bernstein, *A Caring Society: The New Deal, the Worker, and the Great Depression* (Boston: Houghton Mifflin, 1985), 21. Also cited in Studs Terkel, *Hard Times: An Oral History of the Great Depression* (New York: New Press, 2000), 231.

35. Mark Thomas Connelly, *The Response to Prostitution in the Progressive* Era (Chapel Hill: University of North Carolina Press, 1980), 6, quoted in John D'Emilio and Estelle B. Freedman, *Intimate Matters: A History of Sexuality in America* (New York: Harper & Row, 1988), 214. See also Barbara Meil Hobson, *Uneasy Virtue: The Politics Of Prostitution and the American Reform Tradition* (New York: Basic Books, 1987).

36. "Cleaning Up New York's Dance Dives," *Literary Digest* 110 (August 1, 1931): 9–10.

37. "Seabury Commission Report," quoted in *New Republic*, December 30, 1931.

38. Walter C. Reckless, *Vice in Chicago* (Chicago: University of Chicago Press, 1933), viii, 137, 146, 153.

39. Stephanie Golden, *The Women Outside: Myths and Meanings of Homelessness* (Berkeley: University of California Press, 1992), 5.

40. *Hearings on S. 5121, Relief for Unemployed Transients*, U.S. Senate Subcomm. of the Comm. on Manufactures, 72nd Cong., 2nd Sess. (January 13–25, 1933), 45, 76 (statements of A. W. McMillen and Dorothy Wysor).

41. Walter Reckless, "Why Women Become Hoboes," *American Mercury* 31 (February 1934): 180.

42. Thomas Minehan, *Boy and Girl Tramps of America* (New York: Farrar & Rinehart, 1934), 140.

43. *Hearings on S. 5121, Unemployed Transients*, 133 (statement of Senator Edward Costigian).

44. Robert Carter, "Boys Going Nowhere: Notes from the Diary of an American 'Wild Boy,'" *New Republic*, March 8, 1932, 92–95.

45. *Hearings on S. 5121, Unemployed Transients*, 156 (statement of Mary Stewart, executive secretary of the Houston Transient Aid Society).

46. Reckless, "Why Women Become Hoboes," 175.

47. Judith Hicks Stiehm, "The Protected, the Protector, the Defender," *Women's Studies International Forum* 5, no. 3 (1982): 367–76.

48. "Comments on Prostitution in New York City," *New Republic*, December 30, 1931, 172.

49. William H. Matthews to Harry Hopkins, May 23, 1933, Records of the WPA, FERA Old Subject File, R.G. 69, box 17, National Archives, quoted in Martha H. Swain, *Ellen S. Woodward: New Deal Advocate for Women* (Jackson: University Press of Mississippi, 1995), 40.

50. For a comprehensive account of Woodward's administrative tenure, see Swain, *Ellen S. Woodward*.

51. In a memo dated November 14, 1933, Woodward touted the benefits of voluntarism and pledged to "mobilize women's inherent capacities for community housekeeping"; Swain, *Ellen S. Woodward*, 45. Bonnie Schwartz also notes the Women's Division's commitment to residual charity practices.

52. FERA, *Proceedings of Conference on Emergency Needs of Women*, n.d., Records of the WPA, FERA Old Subject File, R.G. 69, National Archives.

53. Ibid.

54. Ibid.

55. Press release, November 16, 1933, FERA Conference on the Emergency Needs of Women, box 83, R.G. 69, National Archives.

56. FERA, *Proceedings of Conference on Emergency Needs of Women*.

57. Ibid.

58. FERA, *Unemployment Relief Census: October, 1933* (Washington, DC: U.S. Government Printing Office, 1934).

59. Swain, *Ellen S. Woodward*, 46–50.

60. Linda Gordon makes this point about the masculine contours of male public works projects in *Pitied but Not Entitled: Single Mothers and the History of Welfare, 1890–1935* (New York: Free Press, 1994).

61. Mayme O'Dow to George Power, March 16, 1934, Records of the WPA, FERA State Series, MS: 453.2, R.G. 69, National Archives, quoted in Swain, *Ellen S. Woodward*, 48.

62. Linda Gordon discusses the term "pantry snooper" in "Social Insurance and Public Assistance: The Influence of Gender in Welfare Thought in the United States," *American Historical Review* 97, no. 1 (1992): 19–54.

63. Marie Dresden Lane and Francis Steegmuller, *America on Relief* (New York: Harcourt, Brace, 1938), 20.

64. Guy Watson, quoted in Bloodworth and Greenwood, *The Personal Side*, 76.

65. Maxine Davis, *They Shall Not Want* (New York: MacMillan, 1937), 84, 76.

66. Lorena Hickok, *One Third of a Nation: Lorena Hickok Reports on the Great Depression*, ed. Richard Lowitt and Maurine Beasley (Urbana: University of Illinois Press, 1981), ix.

67. Mary L. McClure, "Two Letters on Relief," *Commonweal*, January 18, 1935, 332.

68. Genevieve Lloyd, "War, Selfhood, and Masculinity," in *Feminist Challenges: Social and Political Theory*, ed. Carole Pateman and Elizabeth Grosz (New York: Routledge, 2013).

69. Harry Hopkins, "What Is the 'American Way'?," address delivered at the Chatauqua Institution, Chatauqua, NY, July 16, 1938.

70. Harry Hopkins, *Spending to Save: The Complete Story of Relief* (New York: Norton, 1936), 116, 141.

71. Earl G. Harrison, "Women without Work," *The Survey* 70 (March 1934): 73–74.

72. Ibid. See also S. D. Ozer, "Women and Work Relief," classified document, Records of the WPA, Women's Division Files, R.G. 69, National Archives.

73. Nels Anderson, "Are the Unemployed a Caste?," *Survey Graphic* (July 1935): 345–47.

74. "Middletown, Ten Years After," *Business Week*, May 26, 1934, 15–16.

75. Donald S. Howard, *The WPA and Federal Relief Policy* (New York: Russell Sage Foundation, 1943), 284–85.

76. Lane and Steegmuller, *America on Relief*, 28.

77. Ozer, "Women and Work Relief," 28.

78. Jacqueline Jones, "Race and Gender in Modern America," *Reviews in American History* 26, no. 1 (March 1998): 224–25.

79. Alfred Edgar Smith, *WPA and the Negro* (NY State Works Progress Administration, 1936), 2.

80. Jones, "Race and Gender in Modern America," 224–25; Gordon, *Pitied but Not Entitled*, 111–44.

81. Alfred Edgar Smith, *Report of Activities, May 1–30, 1937*, Records of the WPA, General Files, File 102, 1936–37, 7, R.G. 69, National Archives.

82. Alfred Edgar Smith, *Negro Project Workers: 1937 Annual Report*, January 1938, Records of the WPA, General Files, File 102, 1936–37, R.G. 69, National Archives.

83. Smith, *Report of Activities, May 1937*, 8.

84. Alfred Edgar Smith, *Report of Activities, April 1–30, 1937*, Records of the WPA, General Files, File 102, 1936–37, 12, R.G. 69, National Archives.

85. C. C. Spaulding to A. E. Smith, 18 May 1936, in Alfred Edgar Smith, *Report of Activities, June 1–30, 1936*, Records of the WPA, General Files, File 102, 1936–37, 6, R.G. 69, National Archives.

86. Smith, *Report of Activities, April 1–30, 1937*, 9.

87. A Portsmouth, VA, resident to A. E. Smith, March 24, 1937, in Smith, *Report of Activities, April 1–30, 1937*, 11.

88. Ellen S. Woodward to Aubrey Williams, November 21, 1936, quoted in Swain, *Ellen S. Woodward*, 74.

89. Swain, *Ellen S. Woodward*, 82.

90. Press release, WPA Public Information Section, New York City, March 23, 1938, Records of the WPA, Women's Division Files, R.G. 69, National Archives.

91. Ellen S. Woodward, "The WPA Prepares Women for Housework," *Occupations: The Vocational Guidance Magazine*, 17, no. 3 (December 1938): 220–22.

92. Winifred Wandersee, *Women's Work and Family Values, 1920–1940* (Cambridge, MA: Harvard University Press, 1981); Phyllis Palmer, *Domesticity and Dirt: Housewives and Domestic Servants in the United States, 1920–45* (Philadelphia: Temple University Press, 1989).

93. Woodward would be criticized for her emphasis on political outcomes by a close subordinate, Chloe Owings. See Swain, *Ellen S. Woodward*, 77n81.

94. Hopkins, *Spending to Save*, 169.

95. Woodward to Regional Conference, March 19, 1936, cited in Swain, *Ellen S. Woodward*, 73.

96. Hickok, *One Third of a Nation*, 122.

97. Howard, *WPA and Federal Relief Policy*, 279.

98. Suzanne Mettler, *Dividing Citizens: Gender and Federalism in New Deal Public Policy* (Ithaca, NY: Cornell University Press, 1998).

99. Findings of the Conference on the Participation of Negro Women in Federal Welfare Programs, April 4, 1938, White House, Records of the WPA, Women's Division Files, R.G. 69, National Archives.

100. On lukewarm response, see, e.g., memorandum from A. S. Cronin to Mrs. Woodward, "Meeting at White House with Council of Negro Women on April 4th," March 30, 1938, Records of the WPA, Women's Division Files, R.G. 69, National Archives.

101. Alfred E. Smith, "Negro Women Workers," *1937 Annual Report*, Records of the WPA, Women's Division Files, R.G. 69, National Archives.

102. Press release, WPA Public Information Section, New York City, March 23, 1938, Records of the WPA, Women's Division Files, R.G. 69, National Archives.

103. Fredric Jameson, *The Political Unconscious: Narrative as Socially Symbolic Act* (Ithaca, NY: Cornell University Press, 1981), 17–102.

104. Lauren Gail Berlant, *The Female Complaint: The Unfinished Business of Sentimentality in American Culture* (Durham, NC: Duke University Press, 2008), 4.

5. Civilian Protectors and Meddlesome Women

1. "Parade's Prologue Tells War's Story: Its Causes and Tragedies Are Dramatized in a Pageant," *New York Times*, June 14, 1942, 39.

2. "2,000,000 Will See City's War Parade: With 500,000 Taking Part, Tomorrow's Spectacle May Be Biggest Ever Held," *New York Times*, June 12, 1942, 23.

3. "Civilian Defense," *Scientific American* (February 1942): 51.

4. Franklin Delano Roosevelt, Executive Order 8757, Establishing the Office of Civilian Defense, May 20, 1941. *The Public Papers and Addresses of Franklin D. Roosevelt. 1941 Volume*, Samuel Rosenman, ed. (New York: Harper Brothers, 1950), 162.

5. "'Morale Week' for California," *New York Times*, March 1, 1942, XX5; "Bulwark to Civilian Morale Seen as Retailers' War Role," *Washington Post*, January 2, 1942, F11.

6. George Gallup, "Wartime Morale Carefully Studied," *New York Times*, December 20, 1941, 10.

7. "Roosevelt Urges Private Gifts Aid National Morale," *New York Times*, October 14, 1940, 1.

8. See, e.g., "Senator Rags Mrs. Roosevelt: Says Civilian Defense New Social Experiment," *Globe and Mail*, February 11, 1942, 12.

9. Frederick Hazlitt Brennan, "Total War Is . . . Democratic!," *Atlanta Constitution*, April 19, 1942, 2; Josiah W. Bailey, "Our Republic: It Must Be Preserved," CBS Radio address, July 4, 1941, published in *Vital Speeches of the Day*, August 1, 1941, 633.

10. Mark H. Leff, "The Politics of Sacrifice on the American Home Front in World War II," *Journal of American History* 77, no. 4 (March 1991): 1296–1318.

11. Warner and Swasey advertisement, *Newsweek*, November 23, 1942.

12. Ibid.

13. United States Rubber Company advertisement, *Newsweek*, November 9, 1942.

14. Advertisement for the *Chicago Daily News* published in *Newsweek*, October 20, 1942.

15. Marquis W. Childs, *This Is Your War* (Boston: Little, Brown, 1942), 76.

16. Ibid., 96, 148.

17. Louis Wirth, "The Urban Community," *American Society in Wartime*, ed. William Fielding Ogburn (Chicago: University of Chicago Press, 1943), 75.

18. Henry Luce, *The American Century* (New York: Farrar & Rinehart, 1941).

19. Franklin Delano Roosevelt, *The War Message* (Philadelphia: Ritten House, 1942).

20. Rogers Smith, "Beyond Tocqueville, Myrdal and Hartz: The Multiple Traditions in America," *American Political Science Review* (September 1993): 549–66. See also Suzanne Mettler, *Dividing Citizens: Gender and Federalism in New Deal Public Policy* (Ithaca, NY: Cornell University Press, 1998).

21. Susan B. Hirsch and Lewis Erenberg, *The War in American Culture: Society and Consciousness during World War II* (Chicago: University of Chicago Press, 1996), 5.

22. Daniel Kryder, *Divided Arsenal: Race and the American State during World War II* (New York: Cambridge University Press, 2000).

23. Luis Alvarez, *The Power of the Zoot: Youth Culture and Resistance during World War II* (Berkeley: University of California Press, 2009), 200–234.

24. John Dower, *War without Mercy: Race and Power in the Pacific War* (New York: Random House, 1986); Robin Kelley, *Race Rebels: Culture, Politics, and the Black Working Class* (New York: Free Press, 1994); Richard Griswold del Castillo, ed., *World War II and Mexican-American Civil Rights* (Austin: University of Texas Press, 2008); Elizabeth Rachel Escobedo, *From Coveralls to Zoot Suits: The Lives of Mexican American Women on the World War II Home Front* (Chapel Hill: University of North Carolina Press, 2013). See also Kryder, *Divided Arsenal*; Alvarez, *Power of the Zoot*.

25. U.S. Office of Civilian Defense, "Black Market in Meat," a bulletin to directors of Victory Speakers Bureaus, n.d., Publications of the U.S. Government, Addresses File, box 276, R.G. 287, National Archives.

26. Rear Admiral Clark H. Woodward, U.S. Navy, April 9, 1942, address, OCD Conference for the Protection of Workers and Plants, Chicago, Publications of the U.S. Government, Addresses File, box 276, R.G. 287, National Archives.

27. U.S. Office of Civilian Defense, *Introduction to the Army: Suggestions for Pre-Induction Informational Meetings* (Washington, DC: U.S. Government Printing Office, February 1944), 16.

28. Eleanor T. Glueck, "Juvenile Delinquency in Wartime," *The Survey* 78, no. 3 (March 1942): 71.

29. Ernest W. Burgess, "The Family," in Ogburn, *American Society in Wartime*, 17–18.

30. James S. Bossard, "War and the Family," *American Sociological Review* 6 (June 1941): 337.

31. Burgess, "The Family," 27.

32. Glueck, "Juvenile Delinquency in Wartime," 71.

33. J. Edgar Hoover and a juvenile court judge, both cited in Edwin H. Sutherland, "Crime," in Ogburn, *American Society in Wartime*, 187. See also Walter C. Reckless, "The Impact of War on Crime, Delinquency, and Prostitution," *American Journal of Sociology* 48 (November 1942): 378–86.

34. Burgess, "The Family," 34. See also Lewis M. Terman, *Psychological Factors in Marital Happiness* (New York: McGraw-Hill, 1938), 319–24.

35. Kevin Allen Leonard, *The Battle for Los Angeles: Racial Ideology and World War II* (Albuquerque: University of New Mexico Press, 2006).

36. U.S. Bureau of the Census, *Victory*, December 22, 1942, 5, cited in Burgess, "The Family," 21.

37. Emilio Zamora, *Claiming Rights and Righting Wrongs in Texas: Mexican Workers and Job Politics during World War II* (College Station: Texas A&M University Press, 2009).

38. Bossard, "War and the Family," 337. See also Charles P. Taft, "Public Health and the Family in World War II"; Ernest Mowrer, "War and Family Solidarity and Stability," in *The American Family in World War II*, ed. Thomas Sellin (Philadelphia: American Academy of Political and Social Science, 1943), 145–46, 100.

39. Wirth, "The Urban Community," 72.

40. John D'Emilio, *Sexual Politics, Sexual Communities*, 2nd ed. (Chicago: University of Chicago Press, 1998), 23–39. Psychiatrists also implemented new screening procedures to exclude homosexuals and other "mental defectives" from military service. See Harry Stack Sullivan, "Mental Hygiene and National Defense: A Year of Selective Service Psychiatry," *Mental Hygiene* 26, no. 1 (1942): 7–14; Allan Berube, *Coming Out Under Fire: The History of Gay Men and Women in World War II* (New York: Free Press, 1990); Margot Canaday, *The Straight State: Sexuality and Citizenship in Twentieth-Century America* (Princeton, NJ: University of Princeton Press, 2011).

41. James M. Landis, *Address before Civilian Defense Rally under the Auspices of the Metropolitan Cleveland Civilian Defense Committee, Public Auditorium, Cleveland, Ohio, March 31, 1942* (Washington, DC: Office of Civilian Defense, 1942).

42. See Franklin D. Roosevelt, "Radio Address Announcing an Unlimited National Emergency," May 27, 1941 in *The Public Papers and Addresses of Franklin D. Roosevelt*, ed. Samuel Rosenman, 1941 vol. (New York: Harper, 1950), 181–94.

43. Roosevelt, Executive Order 8757, in *The Public Papers and Addresses of Franklin D. Roosevelt*, ed. Samuel Rosenman, 1941 vol. (New York: Harper, 1950), 162–72.

44. "National Family Week," *OCD Newsletter*, April 15, 1943; "Director Praises New V-Home Drive," *OCD Newsletter*, February 20, 1943.

45. Rosenman, *Public Papers and Addresses, 1941 Volume*: 170.

46. "Civilian Defense," 51.

47. "Nearly Ten Million!" *OCD Newsletter*, August 8,1942; Robert Earnest Miller, "The War That Never Came: Civilian Defense in Cincinnati, Ohio, during World War II," *Queen City Heritage* (Winter 1991): 5; Mark Jonathan Harris, Franklin D. Mitchell, and Steven J. Schechter, eds., *The Homefront: America during World War II* (New York: Putnam, 1984), 64, 72.

48. Thomas Scott, quoted in Harris, Mitchell, and Schechter, *The Homefront*, 66.

49. *Oklahoma State Defense Committee Newsletter*, June 15, 1942, quoted in *OCD Newsletter*, June 30, 1942; U.S. Office of Civilian Defense, "Black Markets in Meat."

50. Caryl A. Cooper, "The Chicago Defender: Filling in the Gaps for the Office of Civilian Defense, 1941–1945," *Western Journal of Black Studies* 23, no. 2 (Summer 1999): 111–18.

51. "Army Civil Defense Advisers Say Southland Too Complacent," *Los Angeles Times*, February 20, 1942, 9.

52. "Who Speaks for Lincoln?," *St. Louis Argus*, November 6, 1942, 8, cited in Caryl Ann Cooper, *To Preserve and Serve: African-Americans on the Home Front, 1941–1945, the Office of Civilian Defense and the Black Press* (Columbia: University of Missouri–Columbia, 1996), 112. See also *St. Louis Argus*, November 11, 1942, 2; "Anti-Negro Bias Denied by A.W.V.S.," *New York Times*, February 26, 1941, 16.

53. Miller, "War That Never Came," 12.

54. "Harlem Buzzes with Civilian Defense Tasks," *Life*, June 15, 1942, 90–93.

55. Leonard, *Battle for Los Angeles*, 309–40.

56. Cooper, *To Preserve and Serve*, 59.

57. Miller, "The War That Never Came," 7; FDR, February 17, 1942, press conference, quoted in Harris, Mitchell, and Schechter, *The Home Front*, 63.

58. U.S. Office of Civilian Defense, *Sabotage and Preventive Measures* (Washington, DC: U.S. Government Printing Office, December 1943), 1.

59. Donald A. Ritchie, *James M. Landis, Dean of Regulators* (Cambridge, MA: Harvard University Press, 1980), 109.

60. James M. Bramford, "Listen, Washington! The Local Community Talks Back," *The Survey* (March 1942): 72. Bramford concluded, "Remember that this is America, and that each community still has the privilege, in many things, of making up its own mind."

61. "Confused and Unprepared," *Time*, December 29, 1941, 11.

62. U.S. Office of Civilian Defense, *Organization Outline for Local Defense Councils* (Washington, DC: U.S. Government Printing Office, 1942), 2.

63. "Eleanor's Playmates," *Time*, February 16, 1942, 49.

64. La Guardia's critics often diminished his credibility as a male authority figure by referencing his Italian heritage. Some derisively translated his name as "The Little Flower"; his affect was ethnicized and effeminized as blustery and intemperate; and his short, stout, "foreign" body was contrasted with the wartime ideal of muscular white manhood.

65. James M. Landis, "Morale and Civilian Defense," *American Journal of Sociology* 8, no. 3 (November 1941): 338.

66. Anita Brenner, "What Can I Do to Help Win the War?," *New York Times Magazine*, June 7, 1942, 14.

67. U.S. Office of Civilian Defense, *Introduction to the Army*, n27.

68. "OCD Exodus," *Newsweek*, March 2, 1942, 24.

69. Walter Lippmann, quoted in "Confused and Unprepared," *Time*, December 29, 1941, 11. See also "The Civilian Defense Mess," *Collier's*, February 21, 1942, 62.

70. "Landis to OCD," *Time*, January 19, 1942, 61.

71. See, e.g., Frank Capra, dir., *Prelude to War* (1942) and *Know Your Enemy: Japan* (1945), both produced by the Special Service Division, Army Service Forces, in cooperation with the U.S. Army Signal Corps.

72. U.S. Office of Civilian Defense, *Civilian Protection: Why, What, How, Who, When, Where, When* (Washngton, DC: U.S. Government Printing Office, October 1941), 3.

73. James M. Landis, "The Need for Civilian Protection," speech, CBS Radio, January 1, 1942, *Vital Speeches* 8 (March 1, 1942): 319.

74. Landis, address, March 31, 1942.

75. Colonel R. Ernest Dupay, GSC, and Lieutenant Hodding Carter, FA, "The Citizen Also Fights the War," *American City* (August 1942): 60.

76. Landis address to civilian defense rally, Cleveland, Ohio, May 21, 1942, cited in Ritchie, *James M. Landis*, 110.

77. U.S. Office of Civilian Defense, *What to Do in an Air Raid* (Washington, DC: U.S. Government Printing Office, 1942).

78. U.S. Office of Civilian Defense, *Handbook for Air Raid Wardens* (Washington, DC: U.S. Government Printing Office, January 1943).

79. U.S. Office of Civilian Defense, *Administrative Manual for the Air Raid Wardens Unit* (Washington, DC: U.S. Government Printing Office, October 1943).

80. Ibid.

81. USOCD, *Handbook for Air Raid Wardens*, 7.

82. USOCD, *Administrative Manual for the Air Raid Wardens Unit*, 2.

83. Ibid., 3.

84. U.S. Office of Civilian Defense, *A Handbook for Auxiliary Police* (Washington, DC: U.S. Government Printing Office, August 1942).

85. Perry Duis, "No Time for Privacy: World War II and Chicago's Families," in *The War in American Culture: Society and Consciousness During World War II*, ed. Lewis A. Erenberg and Susan Hirsch (Chicago: University of Chicago Press, 1996), 17–45.

86. Barbara Parmelee, "ARP School, Massachusetts," *New Republic*, March 2, 1942, 298.

87. Barbara Parmelee, "Airplane Spotter," *New Republic*, July 20, 1942, 80.

88. Jack Bechdolt, "Mr. Smith Toughens Up: The Story of How the National Crisis Turned an Average Citizen into an Air-Raid Warden," *New York Times Magazine*, December 21, 1941, 4.

89. Duis, "No Time for Privacy," 17–45.

90. General Electric advertisement, *Saturday Evening Post*, November 23, 1942, 71.

91. Parmelee, "ARP School, Massachusetts," 298; *OCD Newsletter*, May 8, 1942. In this issue, an excerpted speech by President Roosevelt on civilian sacrifice is followed by an article titled "The Treason of Hoarding."

92. Paul V. McNutt, radio broadcast, transcript printed in *OCD Newsletter*, September 19, 1941.

93. Ibid.

94. Miller, "War That Never Came," 13.

95. "The Ladies!," *Time*, January 26, 1942, 61.

96. Maureen Honey, *Creating Rosie the Riveter: Class, Gender, and Propaganda during World War II* (Amherst: University of Massachusetts Press, 1984).

97. "OCD on Fire," *Newsweek*, September 8, 1941, 45–46.

98. *OCD Newsletter*, November 19, 1941. See also Eleanor Roosevelt, "Women in Defense: A Script by Eleanor Roosevelt," *New York Times Magazine*, December 7, 1941, 6–7.

99. Eleanor Roosevelt, *This I Remember* (New York: Harper, 1949), 239.

100. Joanna C. Colcord, "Our Plans for Wartime Welfare," *The Survey* (January 1943): 17. See also William Hodson, "In Case of Enemy Attack," *The Survey* (November 1942): 293–95. Hodson was commissioner of the Welfare Department, New York City.

101. U.S. Office of Civilian Defense, *Civilian War Services: An Operating Guide for Local Defense Councils* (Washington, DC: U.S. Government Printing Office, August 1943), 13.

102. Ibid., 1–2.

103. Ibid., 11.

104. "The Ladies!," 61.

105. Raymond Clapper, "Office of Civilian Defense," *El Paso Herald Post*, February 6, 1942, 8.

106. Raymond Clapper, quoted in "Eleanor's Playmates," *Time*, February 16, 1942, 49.

107. Joanna Colcord, "Our Plans for Wartime Welfare." *Survey Midmonthly*, 79, no. 1 (January 1943): 17.

108. Joanna Colcord, "Social Agencies in the Defense Set-up," *The Survey* (October 1942): 265.

109. Eleanor Roosevelt, *My Day: Her Acclaimed Columns, 1936–1945*, ed. Rochelle Chadakoff (New York: Pharos, 1989), 230.

110. "Throng Hears Mrs. Roosevelt Stress Unity: Says America Cannot Win While Divided," *Atlanta Daily World*, February 21, 1942, 1.

111. Cooper, *To Preserve and Serve*, 59.

112. "Civilian Defense and Protection," *U.S. Municipal News*, March 1, 1942, 38, repr. *American City* 57 (March 1942): 38; "The Civilian Defense Mess," 62.

113. A man who identifies himself as "Riley, a construction worker," quoted in Brenner, "What Can I Do to Help?," 14.

114. Victor Keppler, "Wanted! For Murder" (poster) 1944, Still Picture Branch, College Park, MD, National Archives and Records Administration (hereafter NARA Still Picture Branch).

115. See Judith Hicks's discussion of the "substitutability myth" in "The Protector, the Protected, the Defender," *Women's Studies International Forum* 5, nos. 3–4 (1982): 367–76.

116. See Rosenman, *Public Papers and Addresses*, 1941: 172.

117. Wirth, "The Urban Community," 75.

118. Mary Ryan, "The American Parade: Representations of the Nineteenth-Century Social Order," in *The New Cultural History*, ed. Lynn Hunt (Berkeley: University of California Press, 1989), 131–53.

119. W. Russell Neuman, George E. Marcus, Ann N. Crigler, and Michael MacKuen, eds. *The Affect Effect: Dynamics of Emotion in Political Thinking and Behavior* (Chicago: University of Chicago Press, 2007), 1–20.

120. "Three Counties under Curbs," *New York Times*, June 22, 1943, 7.

121. "Harlem Quiet After Night of Strong Guard," *Christian Science Monitor*, August 3, 1943; "Harlem Looting and Rioting Cause Heavy Casualties," *Christian Science Monitor*, August 2, 1943, 1; "Harlem Lay Blame on War-Strained Emotions," *Christian Science Monitor*, August 3, 1943, 1; "Harlem Is Orderly with Heavy Guard Ready for Trouble," *New York Times*, August 3, 1943, 1.

122. "Race Bias Denied as Rioting Factor," *New York Times*, August 3, 1943, 11.

6. The Citizen-Soldier and the Citizen-Internee

1. Office of the Solicitor, Memorandum on the Validity of Detention, January 4, 1944, Records of the War Relocation Authority (hereinafter WRA), Information, Objectives and Principles, R.G. 210, National Archives.

2. George H. Roeder, Jr., *The Censored War: American Visual Experience during World War II* (New Haven, CT: Yale University Press, 1993), 43–66.

3. Luis Alvarez, *The Power of the Zoot: Youth Culture and Resistance during World War II* (Berkeley: University of California Press, 2008). See also Kevin Allen Leonard, *The Battle for Los Angeles: Racial Ideology and World War II* (Albuquerque: University of New Mexico Press, 2006); Mauricio Mazon, *The Zoot Suit Riots: The Psychology of Symbolic Annihilation* (Austin: University of Texas Press, 1984).

4. Grodzins presents a thorough analysis of letters received by the Justice Department in *Americans Betrayed: Politics and the Japanese American Evacuation* (Chicago: University of Chicago Press, 1949), 415–19.

5. Commission on the Wartime Internment of Civilians, *Personal Justice Denied: Report of the Commission on Wartime Relocation and Internment of Citizens* (Washington, DC: U.S. Government Printing Office, 1982), 4–28. See also Brian Masaru Hayashi, *Democratizing the Enemy: The Japanese American Internment* (Princeton, NJ: Princeton University Press, 2004), 76–79. On the political powerlessness of the Japanese American community, see Henry Ueno's oral history in John Tateishi, *And Justice for All: An Oral History of the Japanese American Detention Camps* (Seattle: University of Washington Press, 1984), 186–207.

6. Otto Brower, dir., *Little Tokyo, U.S.A.*, Twentieth Century Fox, 1942.

7. On *Little Tokyo, U.S.A.*, see Clayton R. Koppes and Gregory D. Black, *Hollywood Goes to War: How Profit, Politics, and Propaganda Shaped World War II Movies* (New York: Free Press, 1987), 72–77.

8. *Hearings*, Select Comm. Investigating National Defense Migration, House of Representatives, 77th Cong., 1st Sess., February 22–23, 1942, pt. 29, p. 11015 (comment by Earl Warren).

9. *Hearings*, Select Comm. Investigating National Defense Migration, pt. 29, p. 10990 (letter from Thomas Whelan, District Attorney, San Diego County, February 19, 1942).

10. *Hearings*, Select Comm. Investigating National Defense Migration, pt. 29, p. 11045 (letter from Hugh Gallagher, Federal Security Agency, Social Security Board, February 17, 1942).

11. Office of the Solicitor, Memorandum on the Validity of Detention.

12. On Nisei military reclassification, see U.S. War Relocation Authority, *Semi-Annual Report, January 1–June 30, 1944*, 13, Records of the WRA, R.G. 210, National Archives.

13. *Hearings*, Select Comm. Investigating National Defense Migration, p. 11138 (statement of Mike Masaoka, national secretary and field executive, Japanese American Citizens League).

14. *Hearings*, Select Comm. Investigating National Defense Migration, p. 11231 (statement of James M. Omura, florist and publisher of *Current Life*).

15. Interview with James M. Omura in Arthur Hansen, ed. *Japanese American WW II Evacuation - Part IV: Resisters*, (Munich, Germany: K.G. Saur 1995), 123–326.

16. See, e.g., Lieutenant Commander K. D. Ringle, USN, Report on the Japanese Problem to the Chief of Naval Operations, December 30, 1941, Serial No. 01742316; *Report of the Committee on Immigration of the Senate*, Senate Report 1496 (77–2), Serial Set 10658.

17. Peter T. Conmy, *The History of California's Japanese Problem and the Part Played by the Native Sons of the Golden West in Its Solution* (San Francisco: Native Sons of the Golden West, 1942). On the Native Sons of the Golden West, see Carey McWilliams, *Prejudice: Japanese Americans—Symbol of Racial Intolerance* (Boston: Little, Brown, 1944), 20–25. See also articles relating to the wartime anti-Japanese racism of the Native Sons of the Golden West in the *San Francisco Call-Bulletin*, May 8, 1942, 8, and the *San Francisco Chronicle*, June 16, 1942, 7.

18. As John Tateishi notes, "non-aliens" was a code word for Japanese American citizens. See Tateishi, *And Justice for All*, xix.

19. See "Preliminary Factors of Information Policy," n.d., Records of the WRA, Washington Office Records, Information, Objectives, and Principles of the WRA, R.G. 210, National Archives; Conference on Evacuation of Enemy Aliens, Newhouse Hotel, Salt Lake City, Utah, April 7, 1942, Records of the WRA, Washington Office Records, Documentary Headquarters Files, Meetings and Conferences, 1942–43, R.G. 210, National Archives; War Relocation Authority, *Quarterly Report of the WRA, March 18 to June 30, 1942* (Washington, DC: U.S. Government Printing Office, 1942).

20. Roger Daniels, *Prisoners without Trial: Japanese Americans in World War II* (New York: Hill & Wang, 1993), 26–48; Dillon S. Myer, *Uprooted Americans: The Japanese Americans and the War Relocation Authority during World War II* (Tucson: University of Arizona Press, 1971), xxii–xxx, 15–26; Page Smith, *Democracy on Trial: The Japanese American Evacuation and Relocation in World War II* (New York: Simon & Schuster, 1995), 89–237.

21. John Dower describes the animal-like conditions that evacuees confronted at coastal relocation centers. See his *War without Mercy: Race and Power in the Pacific War* (New York: Pantheon, 1986), 82–83.

22. See Richard Drinnon, *Keeper of Concentration Camps: Dillon S. Myer and American Racism* (Berkeley: University of California Press, 1989), 7–10.

23. See Arthur Hansen and Nora M. Jesch, eds., *Japanese American Evacuation: An Oral History Project*, vol. 5, *Guards and Townspeople* (Westport, CT: Meckler, 1991).

24. See Arthur Hansen, ed., *Japanese American Evacuation: An Oral History Project*, vol. 3, *Analysts* (Westport, CT: Meckler, 1991).

25. A top wage of $19 a month was established for internees without special skills, which was far lower that the rates provided by CWA and WPA. Participation in the Work Corps was voluntary.

26. Hayashi, *Democratizing the Enemy*, 9.

27. On the Japanese American Citizens League's (JACL's) initial reaction, see Emergency Defense Council, Seattle Chapter, JACL, Report Submitted to the Tolan Committee on National Defense Migration, February 28, 1942.

28. On educational policy in the WRA camps, see Thomas James, *Exile Within: The Schooling of Japanese Americans, 1942–1945* (Cambridge, MA: Harvard University Press, 1987); U.S. Department of the Interior, WRA, *Education Program in the War Relocation Centers* (Washington, DC: U.S. Government Printing Office, 1945).

29. Alexander Leighton, *The Governing of Men: General Principles and Recommendations Based on Experience at a Japanese Relocation Camp* (Princeton, NJ: Princeton University Press, 1945), 77.

30. Conference on Evacuation of Enemy Aliens, Salt Lake City, April 7, 1942, Records of the WRA, Washington Office Records, Documentary Headquarters Files, Meetings and Conferences, 1942–43, R.G. 210, National Archives.

31. Senate Resolution No. 166 on Segregation of Loyal and Disloyal Japanese, Senate Doc. 96 (18–1), 1943, 9 (statement of James F. Byrnes, Director of War Mobilization).

32. John Embree, "Causes of Unrest at Relocation Centers," WRA Community Analysis Section, Community Analysis Report No. 2, 1943, Records of the WRA, Reports Division, R.G. 210, National Archives.

33. On the "old bachelors," see Leighton, *Governing of Men*, 130–31. See also Charles Kikuchi, *The Kikuchi Diary: Chronicle from an American Concentration Camp* (Champagne–Urbana: University of Illinois Press, 1973).

34. John L. DeWitt, *Final Report: Japanese Evacuation from the West Coast, 1942* (Washington, DC: U.S. Government Printing Office, 1943).

35. In a confidential memo to Dillon Myer dated January 14, 1943, Mike Masaoka of the Japanese American Citizens League contributed to this characterization of "troublemakers" in the camps. Myer described protesters similarly in his testimony before the Dies Committee. See http://www.resisters.com/Jan_14_1943_WRA.pdf.

36. War Relocation Authority, "Preliminary Factors of Information," n.d., Records of the WRA, Washington Office Records, Information, Objectives, and Principles of WRA, R.G. 210, National Archives. On the curtailment of judo instruction, see *Semi-Annual Report, January 1–June 30, 1943* (Washington, DC: U.S. Government Printing Office, 1943), 37. This same report discusses the encouragement of participation in American-style organizations like the Boy Scouts.

37. "Japs Petted and Feasted in U.S. While Americans in Nippon Are Tortured," *Denver Post*, April 23, 1943. Similar articles appeared in the paper in the last week of April and the first week of May 1943.

38. War Relocation Authority, Comment on Charges Made by the *Denver Post* in the Issue of April 23: Further Statements Made by the *Denver Post* in a Series of Articles . . . with Comments by Officials of the War Relocation Authority, May 1943,

Records of the WRA, Washington Office Records, Information, Policy, Objectives, R.G. 210, National Archives.

39. "Warren Assails WRA Bungling in Tule Lake Camp: Has Destroyed Faith of Citizens, He Says," *Chicago Daily Tribune,* January 21, 1944, 5; "WRA Called Incompetent at Tule Lake Riot Probe," *Christian Science Monitor,* November 30, 1943, 3; Laurence Burd, "Tule Lake Riot Is Laid to WRA Failure to Act," *Chicago Daily Tribune,* November 30, 1943, 1.

40. Embree, "Causes of Unrest at Relocation Centers."

41. Hayashi, *Democratizing the Enemy,* 45–57.

42. U.S. War Relocation Authority, *Semi-Annual Report, January 1–June 30, 1943,* Records of the WRA, R.G. 210, National Archives. See also U.S. War Relocation Authority, *Semi-Annual Report, January 1–June 30, 1943,* Records of the WRA, R.G. 210, National Archives; *WRA: A Story of Human Conservation* (Washington, DC: U.S. Government Printing Office, 1946), 51–58.

43. "Statement of United States Citizen of Japanese Ancestry," cited in Daniels, *Prisoners without Trial,* 69.

44. WRA, *Semi-Annual Report, January 1–June 30, 1943,* 14.

45. Dillon Myer, director of the WRA, statements at a WRA Conference, Albany Hotel, Denver, Colorado, January 28, 29, and 30, 1943, Records of the WRA, Washington Office Records, Documentary Headquarters Files, Meetings and Conferences, 1942–43, R.G. 210, National Archives.

46. U.S. War Relocation Authority, *Nisei in Uniform* (Washington, DC: U.S. Government Printing Office, 1944).

47. On the WRA media campaign, see press clippings file, including the pamphlet collection titled *Nisei in the War against Japan* (Washington, DC: U.S. Government Printing Office, April 1945). Stilwell's words appeared originally in the *Los Angeles Times,* December 9, 1945, and are cited in Myer, *WRA: A Story of Human Conservation,* 131.

48. WRA, *Semi-Annual Report, January 1–June 30, 1943,* 10–11.

49. WRA, *Nisei in Uniform.* Caption of one photograph reads, "The USO's in the relocation centers are usually kept busy providing entertainment for Nisei boys on leave to visit their parents, wives, and sweethearts."

50. On the Heart Mountain draft resistance, see interviews with Frank Seishi Emi and James M. Omura in *Japanese American World War II Evacuation Oral History Project, Part IV: Resisters,* ed. Arthur Hansen (Munich: K. G. Saur, 1995).

51. Eric L. Muller, *Free to Die for Their Country: The Story of the Japanese-American Draft Resisters during World War II* (Chicago: University of Chicago Press, 2001), 64–99. See also *Hearing before District Court* (transcript), August 31, 1944, U.S. v. Kiyoshi Okamoto et al., 1943–44, Records of District Courts of the United States, 1685–2009, R.G. 21, National Archives at Denver.

52. The camp at Moab, Utah, operated from December 1942 through April 1943, after which inmates were moved to an abandoned Indian Training School at Leupp, Arizona. Henry Ueno describes the camp in an interview with John Tateishi, *And Justice for All,* 203. See also Bruce D. Louthan and Lloyd M. Pierson, "Moab Japanese-American Isolation Center: The Dark Postlude to the History of the Dalton Wells CCC Camp," *Canyon Legacy* 19 (Fall–Winter 1993): 28–31.

53. WRA, *Semi-Annual Report, January 1–June 30, 1943,* 19. WRA administrators called segregation "a sifting of the dangerous minority that need to be detained

from the wholesome majority whose location it is the principal object of the WRA to achieve." Office of the Solicitor, "Memorandum on the Validity of Detention," January 4, 1944.

54. Tolan Committee report, cited in Office of the Solicitor, "A Memorandum on the Validity of Detainment."

55. Myer, *Uprooted Americans*, 54.

56. For a firsthand account of the Kibei experience, see Interview with Harry Yoshio Ueno, in Hansen, ed., *Japanese American WW II Evacuation - Part IV: Resisters*, 3–56. See also Minoru Kiyota, *Beyond Loyalty: The Story of a Kibei* (Honolulu: University of Hawaii Press, 1997).

57. The characterization of Kibei as batlike also resonated with popular racist imagery that depicted the Japanese as vermin during the war. See Dower, *War without Mercy*, 77–93.

58. See Leighton, *Governing of Men*, 68–69.

59. Dillon Myer, cited in Hayashi, *Democratizing the Enemy*, 161–62. See also *Hearings on S. 444, A bill providing for the transfer of certain functions of the WRA to the War Department*, Subcomm. of the Comm. on Military Affairs, November 1943, U.S. Senate, 78th Cong., 1st Sess., pt. 4, p. 24 (statement of Dillon Myer). Myer declared that "a good many [of the Kibei] are bachelors."

60. See Hayashi, *Democratizing the Enemy*, 161–62.

61. David L. Eng, *Racial Castration: Managing Masculinity in Asian America* (Durham, NC: Duke University Press, 2001), 18.

62. Minoru Yasui, as told to Jack Cramer, *Portland Oregonian Sunday Magazine*, February 4, 1940, in Myer, *Uprooted Americans*, 5.

63. Eng, *Racial Castration*, 18.

64. Myer, *WRA: A Story of Human Conservation*, 63–74.

65. See, e.g., the following newspaper articles: Rodney L. Brink, "The Wide Horizon: Back of the Japanese Uprising," *Christian Science Monitor*, December 9, 1942, 26; "The Southland: Interned Japs Allowed Control at Tule Lake," *Los Angeles Times*, June 7, 1943, 9; "Assails WRA Freeing of Japanese Group: Dies Subcommittee Says 73 Had Butoku-Kai Membership," *New York Times*, August 24, 1943, 3; Mary Spargo, "Jap Segregation Plan: Loyal, Disloyal to Be Sorted," *Washington Post*, July 8, 1943, 15.

66. *Hearings on S. 444*, pt. 4, November 24, 1943, p. 246 (statement of Major-General M. G. White).

67. The WRA reported that "for a week or so in early November [1943], Tule Lake displaced the battle fronts in top news interest with the West Coast press"; *Semi-Annual Report, July 1–December 31, 1943*, 23. See, e.g., see Nick Bourne, "Focal Point of Trouble at Camp Was 1200 Kibei," *Los Angeles Times*, November 7, 1943, 11.

68. Carl Mydans, "Tule Lake Segregation Center," *Life*, March 20, 1944, 25–35.

69. Myer, *WRA: A Story of Human Conservation*, 118.

70. Francis Warren, "Tule Director Admits Japs Out of Control," *Los Angeles Times*, December 21, 1943, 1A.

71. On November 5, 1943, the San Francisco *Chronicle* characterized top WRA administrators as "phonies" and "bad public servants." Up to this time, the *Chronicle* had been relatively sympathetic to the WRA.

72. Myer, *Uprooted Americans*, 118.

73. *Hearings on S. 444*, pt. 4, p. 250 (statement of Dillon Myer).

74. Ibid.

75. Photographs of Nisei casualties appear in the WRA publicity pamphlet, *Nisei in Uniform*, 20–21. See also "The Nisei's Fighting Chance," *Christian Science Monitor*, January 29, 1945, 16; "263 Casualties among Nisei in U.S. Forces," *Chicago Daily Tribune*, November 23, 1944, 16.

76. George H. Roeder, *The Censored War: American Visual Experience during World War II* (New Haven, CT: Yale University Press, 1995).

77. Some African Americans commented on this double standard. See Harry McAlpin, "Stimson Raps Jap Jim Crow," *Atlanta Daily World*, December 15, 1944, 1, 6; L. C. Ledrazza, "Jap American Combatants Cited," *Atlanta Daily World*, August 2, 1945, 1.

78. WRA, *Nisei in Uniform*, 20.

79. Minutes of the Special Emergency National Conference, Japanese American Citizens League, November 24, 1942, Salt Lake City, Utah, UCLA Library Special Collection 2010, box 296, cited in Muller, *Free to Die for Their Country*, 42. See also Tateishi, *And Justice for All* (1984), xxiv.

80. White officer, quoted in WRA, *Nisei in Uniform*, 19.

81. U.S. War Relocation Authority, *The Evacuated People: A Quantitative Description* (Washington, DC: U.S. Government Printing Office, 1946), 177–96.

82. Dower, *War without Mercy*, 122–24.

83. Ibid.

84. Peter T. Suzuki, "Anthropologists in the Wartime Camps for Japanese Americans: A Documentary Study," *Dialectical Anthropology* 6 (August 1981): 45–46; Francis McCollum Feeley, *America's Concentration Camps during World War II: Social Science and the Japanese American Internment* (New Orleans, LA: University Press of the South, 1999); Richard H. Minear, "Cross-Cultural Perception and World War II: American Japanists of the 1940s and Their Images of Japan," *International Studies Quarterly* 24, no. 4 (December 1980): 555–80.

85. On the principles of the Community Analysis section, see John F. Embree, "Community Analysis: An Example of Anthropology in Government," *American Anthropologist* 46, no. 3 (July–September, 1944).

86. See, e.g., John F. Embree, *The Japanese Nation: A Social Survey* (New York: Rinehart, 1945); Geoffrey Gorer, "Themes in Japanese Culture," *Transactions of the New York Academy of Sciences*, 2nd ser., 5, no. 1 (November 1943), 106–24, cited in Dower, *War without Mercy*, 124.

87. Anne McClintock, *Imperial Leather: Race, Gender, and Sexuality in the Colonial Conquest* (New York: Routledge, 1995), 358.

Stories of Homecoming

1. Franklin Delano Roosevelt, Fireside Chat, July 28, 1943, in Rosenman, ed. *The Public Papers and Addresses of Franklin D. Roosevelt*, vol. 12 (New York: Random House, 1943), 333.

2. Suzanne Mettler, *Soldiers to Citizens: The G.I. Bill and the Making of the Greatest Generation* (New York: Oxford University Press, 2007); Kathleen J. Frydl, *The GI Bill* (New York: Cambridge University Press, 2011); Margot Canaday, "Building a

Straight State: Sexuality and Social Citizenship under the 1944 G.I. Bill," *Journal of American History* 90 (December 2003): 935–57.

3. David H. Onkst, "'First a Negro . . . Incidentally a Veteran': Black World War II Veterans and the G.I. Bill of Rights in the Deep South, 1944–1948," *Journal of Social History* 31, no. 3 (Spring 1998): 517–43.

4. Steven Rosales, "Fighting the Peace at Home: Mexican American Veterans and the 1944 GI Bill of Rights," *Pacific Historical Review* 80, no. 4 (2011): 597–627.

5. Mettler, *Soldiers to Citizens*, 136–43.

6. Edward Humes, "How the GI Bill Shunted Blacks into Vocational Training," *Journal of Blacks in Higher Education* 53 (Autumn 2006): 92–104.

7. Margot Canaday, "Building a Straight State: Sexuality and Social Citizenship under the 1944 G.I. Bill," *Journal of American History* 90, no. 3 (December 2003): 942; Onkst, "'First a Negro . . . Incidentally a Veteran,'" 520.

8. Allan Berube, *Coming Out Under Fire: The History of Gay Men and Women in World War II* (New York: Plume, 1991).

9. Ira Katznelson, *When Affirmative Action Was White: An Untold History of Racial Inequality in Twentieth-century America* (New York: Norton, 2005), 113–41.

10. "Tuohy Picks Aid to Keep Eye on Service Wives," *Chicago Daily Tribune*, August 3, 1945, 13; "Wife Accused," *Chicago Daily Tribune*, August 7, 1945, 14.

11. "Unfaithful Service Wife Stirs Judge to Blast Morals of Day," *Washington Post*, May 19, 1945, 1.

12. Shortly after returning from overseas, Fred reveals his marital infidelity when, in an intoxicated state, he mistakes Peggy Stephenson (Teresa Wright) for another woman and attempts to pull her into bed.

13. "Divorce Pleas by GIs Rising Sharply Here," *Washington Post*, November 17, 1945, 3.

INDEX

100th Battalion, 185, 197
442nd Combat Team, 185–86, 188
1944 Serviceman's Readjustment Act. *See* GI Bill

able-bodied workers, 28–29, 31, 33, 36–38, 118, 122
Ackerman, Nelson, 104
adultery, 144, 208
African Americans: in CCC, 74, 76, 78–79, 78–81, 84, 91–93; civil rights leaders, 6, 43–45, 72, 144, 149; and CWA, 20; discrimination against, 6, 16–17, 27, 38–47, 123, 144, 147–49; families, 40; and forgotten-man narratives, 13, 27, 43; juvenile delinquents and hoodlums, 144, 168, 205; lynching of, 44–47; in OCD, 146–49, 152, 156, 163–65, 167–68; transients, 49–50, 60; as unemployable, 36, 38–40; in WPA, 32, 36, 38–44; in WWII, 195–96; zoot suiters, 170, 179
African American women: Depression-era stereotypes, 98, 108–9; employment, 98–99, 101–2, 123–25, 129–30; in Harlem race riots, 168; relief for, 43–44, 110–11, 114, 128–30; sewing projects, 123–25, 130
Agricultural Adjustment Administration (AAA), 46
agricultural labor, 27, 36–37, 39, 46, 74, 109, 123–25, 191, 225n19
Ahmed, Sara, 8–9
Aid to Dependent Children, 119, 121, 126
air raid wardens, 152–59, 161–67
Akridge, Garth, 74
Algren, Nelson, 69–70
Alvarez, Luis, 170
American Century, The (Luce), 141, 159
American Federation of Labor, 71
Americanism, 8, 29, 139, 141, 178, 195–96
Americanization, 77–78, 80, 177, 180

American Red Cross, 148
American way of life, 25, 30, 35, 47–48, 157
American Women's Volunteer Services, 148
Anderson, Nels, 52, 120, 220n3, 221n25, 221nn36–37
Andrews, Dana, 207
antimiscegenation laws, 190
Aronson, Julian, 14

bachelors: old, 179, 189–90; working-class subculture, 70, 93
Badger, Anthony, 41
Bailey, Josiah, 45
Baker, Kenneth, "Swimming and Boating on Lake McDonald," 87
Bakke, E. Wight, 18
Banning, Margaret Culkin, 27–28
Battle of Washington, 1–2
Bechdolt, Jack, 158–59
Berlant, Lauren, 3, 213n3, 213n24
Best, Ray, 193
Best Years of Our Lives, The (Wyler), 207–9
Bethune, Mary McLeod, 129
Biggers, John, 101
"Bill Meade: Brass-Tag Man" (Frazer), 22–24
birth control, 117
Blake, Doris, 102–3; "Wielding Club of Authority May Cure the Shrew," 97
Blake, Samuel, 70
Bluebeard's Eighth Wife (Paramount), 97
Bonus veterans, 1–2, 9, 13, 57, 203
Boy Scouts, 147, 180, 241n36
Boys Town (Taurog), 69
Bradley, Omar, 206
Bramford, James M., 236n60
breadwinner ideal (male-headed home), 14, 65, 207, 209; and citizenship, 173, 197, 202. *See also* forgotten man; white male householders
Brock, William, 16, 211n9

247

INDEX

Buffalo Knitting and Sewing Project, 38
Bullard, Robert Lee, 27
Bureau of Indian Affairs, 225n17
Burgess, Ernest W., 143–44
Butoku-kai (Japanese Military Virtue Society), 179

Camp Frontier (transients), 60
Camp Roosevelt (CCC), 74
Canaday, Margot, 5, 53, 206, 224n8
Capra, Frank, 132
Carter, Hodding, 154
Cartier, Joseph, 63–64
CCC. *See* Civilian Conservation Corps
Century of Progress Exposition (Chicago), 96
charity. *See* private charity
Chatfield, Caroline, 97
Chicago, Illinois, 96, 97, 106, 158; South Side, 148
Chicago Daily News, 140
Chicago Daily Tribune, 102
Chicago Defender, 44
Children's Bureau, 52
Childs, Marquis, *This Is Your War*, 140
chiselers, 27, 177
chronically dependent older woman, 120
chronic relief population, 36, 51–52, 57, 59, 120
citizenship, 7–9; and breadwinner ideal, 173, 197, 202; gender and racial dimensions, 71, 91–93, 114, 177–78, 197, 201–2; and heterosexuality, 206–7; Issei, 174, 184; Japanese Americans, 177, 181, 187; martial idealism, 187–88; and masculine youth, 91, 182, 201–2; Nisei soldiers and, 197. *See also* social citizenship
citizen-soldiers: air raid wardens, 152–59, 161–67; gap between soldiers and, 151–52; grimness and determination, 136–38, *138–39*, 152, 172; hostility toward women and racialized others, 136–37, 162, 167, 205. *See also* Office of Civilian Defense
civic myths, 211n7, 213n3
civic preparedness, narratives and rituals of, 136–37. *See also* Office of Civilian Defense
civic stories: civic genres, 3, 99; gender, racial, and sexual aspects of, 2–10, 201–9
Civilian Conservation Corps (CCC), 4, 57, 205–7; African Americans in, 74, 76,
78–81, 84, 91–93; age eligibility, 72–73; compared to WRA, 177, 187–88; establishment of, 71–76; homoeroticism, 70, 93, 224n8; homosociality, 81–87, 201–2; intergenerational relationships, 81–82; loosely-clad forestry worker, image of, 70, 89, 91, 93, 188; Mexican Americans in, 91; militarized U.S. Army camps, 71, 73–74, 76, 80–87, 94; nationalism in, 91–93; Native Americans in, 91, 225n17; and natural landscape, 77, 79–80; physical development narratives, 79, 87–91; popularity of, 70–71, 73, 94, 113; publicity pamphlets, *89*; racial nondiscrimination policy, 72, 74, 91–92; racism and segregation, 72, 74–76, 80–81, 91–93, 226n42; and whiteness, 89, 91; and women's exclusion, 93; working-class youth narratives, 76–80
Civilian Defense Volunteer Office, OCD, 136, 147, 152, 159–66
Civilian Protection, OCD, 136, 147, 152–59, 161–62, 164–65
civil rights leaders, 6, 43–45, 72, 144, 149
Civil Works Administration (CWA), 19–21, 37, 45, 112, 114–16, 118; demobilization of, 24, 28, 118; discrimination against people of color, 20; graft and political corruption, 21, 24–25; and women, 20, 115–16
Civil Works Service (CWS), 20, 115–16
Clapper, Raymond, 163
Clark, Marian, 109
cocktail saboteurs, 147
Colbert, Claudette, 97
Colcord, Joanna C., 163
Collins, Charles, 96
colonial administration, 200
Committee on Mobilization for New York at War, 135
community, 7–9, 204–5; traditional images of, 141, 158–60, 163. *See also* citizenship
Community Analysis section of WRA, 176, 179, 199–201
Community Chest, Reading County, Pennsylvania, 150
Community Welfare section of WRA, 176–77, 200
"concentration camps," 71, 82, 94, 171, 177, 181
Conference on the Emergency Needs of Women, 111–14

Conference on the Participation of Negro Women and Children in Federal Welfare Programs, 129
congregate care, 59, 113
Connery, William P., 71
Connolly, Walter, 97
construction projects, 20, 31–32, 116
Cook, Allen, 85
Cools, Victor, 43
Cooper, Gary, 97, 132
cooperative federalism, 35, 38, 45
Costigian, Edward, 106
Costigian-Wagner antilynching bill, 44–45
Cousins, Norman, 98
Couzens, James, 71, 82
Coyle, David Cushman, 66
cream puffs, 87
Crocker, Holly A., 99
Current Life, 173
Cutting (Senator), 224n9
CWA. *See* Civil Works Administration
CWS. *See* Civil Works Service

Daughters of Spanking Fathers' Club, 97
Davis, Maxine, 117
Davis, Mike, 213n2
D'Emilio, John, 235n40
Democratic Party, Women's Division, 128
Democratic political machine, 26
Denver, Colorado, 175
Denver Post, 180–81
Department of Agriculture, 175
Department of Justice, 153
Department of the Navy, 153
De Priest, Oscar, 72
Dern, George H., 81
Detroit race riots, 167–68
DeWitt, John L., 175
Dies, Martin, 167
Dies Committee, 179–80, 181
direct relief (dole), 29, 110; criticism of, 18–19, *34*; as demoralizing, 18, 22–24, 30–31, 35
disloyalty. *See* political loyalty and disloyalty
Division of Transient Activities (FERA), 52–53
Division of Women's and Professional Projects (WPA), 125–27
divorce, 97–98, 102–3, 208
"Does the World Owe John Doe a Living?" (Wayne), 26
domestic service, 108–9, 123–25, 130
Dower, John, 142, 199, 240n21

Drinnon, Richard, 175
Duis, Perry, 158
Dupay, R. Ernest, 154

Early, Stephen, 83
Eisenhower, Milton S., 175, 177, 178
emasculation: of forgotten man, 22–25, 28, 33, 48, 116–17; by wives, 104–5, 130
Emergency Conservation Work, 226n42
Emergency Work Relief Program, 118
Emergency Works Program (FERA), 25
employables, 36, 118–19
Employment Service office, 206
Eng, David, 190
entitlement, 1, 7, 62, 119, 128, 189, 197–98, 201–2, 209
equality, 91–93
Erenberg, Lewis, 141
espionage, 150, 156, 170, 171
exclusion laws, 190

Fairbanks, Douglas, 96
Fair Play Committee, 187
faithless wives, 208–9
family: African American, 40; heterosexual ideal, 8, 188; traditional ideals of, 141, 158–59; white *vs.* Japanese, 173. *See also* kinship metaphors for national identity; white male householders; wives
Fauset, Crystal Bird, 149, 156, 165
Fechner, Robert H., 71–73, 75–76, 83, 92, 111, 226n42
Federal Arts, Theater and Writing Projects, *30*, 125–26
Federal Bureau of Investigation (FBI), 171
Federal Economy Act (1932), 100
Federal Emergency Relief Administration (FERA), 4, 16–19, 29, 45; data on female transients, 61; Division of Transient Activities, 52–53; Emergency Works Program, 25; guidelines on fraternization in transient camps, 64; racial discrimination, 16–17; service projects, 116; suspension of, 114; transition to WPA, 28; Women's Division, 37, 110–16
federal government: centralized bureaucracy, 48, 66, 120; cooperative federalism, 35, 38, 45; expansion of, 3–4, 12, 27, 50–52, 57, 116, 120, 166, 204; paternalism, 28, 48, 62, 66, 159, 167. *See also* New Deal relief policies; specific government agencies
Federal Security Agency, 173

250 INDEX

Federal Theater Project (FTP), 97
Federal Transient Program (FTP), 18, 53, 57–65, 111, 177, 222n57; establishment in FERA, 52–53, 57; federal nature of, 58–59; homosociality in, 93
FERA. *See* Federal Emergency Relief Administration
fifth columnism, 149, 169–72
Flanagan, Hallie, 125
Fontanne, Lynn, 96
Forestry Service, 74, 76, 78
forestry workers. *See* loosely-clad forestry worker
forgotten man, 3–4, 8, 11–15; affective dimensions, 45–46; civic participation, 3–4, 35; conservative counternarratives, 25–28, 29, 48; in cultural texts, 213n4; demoralization of, 15, 18, 22–24, 30–31, 35, 104; emasculation of, 22–25, 28, 33, 48, 116–17; and federal relief, 15–19, 22–25, 28, 33, 48, 116–17; gender and racial aspects, 22–24; morale-boosting, 104–5; pauperization of, 22, 24–29, 31; popular narratives, 13–15, 21–25; revitalization of, 29, 35, 115–17; subversive homosocial fraternization, 15; unemployables and, 37; as white figure, 17; working wives of, 101–2 (*see also* married women workers); and WPA, 28–35, 118–21. *See also* New Deal relief policies
Forman, Clark, 39
Fort Eustis (transient camp), 221n35
Fort Lauderdale, Florida, 46
Foster, Preston, 172
Foucault, Michel, 9
Frazer, Elizabeth, "Bill Meade: Brass-Tag Man," 22–24
"Fred Salo—Forgotten Man" (Parry), 14–15
fruit tramps, 179, 190
FTP. *See* Federal Theater Project; Federal Transient Program
Fyn, Arthur, 224n5

Gable, Clark, 97
Gallagher, Hugh, 173
Garland, David, 46
gender: and citizenship, 71, 91–93, 114, 177–78, 197, 201–2; and civic stories, 2–10, 201–9; and the forgotten man, 22–24; and national identity and collectivity, 197–98; and New Deal relief policies, 12–13, 47–48, 128; sensational narratives of outlaws, 3–4; and sexual anxieties, 3–6, 114, 135, 141–44; traditional roles, 114, 118–21, 130–31, 137, 154; in U.S. civic culture, 2–10, 135–37; and World War II, 143–45. *See also* masculinity; woman-blaming narratives; women
General Electric, 159
GI Bill (1944 Serviceman's Readjustment Act), 203–4, 206–7, 209
Gillis, Willie, 203
Girl Scouts, 147
Glueck, Eleanor T., 143
Golden, Stephanie, 106
Goleta, California, 169
Gone with the Wind (Mitchell), 98, 108
Good Neighbor Policy, 141, 159
Gordon, Linda, 123, 231n60, 232n62
Great Britain's Home Defense, 149
Great Depression. *See* forgotten man; New Deal relief policies; woman-blaming narratives
Green, William, 71
Groves, Ernest, 62
Guthrie, John Dennett, 79, 82, 84, 88–89

Hagood, Johnson, 83
Handbook for Auxiliary Police, 155
Happy Days (newspaper), 77, 84, 86
Harlem, 148; race riots, 167–68
Harris, Trudier, 46
Harvey, Evelyn, 62
Hawaiians, 185–86
Hayashi, Brian Masaru, 182, 211n9
Hearst editorial cartoons, 137, *138*
Heart Mountain (internment camp), 174, 187
Hell Cat (Columbia), 97
heterosexuality, 8, 188, 206–7
Hickok, Lorena, 117, 128
Higbie, Frank Tobias, 219n1
Hirsch, Susan B., 141
hoarding, 147, 160
hoboes. *See* transients
Hobson, Barbara Meil, 51
home defense, rhetoric of, 145–54. *See also* citizen-soldiers; Office of Civilian Defense
homelessness. *See* transients
homeliness, rhetoric of, 140–41
homosexuality: antihomosexual campaigns, 5; discrimination against veterans, 206–7; exclusion from military service, 235n40; homoeroticism in CCC, 70, 93, 224n8;

INDEX

transient perversion narratives, 48–58, 49–58, 51, 63–64, 67, 69–70, 85, 179, 190, 220n3; wartime migration, 144
homosociality: among Kibei, 189–90, 198; among Nisei, 179–80; among transients, 55–56, 93; in CCC, 81–87, 82–87, 201–2; and the forgotten man, 15; homosocial-fraternal model of community, 8; intergenerational male intimacy, 70; as subversive, 15, 52, 82, 85, 179–80
Honey, Maureen, 162
hoodlums, 168, 191, 194–95, 205
Hoover, Herbert, 1, 13, 19, 219n115
Hoover, J. Edgar, 143
Hoovervilles, 57
Hopkins, Harry, 16–21, 24, 29–32, 36, 64, 111, 113, 115, 118, 120–21, 128; *Spending to Save*, 31, 65, 119, 127
Hot School Lunches program, 122, 126–27
householders. *See* breadwinner ideal; white male householders
Household Workers Training program, 122, 126–27
Housekeeping Aides Project, 122, 126, 130
House Un-American Activities Committee, 167
Howard, Donald S., 37, 121, 128
Hoyt, Ray, 88; *"We Can Take It": A Short Story of the C.C.C.*, 86
Huber, Harold, 171
Hufford, Keith, 86
Humes, Edward, 206
Hurst, Fannie, *Imitation of Life*, 98

Ickes, Harold, 17, 20
idleness, 15–16, 18, 71, 79, 81–84, 87–88, 93, 180, 191
Imitation of Life (Hurst), 98
intergenerational relationships, 3, 52, 55–56, 70, 179, 189–90, 220n3
International Association of Machinists, 71–72
internment camps. *See* War Relocation Authority
interventionism, 135, 137, 166–67, 201, 205
Irvine, Janice, 66, 212n12
Issei, 178, 190; citizenship, 174, 184; internment, 171, 181–82; loyalties, 173
It Happened One Night (Columbia), 97

JACL. *See* Japanese American Citizens League
Jameson, Fredric, 132

Japan: national character, 199–201; postwar occupation of, 201; as U.S. enemy in WWII, 183, 196
Japan Association, 171, 182
Japanese American Citizens League (JACL), 173, 178, 182, 241n35
Japanese Americans, 6, 8–9, 167–68, *192–93*; civil and citizenship rights, 177, 181, 187; dual citizenship, 174; exclusion from war mobilization parade, 135; generational aspects, 178–79, 190; internment in WWII, 169–71, 175–95, 205; loyalties, 169–74, 178; old bachelors, 179, 189–90; public opinion on, 170; and sexuality, 189–90; voluntary resettlement, 175. *See also* Issei; Kibei; Nisei; War Relocation Authority
Japanese Military Virtue Society (Butoku-kai), 179
Jenkins, Burris, Jr., *138*
Jezebels, 108
Jim Crow South, 41, 76, 135
Jones, Jacqueline, 123
Jones, Marion, 46–47
Joyce, Brenda, 172
judo clubs, 179–80
juvenile delinquency, 82, 143–44, 168, 179, 182, 199, 205

Kibei, 5, 7, *193*, 202; as batlike, 189; as disloyal troublemakers, 182–83, 188–95, 197–98, 205–6; expulsion from U.S. Armed Services, 173, 182; as no-no boys, 194; as pressure boys, 191; stereotypes of, 201; stigmatization of, 189–90; as young hoodlums, 194–95
kinship metaphors for national identity, 8–9, 66, 149, 201–2, 213n24
Kolb, Andy and Meri, 103

Labor Department, 74
labor groups, 71–73, 77, 83
La Guardia, Fiorello, 135, 146, 150–51, 154, 161, 168, 236n64
Landis, James M., 146, 151–52, 153–54
Lane, Marie Dresden, 18, 121
Laughlin, Gail, 98
Leigh, Vivien, 108
Leonard, Kevin Allen, 144, 149
Leuchtenberg, William, 35
Lewis, Morris, 59
Leyendecker, J. C., "Southbound Hitchhiker," 49–50, *50*, 53

252 INDEX

Liberty Bond campaign, 134
Life (magazine), 191, *192–93*
Lincoln College, 148
Lindner, Pearl, 38
Lippmann, Walter, 151
Little Tokyo, U.S.A. (Twentieth Century Fox), 171
loafers, 3, 27, 87, 125, 177
local government, relief administration by, 16–17, 28, 35, 118, 124, 206
localism, 32–33, 35, 45, 48, 149, 150
loosely-clad forestry worker, 70, 89, 91, 93, 188
Los Angeles Times, 193
Lost Battalion, 185
loyalty. *See* political loyalty and disloyalty
Luce, Henry, *The American Century*, 141, 159
Lunt, Alfred, 96
lynching, 44–47
Lynd, Helen Merrell, 47
Lynd, Robert Staughton, 47

MacArthur, Douglas, 1
MacRae, Hugh, 63
Maher, Neil, 211n9, 224n8
male-headed home. *See* breadwinner ideal; white male householders
mammy figure, 108
Manzanar (internment camp), 182
married women workers, 99–102, 108–9, 117–20, 130–31
Masaoka, Mike, 173, 241n35
masculinity: and citizenship, 91, 93–95, 182, 201–2; military mobilization of youth, 142–45; and self-reliance, 32; and sexuality, 86–87; socialization of youth, 173–74, 198–99, 202. *See also* emasculation; forgotten man; white male householders
Massachusetts Air Raid Protection School, 160
Masuda, Kazuo, 185–86
Masuda, Mary, 186
Mattosh, Steve, 103
Mayo, Virginia, 207
McClintock, Anne, 202
McDaniel, Hattie, 108
McEntee, James J., 71, 73, 79, 81, 83, 90, 93, 228n85
McGuire, Matthew F., 208
McMillen, A. Wayne, 54
McNutt, Paul V., 160–61

means testing, 18, 19, 115
Mears, H., 84
Meet John Doe (Warner Brothers), 132
Merchant Marines, 207
Mettler, Suzanne, 8, 48
Mexican Americans: and CWA, 20; discrimination in local relief, 16–17, 27, 206; employment discrimination, 144; and federal relief policies, 6; forgotten-man narratives, 13, 27; juvenile delinquency, 144; and OCD, 146, 156; scapegoating of, 205; as unemployable, 38; zoot suiters, 142, 144, 168, 170, 179
Mexican American women: employment, 98, 101–2, 124–25; relief for, 114, 128; sewing projects, 130
migrant laborers, 65–66, 179, 189–90
Miller, Kelly, 41
Miller, Robert Earnest, 148, 161
Miller, Robert L., 85
Minehan, Thomas, 54–55, 106
minuteman, figure of, 155–56
Mitchell, Margaret, *Gone with the Wind*, 98, 108
Mobilization for Human Needs, 1940, 136
Monaghan, Frank, 135
moral panics, 51–53
Mosley, George Van Horn, 92
mothers: mother-blaming narratives, 226n46; single, 38, 119, 126
Moynihan, Patrick, *The Negro Family*, 40
Murphy, J. Prentice, 2, 4, 9
Myer, Dillon S., 175, 184–85, 189, 191–95, 205, 241n35

nagging wives, 99, 102–4, 108–9
National Association for the Advancement of Colored People (NAACP), 167
National Council of Negro Women, 129
National Economy Act of 1932, 37
National Family Week, 146
national identity and collectivity, 8–9; gender and racial aspects, 197–98; and kinship metaphors, 66, 149, 201–2, 213n24. *See also* patriotism
national morale, 20, 75, 136, 146
national recovery, 11, 15, 21, 32, 47, 127; metaphors for, 78, 88, 93–95, 114
National Safety Conference, 102
national unity, 20, 142
National Woman's Party, 98
nativism, 27, 174, 186
Negro Family, The (Moynihan), 40

Negro on Relief, The (Division of Social Research, WPA), 40
"Negro Project Workers, 1936" (Smith), *42, 43*
neighborliness, rhetoric of, 141
New Deal relief policies: administration by state and local governments, 16–17, 28, 35, 118, 124, 206; advent of, 219n115; as a business, 121; compared to WRA, 176–77; criticism of, 18–19, *34,* 120–21, 205–6; as demoralizing, 18, 22–24, 30–31, 35; direct relief, 29, 110; as effeminate, 137, 152, 160; gender and racial dimensions, 12–13, 47–48, 128; nation-saving rhetoric, 114, 120, 131; punitive implications, 37, 94, 99, 110–11, 114, 119, 127, 129, 222n57; sexual politics of, 3–10, 57, 95; social objectives, 163; as threat to civic ideals, 27–28; and women, 109–18; work relief, 110. *See also* Civilian Conservation Corps; Civil Works Administration; Federal Emergency Relief Administration; forgotten man; GI Bill; Works Progress Administration
New England home life, 157–60
New Republic, 106, 157, 159–60
New York at War Parade, 134–35, 168
New York City, 110–11, 148, 167–68
Nisei, 177–82, 202; animosity against, 171–74, 177; draft resisters, 174, 187; loyalty of, 171–74, 182–87; soldiers, 183–87, 195–98
no-no boys, 194
Nordstrom, Nels Francis, 15
November incidents, 191–95
Nylander, Towne, 55–56

obligation, 7, 56, 62, 78, 118, 131, 136, 158–59, 173–74, 183, 187–88, 195, 198, 201–2
OCD. *See* Office of Civilian Defense
OCD Newsletter, 159–60
Office of Civilian Defense (OCD), 4, 135–39, 145–52, 166–68, 205, 207; African Americans in, 146–49, 152, 156, 163–65, 167–68; air raid wardens, 152–59, 161–67; Mexican Americans in, 146, 156; nonprotective branch, 136, 147, 152, 159–66; protective branch, 136, 147, 152–59, 161–62, 164–65; publicity, 150; racial segregation, 146, 147–49; sex segregation in, 161; total war rhetoric, 137–47; women in, 152, 159–66

Office of Education, 74, 77
Okamoto, Kiyoshi, 187
Oklahoma State Defense Council, 147
old bachelors, 179, 189–90
Omiya, Yoshinao, 195–96, *196*
Omura, James M., 173–74
Onkst, David H., 206
Our Job with the WPA (handbook), 32–35, *34*
Outland, George, 58
Owings, Chloe, 233n93
Ozer, S. D., 121–22

pansies, 87, 94
pantry-snoopers, 18, 24, 25, 115, 116–18, 232n62
Parmalee, Barbara, 157, 159–60
Parry, Tom Jones, "Fred Salo—Forgotten Man," 14–15
paternalism in federal government, 28, 48, 62, 66, 159, 167
Patman Bonus Bill, 1. *See also* Bonus veterans
patriarchal power, 8, 137, 197. *See also* breadwinner ideal; white male householders
patriotism, 78, 83–84, 87, 94, 136, 138, 140, 156, 166, 170, 178, 184, 197
Pearl Harbor, 137, 141, 151, 152, 159, 163, 171, 172
Pender County, North Carolina, 63
Perkins, Frances, 75
Perkins, Jackson, 96
perversion: and old bachelors, 189–90; transient homosexual perversion narratives, 49–58, 63–64, 67, 69–70, 85, 179, 220n3
Phillips, Norman, Jr., 208
Pickford, Mary, 96
pin money, 100, 102, 109
pioneer era, 77, 80
Plunkert, William J., 59, 62; "The Transient Program," 60
political loyalty and disloyalty, 153, 162, 170–74, 182–95, 197–98, 201, 205–6; War Department loyalty questionnaire, 183–84, 187–88
political protests: by Japanese American internees, 190–95; in support of CWA, 21, 24
Poston (internment camp), 182
Potter, Ellen C., 53, 59
private charity, 14, 38, 111–13, 118, 120, 163, 231n51

INDEX

promiscuity, 5, 99, 107–9, 112, 131
prostitutes, 5, 105–9, 112
Public Works Administration, 19

race: and citizenship, 71, 91–93, 114, 177–78, 197, 201–2; and citizen-soldiers, 136–37, 162, 167, 205; and the forgotten man, 22–24; interracial aspects among transients, 224n7; and national identity and collectivity, 197–98; and New Deal relief policies, 12–13, 47–48, 128; in U.S. civic culture, 2–10, 135–37, 141–42, 198, 201–9; wartime politics of, 195–96. *See also* African Americans; Japanese Americans; Mexican Americans; whites
Race Relations Division, OCD, 149
race riots, 167–68
racial segregation, 72, 123, 148–49; in CCC, 72, 74–76, 80–81, 91–93, 226n42; and civic defense, 156; in Jim Crow South, 41, 76, 135; in military units, 141–42; in OCD, 146, 147–49; in women's work relief, 110–11
racism and racial discrimination, 13, 44, 114, 147–49, 174, 199, 236n64, 243n57; CCC nondiscrimination policy, 72, 74, 91–92; Federal Emergency Relief Administration (FERA), 16–17; in GI Bill, 205; against Japanese Americans, 171, 189; Roosevelt, Franklin on, 40–41; Southern white racial practices, 39–40, 123–24, 149, 206
Rawick, George, 92
Reade, J. O., 62, 222n57, 222n61
Reckless, Walter, 106–7
Reed, Ellery, 60
Reid, Carl Benton, 96
Reitman, Ben, 61
relief: old-style poor, 16, 120, 217n60. *See also* New Deal relief policies; private charity
relief dependency, 18–19, 22, 25–26, 81, 116, 122, 181
Republicans, 47, 71; criticism of Roosevelt administration, 62, 64, 66–67
Rockwell, Norman, 157, 203, *204*
Roeder, George H. Jr., 195
Ronald, James, *This Way Out*, 103
Roosevelt, Eleanor, 38, 205; in OCD, 146, 148–52, 161–65; and women's relief programs, 111–13
Roosevelt, Franklin: and CCC, 71–73, 93; on civilian defense, 153, 166; on dependency, 19; Executive Order 9066, 175; on federal relief, 28, 36; on forgotten man, 11, 13, 17, 203–4; on national morale, 136; on neighborliness, 141; on racial discrimination, 40–41; on threat of enemy attack, 150; "Three Essentials for Unemployment Relief," 16; on transient relief, 65; on WPA, 29
Roosevelt administration: criticism of, 66–67; Good Neighbor Policy, 141, 159; mobilization for war, 136–37; as political machine, 21; transient policy, 52–53; and women's relief programs, 110, 127–29; and WRA, 176, 201. *See also* New Deal relief policies
Rosales, Steven, 206
Rosenman, Samuel, 147
Ross, James A., "What WPA Means to the Negro Worker in New York State," 42
Russell Sage Foundation, 121; Charity Organization Department, 163
Ryan, Mary, 166

sabotage, 147, 150, 156, 170
Salt Lake City, Utah, 175
Saturday Evening Post, 49, *50*, 203, *204*
scapegoating, 3, 24, 177, 190; and national identity, 8–9; of Nisei and Kibei youth, 177; of prostitutes and female hoboes, 105, 106–8; of women for economic crisis, 98, 100, 122, 125, 131; of women in reconversion period, 207–9; during World War II, 137, 205. *See also* woman-blaming narratives
Schneidermann, Rose, 112–13
Schwartz, Bonnie, 231n51
Scientific American, 147
Scott, Thomas, 147
Seabury Commission, 105–6
Sedgwick, Eve, 4
Selective Service System, 151, 173
self-reliance, 18, 26, 30, 32, 36–37, 116
Selling, L., 103
sensationalism, 2–4, 50–51, 55–56, 63, 67, 100, 107, 177, 205
service projects, 32, 108, 116, 122
sewing rooms, 121–27, 129–30
sex panic, 5, 51–52, 66, 212n12
sexuality: discourses of sexual deviance, 9; female sex delinquency, 144; of female transients, 106–7, 109; of masculine youth in CCC, 86–87; of prostitutes, 106–7, 109; sexually promiscuous woman alone, 99, 107–9, 112, 131. *See also*

INDEX

heterosexuality; homosexuality; perversion
sexual predators: African Americans as, 50; transient "wolves," 3, 52, 55–56, 70, 220n3
Shakespeare, William, *The Taming of the Shrew*, 96–97, 132
Simkhovitch, Mary, 38
Sioux Falls, North Dakota, 97
Smith, Alfred Edgar, "Negro Project Workers, 1936," 42, 43
Smith, Rogers, 8, 48, 141, 211n7, 213n3
social citizenship, 3, 5, 7, 41, 71, 206–7
Social Security Act of 1935, 38, 126
social workers, 115, 163; female, 16, 18, 22–24; professional standards, 17; on unemployables, 36
soldiers, 203; gap between civilians and, 151–52; Nisei, 183–87, 195–98; valorization of, 142. *See also* GI Bill; veterans
Somebody in Boots (Algren), 69–70
"Southbound Hitchhiker" (Leyendecker), 49–50, *50,* 53
Southern Democrats, 6, 17, 45, 72
Southern white racial practices, 39–41, 76, 123–24, 135, 149, 206
spanking, of wives, 97–98, 132
Spending to Save (Hopkins), 31, 65, 119, 127
Springer, Gertrude, 24, 59
Stacy, Rubin, 46–47
Stanwyck, Barbara, 132
State Department, 200
state government, relief administration by, 16–17, 28, 35, 118, 124, 206
Steegmuller, Francis, 18, 121
Stilwell, Joseph, 186
St. Louis Community Council, Committee on Migrant Boys, 56
Swain, Martha, 128, 211n9
"Swimming and Boating on Lake McDonald" (Baker), 87

Taming of the Shrew, The (Shakespeare), 96–97, 132
Taurog, Norman, 69
This Is Your War (Childs), 140
This Way Out (Ronald), 103
Thomas, Howard, 64
Thompson, "Boxcar Bertha," 60–61
"Three Essentials for Unemployment Relief" (Roosevelt), 16
Tolan Committee hearings, 172–74, 182, 188

total war, rhetoric of, 137–47, 149, 154, 156, 159–61, 175
"Transient Program, The," Plunkert, William J., 60
transients (tramps): African American, 49–50, 60; Camp Frontier, 60; camps, 60–65; chronic hoboes, 51–52, 57, 59; female, 60–61, 105–7, 112, 131; Fort Eustis, 221n35; fruit tramps, 179, 190; hobo jungles, 52; homosexual perversion narratives, 3, 5, 48–58, 49–58, 51, 63–64, 66–67, 69–70, 85, 179, 190, 220n3; interracial aspects, 224n7; local relief agencies, 59; old bachelors, 179, 189–90; older men as sexual predators or "wolves," 3, 52, 55–56, 70, 220n3; sensational stories on, 50–51, 55–56, 63, 67; tension between camps and white male householders, 63; Uncle Sam's Wayside Inns, 62–64, 67; as unemployable, 65; wandering youth, 50–56, 64–65, 68–71, 75, 223n2. *See also* Federal Transient Program; migrant laborers
Truman, Harry, 166, 206
Tule Lake Segregation Center (internment camp), 187, *192–93,* 200; political protests by internees, 190–95
Tuohy, William, 208

Ueno, Henry, 242n52
Uncle Sam: grim and determined, 137–38, *138–39;* Uncle Sam's Wayside Inns, 62–64, 67
unemployables, 36–40, 65, 118–20, 122
unemployment. *See* forgotten man; New Deal relief policies
unemployment census, 101
United Service Organization (USO), 186
United States Rubber Company, 139
U.S. Army: CCC work camp administration, 71, 73–74, 76, 81; segregation in, 185; takeover of Tule Lake Segregation Camp, 191–93; Western Defense Command, 175. *See also* War Department

venereal disease, 225n19
veterans, 203–9
Veterans Administration (VA), 206
Victory Gardens, 147, 160
Victory Homes, 146
voluntarism, 231n51
Volunteer Participation Committee, OCD, 146, 149, 161–63

wandering youth, 50–56, 64–65, 68–71, 75, 223n2. *See also* transients

War Department, 151–52, 153, 168; and administration of internment program, 194; all-Nisei combat team, 183–87; expulsion of Kibei from U.S. Armed Services, 182; loyalty questionnaire, 183–84, 187–88; Pre-Induction Training Branch, 151. *See also* U.S. Army; World War II

Warner, Michael, 213n24

War Relocation Authority (WRA), 4, 168–71, 175–202, 205, 207; Community Analysis section, 176, 179, 199–201; Community Welfare section, 176–77, 200; compared to CCC, 187–88; conflicts with camp residents, 191–95; criticism of, 180–81; ethics of internment, 175; fall 1942 disturbances, 182–83; Heart Mountain camp, 174, 187; internment camp administration, 175–77; leave clearance, 182–83; Manzanar camp, 182; political protests by internees, 190–95; Poston camp, 182; Work Corps, 177, 241n25. *See also* Issei; Kibei; Nisei; Tule Lake Segregation Center

Warren, Earl, 172

Washington, Forrester B., 17

Wayne, Priscilla, "Does the World Owe John Doe a Living?," 26

We Are Not Alone (Warner Brothers), 104

Webb, John N., 56, 58, 60, 61

We Can Take It: A Short Story of the CCC (Hoyt), 86

welfare state: advocacy for, 163; citizenship and, 7; professionals, 217n60; sexual politics of, 3–5, 57, 131. *See also* federal government; New Deal relief policies; social workers

Wellman, William, 68

Wendelin, Rudy, *Woodsmanship for the Civilian Conservation Corps*, 89

What to Do in an Air Raid (OCD), 137, *139*, 154

"What WPA Means to the Negro Worker in New York State" (Ross), 42

When Strangers Marry (Columbia), 97

white male householders: authority in the home, 4, 18, 32–33, 35, 46, 48, 105; civic authority, 3, 7–8, 26, 137–40, 150, 153–59, 163; moral authority, 138–40; New Deal officials and, 66–67; in OCD, 147; tension between transient camps and, 63. *See also* forgotten man

whiteness, 7–8, 17, 91; as metaphor for nationhood, 93–95

whites: Southern, racial practices of, 39–40, 123–24, 149, 206. *See also* white male householders; whiteness; white women

white women: reconstruction of, 129–30; as sexually promiscuous, 107–8; as transgressive, 98–99

Wickenden, Elizabeth, 59, 61

"Wielding Club of Authority May Cure the Shrew" (Blake), 97

Wild Boys of the Road (Wellman), 68–69

Willkie, Wendell, 47

Wirth, Louis, 140, 144

wives: emasculating, 104–5, 130; faithless, 208–9; nagging, 99, 102–4, 108–9; wife spanking, 97–98, 132. *See also* married women workers

Wives of Spanking Husbands' Club, 97–98

woman-blaming narratives: in Great Depression and New Deal rhetoric, 98–109, 116, 127, 131–33; and women of color, 108–9; in World War II, 165–66; and WPA, 122

women: delinquency, 144; discrimination against, 37, 109, 128–29; domestic roles, 107, 126–27, 160, 162; employment, 98–99, 109 (*see also* married women workers); exclusion from wartime civic ideals, 202; and GI Bill, 207; moral weakness of, 100, 106–7, 113, 118, 166; as mothers, 38, 119, 126, 226n46; in OCD, 152, 159–66; in public sphere, 107; relief policies for, 43–44, 109–18, 127–29; sex delinquency, 144; single, 38, 112–14, 113, 119, 126; as social workers, 16, 18, 22–24; as submissive, 99, 119, 132; unemployment, 37, 105, 109, 119–20. *See also* African American women; Mexican American women; white women

Women's Air Force Service Pilots, 207

Women's Division (Democratic Party), 128

Women's Division (FERA), 37, 110–16

Women's Division (WPA), 32, 126, 128

Wood, Amy Louise, 46

Woodring, Henry, 82–83

Woodsmanship for the Civilian Conservation Corps (Wendelin), *89*

Woodward, Ellen S., 30, 111–12, 122, 126–28, 231n51

workers: able-bodied, 28–29, 31, 33, 36–38, 118, 122; loosely-clad forestry worker,

70, 89, 91, 93, 188; married women, 99–102, 108–9, 117–20, 130–31; migrants, 65–66, 179, 189–90; unemployable, 36–40, 65, 118–20, 122

working-class: bachelor subculture, 70, 93; youth in CCC, 76–80

Works Progress Administration (WPA), 4, *30,* 89, 207, 217n60; abolition of, 205–6; African Americans and, 32, 36, 38–44; construction programs, 31–32, 34–35; Division of Women's and Professional Projects, 125–27; eligibility criteria, 35–40, 118–19; and the forgotten man, 28–35, 118–21; *The Negro on Relief* (Division of Social Research), 40; Office of Information, 29; *Our Job with the WPA* (handbook), 32–35, *34;* publicity and public relations, 29, 34, 43, 217n62; unemployable workers and, 36–40; women and, 33, 37–38, 43–44, 118–30; Women's Division, 32, 126, 128

World War II: employment opportunities, 144; military mobilization, gender and sexual anxieties, 143–45; mobilization parades, 134–35, 168; racism in images of combat and military life, 195–96; rhetoric of total war, 137–47, 149, 154, 156, 159–61, 175. *See also* Japanese Americans; Office of Civilian Defense; War Department; War Relocation Authority

WPA. *See* Works Progress Administration

Wright, Teresa, 209

Wyler, William, *The Best Years of Our Lives,* 207–9

Young, Pauline, 14, 15

youth, masculine. *See also* juvenile delinquency; transients; wandering youth: and citizenship, 91, 182, 201–2; degeneration of, 90; homeless, 68–70, 82; military mobilization, 142–45; scapegoating of Nisei and Kibei youth, 177; sexuality, in CCC, 86–87; socialization of, 173–74, 198–99, 202; unemployed, 223n2; working-class, in CCC, 76–80, 86–87

zoot suiters, 142, 144, 168, 170, 179